Tales of a Cultural Conduit

ALSO FROM TIGER OF THE STRIPE

Landesmania!
Philip Trevena

The Bibliomania or Book-Madness
Thomas Frognall Dibdin

Tales of a

Cultural

Conduit

———— & ————

The Nervous Set

JAY LANDESMAN

TIGER OF THE STRIPE · RICHMOND · MMVI

First published in 2006 by
Tiger of the Stripe
50 Albert Road
Richmond
Surrey TW10 6DP
United Kingdom

ISBN 1 904799 08 6

Printed in the US and UK by
Lightning Source

Contents

૭ℐ

Introduction

BY JOHN CLELLON HOLMES

WHENEVER I MET JAY LANDESMAN in a bar in the old days, I always seemed to arrive first. I waited around and far from being piqued I discovered that I was experiencing a pleasant little ping-ping-ping of anticipation. What I was anticipating was laughter.

Black laughter. Like the idea of a cigarette smoking a man, or *Dr Strangelove*. Absurd laughter. Oh – like a camel in sneakers, beaded Art Nouveau lamps that play 'Valencia', Andy Warhol. Pertinent laughter. You know, like, 'Laugh? I thought I'd *die*,' the cobalt bomb, Lenny Bruce. Laughter accompanied by the sound of hot air escaping from reality's punctured balloons.

When I think of things like this, I always think of Landesman. Not because he was a wit. There wasn't a proper epigram in him. Nor one of those living room Berles, machine-gunning everyone with gags. It was that he saw everything on the bias. It was that everything he did had an air of elaborate burlesque about it.

For instance, his six-button jackets with the multiple vents and triple lapels. His stuffed alligator with the lamp in its jaws. His study in St Louis that was a facsimile of an old Von Sternberg set in all its claustrophobic proliferation of unrelated dreck. *Neurotica*, for instance – so outrageous in its time that you automatically assumed he must have started it for the same reason that other people suddenly decide to throw a wild party. It was like daring the *Partisan Review*-niks to go skinny-dipping. Or ASCA (Advanced School of Cultural Analysis), with all those spoofing lectures on sports cars, drinking, jazz, conformity and other aspects, which seemed to be nothing more than a deadpan excuse for Sunday afternoon cocktail parties. Or the Crystal Palace Cabaret Theater in St Louis, created by Landesman and his brother for the simple reason (one couldn't help but feel) that it didn't already exist, and they needed an arena in which to 'make things hot'. Or Landesman's musical, *The Nervous Set*, that got to Broadway, perhaps too soon, and died – funny, irreverent, a parody of the Beat Generation. Or was it? You kept remembering lines from it, you kept humming those songs. And you laughed.

You did. You laughed at all this. You said, 'Good old Jay. What the hell kind of wild stunt will he pull off next?' You always looked forward to seeing him, and what he pulled off next was always more outlandish than you had anticipated. A 'Twist Room' that must have been one of the first authentic discotheques in America. Or a TV gab show that opened with a shot of Landesman's firehouse shoes, and then panned up to a wry smile that suddenly admitted, 'Talk is cheap.' Or a musical version of *Dracula*.

A million laughs, all right. A hip, sardonic mind behind it. No doubt of that. Landesmania, his friends called it. A life style that was a wacky amalgam of Hellzapoppin, Theatre of the Absurd and Pop Art. But serious? You must be kidding. I mean, I once saw him wear magenta Bermudas and a pith helmet. He planned a lecture entitled 'Abortive Attempts at Middle Class Rebellion.' He was often heard to say things like, 'George Raft in a dinner jacket looks like a stolen Bentley.' And take his parties! There was something fiendish about them. Chandler Brossard and James Jones in the same room. Hostility games. Come as your favourite perversion. Confess your first homosexual experience. He was a wrecker, he was frivolous, he was – well, just think of going up to Dorothy Kilgallen on Madison Avenue and saying, 'This is Sin Street, Madam, get off it!' Or naming your kids Cosmo and Miles Davis. It was all prankishness, eccentricity, maladjusted *chutzpah*. And yet –

And yet there was that damn under layer to it all. His projects all seemed to have a disturbing half-life that lingered in the mind like strontium-90 in the bone. His personal preoccupations had the maddening habit of becoming cultural tendencies ten years later. You never took him seriously at the time and you were never sure that he did either, and then all of a sudden everywhere you went in New York during the sixties there was a sort of public version of Landesmania. But where was Landesman? He had moved to England, and he wrote back mysteriously, 'I see a kind of blurring of the sexual lines... But no matter how you slice it, ducks, it's all love... ' And you started to keep your eyes open, craftily, for that one to reach the surface.

After knowing Landesman for seventeen years, I still find it difficult to explain him to a stranger. A tall, shambling man, who has the warm, inquisitive dark eyes and the self-mocking smile of a secret idealist; who speaks in a glib, exaggerated *patois* of show biz lingo, psychiatric gobbledy-gook, and Negro and Yiddish slang, all blended into a contagious argot of his own, Landesman has been variously described as 'a puppetmaster with an aggressive *lack* of talent', 'the Mike Todd of dying cities', and 'a genie with a certain sense of merchandising.' There is a bit of truth in all these estimates, but the whole truth is not there.

For myself, I would say that Landesman possessed, years before it was either chic or marketable, what would now be called the 'Pop Imagination'. In a culture where everything is mass produced, quick-frozen, ready-made, pre-cooked or painted-by-numbers, he was the first person I knew who refused such a society's categorical choice of either remaining an aesthete or becoming a vulgarian. For any and all evidences of a unique and unconventional point of view interested him and he looked for these evidences in junk shops, movie houses and newsstands (wherever his own quirky eye led him), as well as in bookstores, art galleries and theaters. In that Stone Age (ten or fifteen years back) when enlightened people sat in their Eames chairs, under their Calders, talking about T. S. Eliot, Landesman was already living in a thicket of Victorian bric-à-brac and publishing Allen Ginsberg. I suspect his reasons for doing both were very much the same: he believed in indulging his own curiosity and only things that were counter, wry, eccentric, special and excessive stimulated him.

Having grown up into and through a family antique business, Landesman believed that artefacts were sometimes more evocative of their times than ideas. Things had an uncanny aura to him and clutter made him feel at ease. The first sight that confronted you on entering his New York apartment was a huge sculpture of Noah's ark fashioned from half the gunwhale of a catboat. Over his desk in St Louis hung a spray-painted jock strap in a gilt frame, and he always worked warmly insulated behind mountains of books, magazines, record albums, and any other nameless effluvia that had caught his eye. As a consequence, it was impossible to imagine him living for long in the functional Gobi of a modern house, and he could be painfully hilarious when a guest in one.

Equally, eccentricity of attire was evidence of soul to him, and one ceased being surprised when he turned up in horrible candy-striped seersuckers and a string tie that hung down to his crotch, or sporting a denim sack suit in an advanced state of rumple. Such props were as expressive of his personal vision of things as anything he said, for, as he once confided with a dim smile, 'Every time I see a man in jodhpurs and an opera hat – and it only happens two or three times a month these days, I always go up and speak to him, because that man isn't going to hang you up about the weather.' Sometimes this flair for the eccentric was only inches this side of outright perversity ('the three-lapel jacket – yes, that was a very important project'), but most of the time Landesman was that unique phenomenon in a status-drunk society: a man who knew that the only really hip style is the next one, the one that hasn't been established yet.

He had an omnivorous interest in popular culture, and long before it was high camp to collect back issues of *Batman* and idolize the horror movies of Tod Browning, he was publishing articles that anatomized the one, and scouring the most dismal reaches of Brooklyn for screenings of the other. Like many of us in the late forties he felt that the fine arts were so tyrannized by one or other version of the New Criticism that they had become little more than lifeless appendages of it, but, unlike a lot of people in later years he shifted his attention to the popular arts without sacrificing his sense of the culture as a whole.

The idea that there is something intrinsically worthwhile about the soup cans, science fiction movies, mammoth billboards and electronic noise that inundates our civilization (an extremely fashionable idea just recently) would have struck Landesman as being hopelessly frivolous. These things were interesting to him only insofar as they indicated the condition of our imaginations, a condition that could not be perceived as we celebrated the signs of its poverty merely for themselves. 'Popular culture never lies,' he used to say. 'Not about the people who consume it,' among whom I'm sure he would have included Susan Sontag as well as the stenographer down the hall.

For it was popular culture's unconscious embodiment of inner fantasies that attracted Landesman. He revelled in it, he let it stimulate his rarer appetites for the bizarre, but he never patronized it in the manner of camp and his ear was always cocked for the psychic throb within it – seismographic evidences of which filled the pages of *Neurotica*.

As its editor, Landesman's greatest gift probably lay in getting other people to track down and amplify the whispers he had heard. This wasn't laziness, nor inability to do the job himself, but simply a canny understanding that what he could best contribute to the magazine was a general intuition about the culture, and a Hawkshaw-knack for ferreting out people who could particularize that intuition into usable knowledge. Though there were several assistant editors, all of whom did most of the comma-shifting and phrase-haggling, the magazine showed little of their influence – with the single exception of Legman. For Landesman knew precisely what he wanted from the start. He wanted articles like 'The World of the Borderline Fetishist', and 'Psychiatrist: God or Demitasse?' and 'The Unique Mores of the Bar and Tavern Social Milieu' - all of which existed in the beginning only as titles, to which the articles themselves were more or less jerry-written by other people later.

Also he knew the audience he was trying to reach. 'I'm not publishing for the three dozen hard-core scatologists along Forty Second Street or the little magazine crowd that tells their shrinks that, of *course*, they consider *Neurotica* too sick to read. I want to get to the five thousand people who really make this society go – the opinion makers, the guys with the crazy power, the sell-outs who are responsible for running the mess in the first place.'

It is highly debatable whether *Neurotica* ever succeeded in achieving this aim (despite the fact that to my knowledge, it is the only little magazine whose entire run of issues was republished in book form a full decade after its demise), but certainly, in Legman, Landesman found someone with the same muck-raking appetites, and they worked together like a couple of unemployed dynamiters trying to blow up the Time-Life Building with a firecracker. I tagged along behind them, as did others.

But for all the barefoot crusades of those *Neurotica* days, it is the sheer excitement, the high pitch of fun, that I have remembered longest. It is the laughter that rose through the smoke to the ten foot ceiling of Landesman's brownstone apartment on West Fifty-Third Street where we worked together through the late mornings, writing 'Alfred Towne's' exposés of homosexuality in American culture. It is Landesman in his undershirt deciding that we should describe Towne as a 'midwesterner who has left the country', and the afternoons we fuelled our gleeful outrage (at what Towne humourlessly insisted on calling 'the effeminization of values') with lunchtime gin and staggering corned beef sandwiches from the Stage Delicatessen around the corner. It is remembering how laboriously we fashioned our mile-wide hints about such-and-such a conductor; and how lecherously we stripped our scandalous aspersions (concerning so-and-so's penchant for drag) down to their last veil; and with what giggling thoroughness we mapped that murky territory of innuendo just this side of libel.

It all seems a little silly today, a little far-fetched (though fearless articles almost identical to those Alfred Towne published in *Neu-*

rotica and *The American Mercury* still appear all these fifteen years later) and yet from those hoarse and smoky afternoons I think we both distilled, for ourselves at least, a sense that we were engaging the real scene that lay buried somewhere under the glum hypocrisies and lofty nonsense that passed for a serious culture then.

And anyway, those afternoons led inevitably toward five o'clock, and five o'clock inevitably brought people; Anatole Broyard with that week's facsimile of the Broyard-girl – blonde, tooled, wordless – changing as little, version to version, as Anatole changed from year to year; Robert Lowry as big and bearish in his corduroys as a grizzly with the face of a panda; Marshall McLuhan (when he was in town) improvising ideas like a combination Spengler, Picasso, and Mort Sahl; little, zany William Poster with his clear, darting eye for subtle values; Chandler Brossard as difficult to crack as a horse chestnut and just as tart when you did; Paul Mazursky doing his funny Brando imitations while Stanley Radulovich did his serious ones; Carl Solomon yoinking around so frenziedly on a pogo stick that one night he put the end of it right through the floor into the restaurant below – and all their girls, and their friends' girls, and their friends' friends, and even nameless others who may have just heard the hubbub and walked in the door.

These five o'clocks always got to be ten o'clocks somehow, and we found ourselves in Birdland, or up at the Park Palace in Spanish Harlem, or in Glennon's practising what Landesman called 'futility rites' or down at Louis' in the Village. Landesman was table-hopping, or mamboing with great flung feet and stabbing hands. Landesman was ankling off to phone, or being loudly paged by the bartender, having told half a dozen people just where he would be and when to call.

Mostly, he was always somewhere near the center of a throng of people when I saw him, but one night I found him alone in his apartment, except for a dark-gold girl named Fran, her face luminous with the hip chick's soulfulness; a girl who bore astonishing resemblance to Zelda Fitzgerald – only lovelier, softer, more remote; a girl who looked as if she had been tagged early, and *become* herself in the act of surviving it; the kind of girl with a certain pang behind her intelligence and her chic; the kind of girl you marry if you know your own hang-ups well enough. A month or so later, Landesman did just that, and almost immediately they became 'Jay and Fran' to everyone who new them, one name all but unpronounceable without the other.

Soon after this, Landesman grew bored with hunting the culture's various psychic snarks, for, unlike Legman, he was not imprisoned by a single perception, and world-changing was not his wine. That singular Geiger counter in his head was geared to himself and his personal interests (which he took to be representative) and when there was no click in his current life, he always began to look elsewhere.

Also, by 1951, there was Fran, and their marriage; there was a growing need for a setting where the results of an action could be immediately seen, and there was New York that is never hospitable to this need. In one of those abrupt decisions that make us look at our friends through new eyes, Landesman gave *Neurotica* to Legman, and he and Fran moved back to St Louis.

Thereafter, the trait that had distinguished everything that Landesman had done surfaced in him rapidly until it became clear that what drove him (and drives the Pop Imagination generally) was an overriding theatrical sense – a sense of how to put a point of view on display, how to isolate a falsehood so that it could be seen, how to reveal a subtle truth through sheer exaggeration. Landesman's need was to enliven life by staging it, to strike creative sparks by rubbing people and ideas together and, above all, to satisfy a curiosity that was as gluttonous as a Dempster Dumpster. To Landesman, existence was a series of happenings, or he got glum. Ultimately, his need was for a theater, and St Louis became that theater for him.

What followed was the Crystal Palace ('the most gorgeous saloon in America'), and the plays, ASCA, and the TV show. What followed where the lyrics that Fran began to write one day that were set to music by Tommy Woolf, Alec Wilder, and Roy Kral (those sad, wry, sexy lieder – like 'Listen Little Girl', 'Fun Life' and 'Spring Can Really Hang You Up The Most' - that resembled nothing so much as the fragrant, whimsical, intimate contents of an evening purse, belonging to a girl who is as interesting to talk to as to lie with, spilled out on the dressing table of another, inevitable dawn) and the need for a showcase in which these songs could be displayed. And what followed that was *The Nervous Set*, with book by Landesman, and all the other shows that made St Louis, for a brief few years, a town that people visited for more than beer and baseball.

When I conjure up such a visit, I am sitting in Landesman's living room, or in the patio behind his house, or in any one of a dozen apartments nearby that he and his brother kept for their people; music is providing its throbbing insulation against the discordant world outside (more than likely little-known show tunes, or bossa nova or good rock); martinis are being stirred in a huge pitcher, making that velvety sound of ice cushioned by gin; there are half a dozen people around, all of whom give off the indescribable air of being members of Landesman's *troupe*; children yodel at a TV programme upstairs; later there will be a dinner party somewhere under a chandelier or among enormous imitation trees during which everyone will be brighter and wittier and sexier than he really is, and later still, Gaslight Square and the Palace, Lenny Bruce or Samuel Beckett, and crowds of people who seem to know me simply because I knew Landesman.

I am sitting there, nicely mulled, astonished by the realization that I am in the midst of a community within a community – a community with its own theaters, bars, restaurants, apartments and galleries, all reflecting the same life style, the same brand of restless and bizarre intelligence. I am amazed, because I have never known its exact like before but I am also happily expectant (the way I used to be at Billy Wilder movies, the way I still am when I listen to Thelonius), for I know that no matter what happens in the hours ahead, it will be funny, hip, mordant, noisy, and meaningful: the stuff of a good memory.

Landesman's sense of theater permeated this whole community and infected anything he spent five minutes on. He always answered the phone with a crisp, 'Jay L-a-n-d-e-s-m-a-n here!' lingering sonorously on his own name, as one does every time one says a name like Walther von der Vogelweide. He introduced outlandish soubriquets for everyone, some of them so maddeningly adhesive that they simply absorbed the actual person, like a kind of verbal Venus flytrap. I remember for instance a five-foot-two chutney salesman who was known to me only as 'The Lord God,' a buxom flip of a girl from the Ozarks called 'Dearest Little' and a hip-talking layout man invariably referred to as 'F. Scott Fredsegal.'

The cocktail hour was orchestrated like an *opéra bouffe* – music, and booze, and just the right mix of jarring people, all of it calculated to produce an unexpected and sometimes scandalous *dénouement*. Gossip flitted around the room in a balletic counterpoint that intensified the odd feeling of theatricality. There was something overheated and incestuous about these liquid twilights, for Landesman believed that strong personalities, acting on one another in an artificial setting, inevitably would generate the kind of drama out of which recognition came, and he frankly manipulated his people towards this end.

There were animosities a-plenty; there was a more or less continual game of musical beds going on; new stars were taken up, old ones dropped; games of charades somehow always ended in group therapy sessions; parties quickly became psychodramas and there are people from those days who probably have no desire to ever hear the name Landesman again. In my opinion, however, Landesman's habit of playing the social Diaghilev was ultimately more creative than destructive (how thin the line!). For its spur was not merely boredom, but rather a desire to break through all the masks, and heighten his sense of life as being open-ended, dangerous with possibilities, free; a sense that later drew him naturally through Zen, LSD, and consciousness expansion in general. In any case, people seemed to perform a little beyond their usual talents when they were around

Landesman. At least, most of them still refer to those days with the unmistakeable accents we reserve for the description of an enlarging experience, and Landesman spoke to a vein of ironical decadence which, in those pious, prosperous years, ran deep in all of us. For, in the struggle of progress versus decay, Landesman frankly opted for the latter, and this, I believe, was the closest he came to having a guiding principle. It was also the dark secret of his appeal.

Out of the loftiest of intentions, the lust for progress has created the shallowest of worlds, and even the most optimistic of social engineers must sometimes wake up after midnight, disturbed by a vague but persistent nostalgia for something that is not covered in the manuals. As a result, people of my generation instinctively gravitated to the margins, the corners, the backstreets of contemporary experience, hoping to gain a little human time before the automated bulldozers of the future arrived. A lot of us felt twinges of guilt about this, but there was no arguing with the fact that, though we were *for* progress, it profoundly depressed us; and as the steel and glass environments went up, we tended to withdraw to whatever neighbourhoods were left.

Landesman was usually there before us, getting out the gin and busily poking at the pomposities of a culture so traduced that it equated the good only with the useful. This was why he had gone back to St Louis in the first place, for St Louis in the fifties was a dying city (hopelessly stratified by outmoded distinctions, its growth paralyzed by civic ordinances that were as hoary as its architecture), and its prevailing mood can best be compared to the mood of pre-Castro Havana: lethargy, somnolence, and a faint whiff of corruption hung in the air that wafted off the big river. It was precisely the sort of scene in which a canny and energetic provocateur could make his move, and almost before they knew it, the burgher and the debutantes found a minor, but authentic, cultural renaissance flourishing under their very noses – *Krapp's Last Tape* instead of the usual *South Pacific*, and 'Squareville U.S.A: A New Look at Main Street' in place of the standard lecture on rubbernecking in Angkor Wat.

For a while a few luxuriant poinsettias bloomed among the crumbling buildings and the blistered streets. But cultural renaissances cannot hold out for long against America's twin fixations of the moment – urban renewal and civic betterment – and St Louis eventually voted for progress as represented by the wrecker's ball and the touring company. You *knew* a Broadway Musical was good (hadn't you read about it in *The New Yorker*?) and every city, with any pride in itself, was erecting those distinctive air-conditioned saltine boxes. But how did you *know* what to feel about the murky and controversial plays the Landesmans put on? And those old waterfront buildings, some of them going back a hundred and fifty years or more – they were only eyesores that never ceased to remind you that you lived in a backward little city in Hicksville. So as the Saarinen Arch (The Gateway to the West) relentlessly went up, Landesman's flamboyant banner, on which might have been emblazoned the frank admonition, 'Onward and Downward!', fluttered to the pavement. And in another of those abrupt uprootings, which were the surest sign that it was never comfort that he prized, but creative *room*, he went east. All the way east. All the way to London.

Landesman chose decay, I firmly believe, because of what he knew. He knew himself, and he knew what interested him, and he knew in what exotic mulch those interests had a chance of coming to full flower. Also he knew precisely how he had to live to prevent the contradictions in his nature (an artist's nature, even though he sometimes lacked an art – that is to say, a reckless, inquisitive, ultimately unsatisfiable nature) from becoming stalemated in a struggle that he knew he could only *lose*. For underlying his imagination, his theatricality, and his decadence, was something considerably more rare: a man cursed with a keenly contemporary sensibility and all its exaggerated appetites, living out, in himself, most of the psychic displacements and realignments, which, in this time, often suggest that a new and wider human consciousness is on the road to its Bethlehem to be born.

Beyond this, one can only speculate, but my speculation tells me that it was a radical notion of sex that stood behind most of Landesman's projects. For when I think of him, I always think of that black, iconoclastic humour that we all possessed, or at least recognized instantly, in those days; that humour which said, 'It isn't that way. That isn't the way it is. We all know how it *really* is'; that humour dubbed 'sick' by a society so Orwellian that it actually confused the diagnosis with the disease. I think Landesman knew, as well, that in a situation so existentially false that black humour is the only intelligent saving response, that humour always tends to reflect the secret intuition that sexuality is somehow the last sanctuary of the real; a final frontier that no passports, visas or customs can prevent us from crossing in order to discover in the danger and the dark on the other side what it is like to be fully and mysteriously alive. I think Landesman ceaselessly experimented, dared to act out, engineered new and disturbing situations and always put himself on the line because he worked at his life the way writers work at a book, and always assumed, often wrongly, that everyone else was as seriously involved in the search as he.

For above all I think he *was* serious. He was serious about marriage, for instance – so serious that he tried to discover a new sort of basis on which it could survive in an age of Splitsville, a basis that would embody *all* the contradictory urges of love and power, ego and self, which (far from representing abnormality in our century) are the very norm from which we must begin; and his marriage to Fran, which survived enough upheavals to wreck any relationship with the slightest bit of deceit in it, was probably the single marriage that I knew about that I would have made book would last. If, as he got older, he was less and less concerned with challenging the powers that be, influencing the age and competing in the arena (hadn't we all seen the issues come and go, despite the tireless energy and high hopes that were expended on them?), it was probably because he eventually came to believe that there was no direction left for us to take, except down into the cavern of ourselves where all the issues start. And if he became more hedonistic, less success-driven, and occasionally an advocate of avant-garde sex mores, I think it was because he suspected that the most far-reaching revolution of our generation would probably turn out to be the Sexual Revolution – predicated, as it was, on a conception of the totally unsuppressed human being, and promising, as it did, an end to the duality of which all the issues were only the bitter, cerebral end products.

'What I really want,' he once said, 'is reasonably simple. I want economic security, I want to be around beautiful women who smell good, and I want to stay creative. It seems to me, more and more, that this means adjusting, not to the society, but to the springs of life itself – insofar as you can know them by knowing yourself. Beyond that, I guess what I want is to do everything twice.' Knowing him, there is nothing very unreasonable in this.

To me, Landesman represented a side of my generation, and its experience, that I have only come to fully appreciate as we have all gotten older and less amusing. The game-playing, style-enamoured, pomposity-puncturing side. The side that practised its futility rites with so much energy, and wit, and unconscious courage. The funny, hip, mordant, noisy, meaningful side. Not the deepest side perhaps; too impatient and too facile, too continually *aware* of everything, to pause for the probe to ultimate causes. But a side that lived intensely up to its times, nevertheless.

In any case, on those flawless spring mornings when anxiety or exhilaration makes me feel that only a drink in a sunny, uncrowded, old-fashioned barroom will put an egg in my day, I always think of phoning Landesman and urging a lunch. The talk won't be solemn or profound, but its surface will shimmer with a mind that knows where we have been, and where we are now; a mind that has always found life interesting and a little absurd, but has never lost its taste for the adventure. The people who will turn up later are likely to be tough-minded, attractive and up on things. They will carefully consider what to drink and make the smart decision. They will pull their own weight and won't have to have anything explained to them. And for a few hours, I will have a very keen sense of all of us there together – heirs of a fairly bad world, who have lived through it with some grace, and not made it any worse.

Sometimes during those hours, Landesman is bound to say to me, 'We've got us a big talk coming one of these days, Johnnie...' always a sign to me that he is feeling warm, expansive, hurried and affectionate. And I will think (as I always do) that we really have no need of that talk. I know where he is going, and I know why. His restless eye – for the fun, and the nerves, and the girls of his time – has always given him away.

PUBLISHER'S NOTE

John Clellon Holmes wrote this Introduction in 1968.

Tales of a
Cultural
Conduit

JAY LANDESMAN

1

B Y THE STANDARDS OF ANY DAY, my mother, Cutie, was a remarkable woman. Youngest and plainest of six children born to poor New York immigrant parents, she was a petite, beaky, cross-eyed Jewish Cinderella who stayed home to do the housework while her mother looked for husbands for her two older sisters. It never seemed possible to Grandma that she could find a husband for Cutie until a handsome young artist from Berlin knocked on the door of their Hester Street flat.

'My name is Benjamin Landesman. In the directory I see your name is Landsman without the "e". Are we related?'

'Are you married?' Grandma asked.

When he said no, she grabbed him by the lapels of his tight-fitting suit and sat him down in the kitchen with a nice cup of hot coffee. His first sight of Cutie was of her on her hands and knees scrubbing the floor. Benjamin was impressed; he knew a worker when he saw one.

He was on his way to St Louis, commissioned by the German government to decorate their pavilion at the 1904 World's Fair. Over the next three years he established something of a reputation in St Louis as a muralist, specializing in Teutonic cherubs and playful nymphs. But he didn't forget Cutie. He returned to New York to collect her and the gold watch Grandma had promised he could have when they got married. He never got the gold watch, but he won a 24-carat bargain with a heart of steel – my mother.

I was the youngest child, and determined not to be ignored. I was also the noisiest, making demands upon Cutie's busy life out of all proportion to my size and status. At an early age I had to invent new techniques to get attention and I continued to do so for the rest of my life. It was a necessity during childhood, a mission through adolescence and, in later life, my only hobby.

By 1940, the threat of war and the registration for the draft were preventing me from taking anything too seriously. I found an empty store on Bed Bug Row, a parade of bizarre, run-down shops that was considered an eyesore by the more respectable elements in the neighbourhood. It was my favourite section of town, the source of many colourful stories. Above the shops there used to be brothels, regularly visited by the star baseball players when they were in town. The whores were gone, but there remained a sense of camaraderie among the few artists, ex-pimps, interior decorators and antique dealers that inhabited the area. The antique dealers were a special breed of eccentrics, fiercely independent, congenially lazy, hustling in a relaxed atmosphere that suited me perfectly.

My shop was on the side of the street with a wide sidewalk that enabled me to display my stock al fresco. It was hardly worth bringing in at the close of the day and frequently I didn't bother. I called the shop 'Jay Irving's', having added the name Jay after reading Fitzgerald's *The Great Gatsby*. It was the perfect name for a nightclub, and that's the way I ran the business. I always had a drink ready for any patron or friend who happened to drop by because they had no other place to go in the middle of the day. I conducted most of my business from a reclining position on a decrepit chaise-longue on the sidewalk, providing a visual treat for the passing motorist and passengers on the University streetcar line. It was a happy time, lying in the sun with a cold drink in hand, reading *Remembrance of Things Past* to the music of the juke box in the sleazy tavern next door.

The experience of combining business with pleasure proved so compatible with my temperament that I was totally committed to it as a way of life. Naturally, I withheld this information from Cutie, who was insisting I rejoin her in the growing business, promising a partnership if things went well. I capitulated, expecting my draft call-up any day.

If I couldn't handle the simple authority problems of school, how was I to accept the regimentation of army life? There was a part of me that wanted to get drafted, if only to get away from Cutie.

What would the Army do with a one-hundred-and-twelve pound, six-foot weakling with a certifiable Oedipus complex? In a letter to my father, I suggested that Gert, my sister, would be the Landesmans' best bet for the army. Rejection by all his sons nearly broke my father's heart.

I decided that the war effort would best be served by my joining Cutie in the antique business to raise the morale on the decorative home front. Like the good sons we'd been raised to be, Fred, Gene and I explained that times had changed. Her nickel-and-dime philosophy in business was through. We saw a boom ahead for antiques.

With the aid of Fred's artistic supervision, Gene's construction skills and my knowledge of genuine antiques, the shop was transformed into a showplace. Poor Cutie wandered around its exquisitely decorated rooms lost and confused.

She retaliated by pouring out her scorn with ironic comments on our upmarket methods. Her favourite stock was relegated to a small area in the rear of the galleries; little did anyone suspect that her collection of nineteenth-century utilitarian cut glass for which we had such disdain would be the basis of Landesman Galleries' great success.

During the war, lighting fixtures were no longer manufactured. Crystal chandeliers, one of our specialities, could not be found. The demand was enormous and Fred rose to the occasion with an ingenious piece of *ad hoc* designing. Since glass was the main ingredient of a chandelier, he used Cutie's collection of cut-glass carafes, water tumblers, flower vases, dessert dishes, hair receivers, finger bowls and lamp bases, inverting them to disguise their original purpose. The Landesman chandelier was a masterpiece of ingenuity in a war-torn world and we managed to bring a few laughs into a time devoid of any humour.

I proposed to my girlfriend, Pat, the day the bomb dropped on Hiroshima. The idea of getting married was considerably less dramatic. As they were saying about the bomb: 'Something good may come out of it.' If there was ever a time in history when a light touch was necessary, it was then. Our honeymoon in New Orleans provided the combination of comedy and pathos that was later to characterise the marriage. Her real father, who had deserted her when she was a baby, was living in a trailer camp with his young wife, a few years older than Pat. He was working in a strip joint on Bourbon Street as a singing master of ceremonies. He was perfect for the part: tall, greasy, with a pencil-thin moustache that dated him as early Ramon Navarro. I liked him at first sight. He would reminisce about his days as a promising tenor with a travelling musical stock company, when he'd lived with Pat's mother in a little house with a garden and a dog. It was music to my ears. I admired people who had fallen from grace and were still willing to talk about it. 'It's only temporary, honey,' he told Pat. 'I'll be going to Las Vegas next winter where they recognise real class.' It gave me the feeling that, even if I hadn't chosen the right girl for a wife, I had at least chosen the right father-in-law.

We had decided to set up home in Fred's warehouse, a few doors down from the Galleries. His wedding present to us was the choice of anything we wanted to use. No one in their right mind would ever have picked the Cardinal Richelieu bed to start married life upon. It was a monstrous piece of medieval fantasy, with dwarfs holding up the canopy and a mattress that could sleep six Cardinals, if they happened to be very much in love. Every act of lovemaking could have been our last. I insisted that all marriages needed an element of danger.

Once we were settled, our open house hospitality attracted the best collection of rejects St Louis' literary, artistic and musical life had to offer. The only price of admission was a healthy maladjustment to society; an interesting neurosis was an added bonus. 'Square' was the dreaded word. To be 'serious' was to leave yourself open to attack without chance of survival.

I did some serious thinking about the idea of starting a magazine. It occurred to me that my life lacked decent stationery. Nobody was going to be impressed with answers to the major themes of life written on a letterhead that proclaimed to the world that I bought and sold antiques.

When ordering some new stationery for the Galleries, as a joke, I had some cards printed up announcing the existence of a new magazine: '*Neurotica*, A Quarterly Journal: Publisher Jay Irving Landesman.' The title said it all. A magazine for and about neurotics, written by neurotics.

I was determined to bring the best and most original minds of our generation to *Neurotica*. I eventually brought together an unholy alliance of existentialists, surrealists, radical sociologists, psychoanalysts, playwrights and musicians to create the first underground critique of American life.

I received a letter from my old friend, Dorothy, who now worked at the Four Seasons Bookshop in Greenwich Village, urging me to come to New York and promote the second issue. I arrived in New York in a black button-down shirt, a yellow hand-painted tie, a crumpled seersucker suit and a new pair of Clarks desert boots. It didn't matter that our reservation at the Marlton Hotel in the heart of the village turned out to be a converted elevator shaft, with the soot of a hundred parties still on the walls. The room began to look good once I'd stocked it with a few bottles of gin, a tray of pastrami sandwiches, and some people who could help me make my blitz on New York's literary scene a success.

While I was thinking about the need for some fresh outlooks, a call came from Beka Dougherty, a friend from St Louis who was working for *Time* magazine.

'I think *Neurotica* is terrific,' she said in her cool *Time* manner. 'I put them on to you for the feature on Little Mags. You owe me a dinner.' When I told her what I was looking for in New York, she said she knew the perfect man to write for *Neurotica*.

'He's absolutely unprintable, but exactly what you need.' It turned out his name was Gershon Legman, which I thought was a joke name, but she assured me that he was no joke.

I made a quick call to check Legman out. After I introduced myself as the editor of *Neurotica*, he cut me short.

'It's a piece of garbage.'

I laughed at the nerve of the guy. He didn't sound enthusiastic about meeting me, but said I could come up to the Bronx and talk to him. 'There's nothing here to eat or drink,' he added, 'so bring your own refreshments.'

By the time we left for the Bronx, I'd collected quite a party: John Clellon Holmes, a quiet professorial type who had contributed a short story to the second issue; Herb Benjamin, who was writing an article on psychiatrists entitled *God or Demi-Tasse?*; and an attractive young student doing a thesis on the American penal system. We embarked, en masse, a noisy, playful bunch, as if we were going to a picnic. In the shadows at the end of the journey stood a lonely figure; I knew immediately who it was.

'Are you Landesman? I'm Legman.' The tone of the voice was sinister. As he stepped out of the shadows, I saw a heavily moustached, portly figure with a wild shock of hair that made me think of a young Balzac. I knew immediately there weren't going to be any laughs in the Bronx that night. By the light of the platform, I saw the lines of thwarted ambition around his mouth, evoking a permanent sense of rage.

Legman's house was a little cottage, possibly the only one left in the Bronx, with a distressed picket fence going all around the place, trying to hide the shoddy patches of grass. Inside, it reeked of old herring bones. I noticed that Legman himself smelled of musty books. Books were everywhere; stacked in the halls, used as furniture. What little furniture he had was upholstered in books. Books were marching menacingly out of the closets and trickling out of the toilet, and, from the smell of the place, I suspected they were being cooked on a back burner for a late-night snack of glue pudding.

Legman introduced his wife, Beverly, who was administering what looked like mouth-to-mouth resuscitation to one of the dozen cats loitering in the kitchen, waiting, as far as I could figure, to be read to. Beverly was more shy than the cats, but much plainer. For the next two hours, Legman gave us a whirlwind tour of his one-man fight against censorship of social and sexual expression. He had been compiling evidence for years and it was all stored in files or staring at us from every nook and cranny. He started out with comic books, disappearing from time to time to throw examples of them on the table to prove how insidious they were.

'You know, Landesman,' he said, '*Neurotica* could be something if you got rid of all that poetry and fake psychiatric prose. You've got a good idea there, the best that's come along in some time. It shouldn't be trusted to a dilettante like you.' He tried hard to smile when he said that, but the grin froze halfway through.

On the subway ride home, I started reading the manuscript Legman had given me, passing the pages to Holmes as I finished them. We were cracking up with dismay and laughter at Legman's outrageous indictment of the Western world.

'What if Legman's right?' Holmes asked. We looked at each other, shaking our heads in disbelief at what we had experienced that night.

'My God, Johnny, do you realise we've found an honest man?'

'And not a minute too soon,' Holmes added.

I made Legman sub-editor of *Neurotica* and after a hard day fighting with him I would occasionally drop by Holmes's pad. It was like Grand Central Station with characters dropping in at all hours of the day and night. On one of my visits, I found Jack Kerouac sleeping on the floor and Holmes and his wife wondering what to do with the body. 'Let's go out and get a drink,' I suggested.

At the mention of the word drink, Kerouac came to life. He had to meet someone in Times Square and asked us to join him. When we got there, he was like a kid in a circus, pointing out all the freaks hanging around the Pokorino hot dog stand, only he didn't see them as freaks. 'Dig how those cats operate.' He pointed to a couple of hipsters holding up a wall, 'Aren't they cool.' His enthusiasm grew as we went from bar to bar where everybody took on special 'angelic' qualities in his eyes.

I hadn't been in New York two months when I got a call from Beka Dougherty, who still worked for *Time* magazine.

'Are you seated?' She paused. 'What I am going to tell you you won't believe. Henry Luce is interested in buying *Neurotica*.'

The publisher of *Time, Life* and *Fortune* interested in taking over *Neurotica*? It was too much to take over the phone.

'You're kidding.' I accused her of toying with my nerves.

'I kid you not,' she flatly answered. 'Henry has been wanting to publish a mass psychological magazine for years and guess what? He likes Legman's style. Didn't I tell you Legman was right for you? His piece on comics did the job.'

I replied, 'There's no doubt he's the most remarkable writer on the American scene, but he's too difficult to deal with.'

'Try having a love affair with him sometime. He's the most wonderful lover in the world.'

'Well, Beka, I divorced my wife, gave up the antique business, left my family, and moved to New York to work with him. If you don't call that a love affair, then what is it?' She laughed again, this time longer and louder.

I didn't hold my breath waiting to hear from Luce. In the meantime Marshall McLuhan sent in his piece on *The Psychopathology of Time and Life.* In his first paragraph, McLuhan hinted at Luce's interest in starting a fourth magazine, aimed to be a monthly for the literary gourmet, the intellectually indulgent, the well-read, the erudite, who sometimes preferred to smile superciliously rather than laugh outright. Did he know of Luce's interest in *Neurotica*? His article was a devastating attack that I would have published with unsuppressed joy, but I certainly wasn't going to print it if there was a chance that Luce was serious about buying *Neurotica*. Legman became suspicious the moment I mentioned that maybe we ought to save it for a future issue.

I was still counting on Luce's call to set something up. It came just in time. He had arranged for his henchman, Noel Busch, to meet me.

Busch's call was overly friendly, but there was no talk about buying *Neurotica* or about Luce. I assumed he was being cagey.

Legman turned pale as I told him Luce wanted to open negotiations, silently brooding over my 'treachery'. His fingers began to smooth the stray hairs of his walrus moustache. His mouth was in a locked position, as if he were a dog with rabies.

'You don't want to work with those people, Irving.' It was the first time he had ever called me by my real name. Was he trying to remind me that we were just a couple of Jewish boys in a fight against the *goyim*? 'They are the scum of the earth. They will crush us into little pieces before we even got around to working the first issue.'

'What's new? You've been trying to do that since we met.'

'Landesman, please, I'm your friend. You're too smart to fall for the bullshit that lackey Busch brought us. What scum! *Neurotica* is just beginning to have impact. The proof? What other magazine is so universally hated by the Establishment? Landesman, stick with me and I'll make you memorable.'

He hit a nerve. It was very clever of him not to come out with my real reason – wanting to work with Luce - but he suspected that it had something to do with wanting to be a success in Cutie's eyes.

'Your mother wouldn't want you to work with all those gentiles,' was his idea of a good joke. I gave a little laugh.

'Come on, let's be serious. With me you're going to end up a footnote in history. I promise you that.'

In one of those quick dramatic decisions that I was addicted to, I told him to go ahead and print the McLuhan piece. Legman was right: it was better to go down fighting than to sink without a mention in the history books.

Issue number five was banned. I had to pay a modest fine and everybody was happy except Legman. In my close association with him I learned to distrust experts, do-gooders, my former heroes, liberal tendencies, and success. I was going to need something very powerful to believe in if I were to survive.

A week later, New York rushed the season with a sunny spell of weather that had everyone gravitating toward the Washington Square fountain to get the first taste of the sun. I was there with Anatole Broyard, taking in the scene of Morris dancers, throbbing bongos and 12-string guitars entertaining the assorted audience in an impromptu amateur night variety show. A girl was sunning herself in the empty fountain not a yard away. I noticed her and Broyard said 'Hello' to her. 'This is Jay Irving Landesman, the editor of *Neurotica* and a very good mambo dancer.'

She suddenly flashed a smile that told me she might have been waiting to meet me all of her life. It was careless of me, I know, but I returned a smile that said the same thing. I delighted in her dirty fingernails, expensive blonde hair, beautiful teeth and perfect gum line. 'Don't think I'm crazy,' she said, 'but could we go to my place? My folks are away.'

She lived in The Kenilworth on Central Park West at 75th Street. We entered the apartment together but she went to the bathroom leaving me in a large room that smelled of beeswax. It reminded me of Landesman Galleries. I sat down in a Chippendale wing chair, facing windows that looked over Central Park. The light was just beginning to glow in the windows of Fifth Avenue. It looked so unreal, like a Hollywood version of a Manhattan skyline.

When she returned, she put her arm around my neck, kissing me lightly. 'When I was a kid I used to sit on the ledge of this window with my feet hanging over the side and look down at all the little figures below me. Sometimes I wanted to join them with the big leap. I often think about death – do you?' she said, in a lonely, lost voice. I hugged her like I never hugged anyone. Neither of us said a word. We kissed again, and I followed her into an almost bare room. The time between the foreplay and the post-coital cigarette had been well spent. She said she had a lot of things to do, so I split.

When I got home, I wrote a letter to Cutie:

Dear Cutie
Today I saw New York's fabulous skyline from a penthouse on Central

28

Park West. A pretty girl lives there who is as crazy as I am. I think I'm going to marry her. I miss you.
Love and kisses. Jay
PS What you wouldn't give to get your hands on some of the antiques that are in her house.

Four months later we were married. I decided the best thing to do was return to St Louis and go back into the business world. How could I break it to Fran? I knew she loved New York, but what was more important – making some kind of life together in the sticks or drifting apart in the Big Apple?

When I put it to her, she looked like someone who had just been handed a death sentence, with no appeal. I told her that if she didn't like it in St Louis she could always return to her mother and father. The thought of that knocked all the fight out of her and she accepted the inevitable.

Back in St Louis, my brother Fred talked of opening a nightclub. I didn't hear any more until a few months after the New Year when Fred asked me to look at a place that had just come on the market. 'It's the old queer bar, Dante's Inferno, on Olive Street. It's got such a reputation that it's going for a song.' He could never resist a bargain. The whole place was frozen the night it closed, looking like a painting by one of the Albright brothers – all that was missing was Dorian Gray.

Fred bought the place that afternoon. Out went all the Formica, in went the marble. Out went the neon lighting, in went the chandeliers. Fred used many of his favourite things, marvellous bits that he had saved for years, waiting for just such an occasion. He used drugstore chairs, doors of etched glass, elevator grills, marble busts, gold leaf pier mirrors, marble top tables from an old soda fountain, a pair of life-size brass monkeys; to top it all, behind the bar he put a mirror so seductive it made ugly people look handsome.

Hiring a bartender was a snap. The first person I interviewed had qualifications too good to ignore. He was Irish, big and looked like a young Charles Laughton. His background was impressive, but not necessarily helpful to a bartender. He had been an underground agent for the Anti-Defamation League, a part-time instructor of sociology at Washington University, a member of the local Fascist party and before that a Trotskyite political activist. The fact that he knew how to make cocktails was incidental.

'What kind of place is it going to be?' Jack O'Neil asked after we settled on the salary and working conditions. 'Queer, straight, posh or neurotic? Upper class, upper middle or lower upper?'

Anyone dropping into the Crystal Palace half an hour earlier than official opening time would not have believed it was going to open at all. Fred was still on a ladder adjusting the lights, workers were still painting, chairs were being dried under sun lamps. It all came together magically a few minutes before opening time.

You could sit next to anyone at the cocktail hour and never be bored with mindless conversation. Women were allowed at the bar, but it was known that O'Neil preferred to run a club for gentlemen preoccupied with the art of drinking and keeping him amused. All that O'Neil asked in return was that they share their victory or humiliation with him. Once his superiority over his customer was firmly established, O'Neil was free to engage in probing their weaknesses, but he was so charming his customers were flattered by his sadistic meddling.

The Crystal Palace was a stunning success. Couples came regularly, the way they might have gone to church in the old days, seeking absolution. They were people you always knew existed but had never found. If it is true that culture is only alive in a town that has a good bar, St Louis was heading for a renaissance.

Fran and I now had two children, Cosmo and Miles. By the time a man reaches the age of forty, his children can usually answer the question, 'What does your father do for a living?' Neither of mine could. Starting out with an identity problem in the forties, I had moved from antique dealer to publisher, editor, novelist, playwright, TV personality, entrepreneur, theatrical producer and urban renewal expert. When Cosmo's teacher asked the question, he answered, triumphantly, 'Bigshot!'

The crowds coming to the Crystal Palace had changed considerably: they wanted to be entertained. I was fighting against the tide by bringing original plays to an audience more interested in playing than plays. But I couldn't resist experimenting: that was what we originally created the new Crystal Palace for. Doing Mailer's *Deer Park*, Shaw's *Don Juan in Hell*, Ionesco's *The Chairs*, Beckett's *Krapp's Last Tape* and Brossard's quirky one-acters was simply more challenging and a lot of fun.

No one represented that change more than Lenny Bruce. There were those who said the Palace would die with his act and there were those who saw it as a courageous piece of booking. But I had seen him in a basement club in Chicago on his way up and knew he was a genius. It was a shock to my nervous system to pay three thousand dollars to Lenny Bruce in the days before he was famous, but I took a chance.

Bruce had played a lot of clubs on his way to the top, but he wasn't prepared for the Crystal Palace. 'This looks like a church that's gone bad,' he said. 'I've never worked in a church but I'll try not to let it inhibit me.' He didn't let his audience down. The dirtier he got, the better they responded.

The respect and recognition I got in the nightclub world led to my election as vice-president of an organization of nightclubs, formed to raise the standards of entertainment nationally. On visits to other clubs in New York I acted as if they were indeed my own club. Working a room, as it was called, was a fine art. These were valuable trips, a constant source of new talent and agents who were handling it. Irvin Arthur was the only agent I took seriously. He was always trying to get his favourite acts work.

'You've got to see this one, Jay. She's just your style, crazy and cheap, and I'll give you options when she's a star. Get her now while she's available. Her name is Barbra Streisand.'

'What an awful name,' I said. 'She'll never make it with a name like that.'

Arthur smiled, 'The name is nothing. You should see the nose! Ah, but when she sings, you forget the face. She sings the kind of stuff you like, obscure numbers nobody ever heard of. She'll even do your wife's songs. The kid can do anything.'

I was interested, but couldn't afford to show too much – his price would leap at any sign of acceptance. The eighteen-year-old singer with a nose and name problem hadn't worked since her appearance on the Paar Show, which wasn't a good sign.

'Trust me,' he pleaded. 'The kid's going to make it. How could you go wrong? Paar wants her back.'

The Smothers Brothers were the stars of the show. Inspired by them, Streisand began to do their sort of patter, but with a Fanny Brice accent that left something to be desired. I thought her heavy Jewish material detracted from the mood and delivery of the subtle songs that followed.

After a few nights of this, I called her into the office for a little fatherly advice.

'Why don't you do the show like on opening night? You can't improve on that performance. Everybody loved you. All your terrible jokes are ruining the effectiveness of your songs. My advice is to cut them out.'

'I get bored doing the same thing every night.'

'You've been in show business two weeks and you're bored already?' I found myself imitating her Brooklyn accent. I was beginning to like her.

'You think I'm funny when I talk in your living room,' she replied. 'I talk the same way on stage.' She started to get that petulant, deprived-kid-from-Brooklyn look.

'That's the trouble,' I told her. 'The stage is no place to be natural. It's a glamorous moment that shouldn't be tampered with.'

She moaned at my explanation. 'I want to do Shakespeare. I'm really an actress.'

Infuriated at her presumptuousness, I gave her a little innocent push that she made into a drama, falling over a couple of chairs and landing on the floor spreadeagled. She really was an actress.

Cutie, an acid critic of all my productions, wrote on the back of the programme of *Caught in the Act*: 'This got a wonderful reception. The house just vibrated with laughter and applause. I didn't like it. The young girl talked too much.'

It was one of those rare occasions on which I had to agree with Cutie.

I went back to producing the kind of shows that I knew something about – satirical revues on marriage, the family, careers, sex, politics and success. One of the most successful was *Stars of Tomorrow*, with the nervous, analytical Woody Allen; a shy, short, red-headed man with a pale green complexion almost obscured by his large horn- rimmed glasses. He was here to break in his act as a stand-up comic, but he had his doubts.

After each show, he would put in an emergency call to his New York psychoanalyst from the public phone on the wall between the men's and ladies' rooms. Anybody waiting to use the toilet would be treated to the intimate confessions of a patient to his analyst. Sometimes it was even funnier than the material he had done on stage. The laughs from the toilet queues encouraged him somewhat, but he would have preferred to be back on the couch instead of on the phone. 'For one thing, it's a lot cheaper than these long distance phone calls,' he explained to me.

On a really bad night, when he felt his performance had made the world forget about sunrise, he would call both his analyst and his girlfriend, begging either or both of them to come out to St Louis to save him from committing suicide on stage. I encouraged him to develop the suicide line in his act.

At the end of the first week he didn't want to accept his salary. 'No, Jay, I haven't earned it. I was lousy. Keep it. I'll try to do better next week, but I think I'm hopeless as a comic. Give the cheque to the Afro-Cuban band – they were a lot better.'

I insisted he take it if only to help defray his phone bill.

'I suppose you're right,' he said, pocketing the cheque. 'I'm ashamed of myself for being able to hold out against the phone company.'

It was obvious even to me that the Crystal Palace could no longer afford to experiment with serious theatre. If laughs were what they wanted, I would give them a season of controlled hysteria. The idea was sparked off by a phone call from Lenny Bruce asking for a date. It was a different Lenny from the cool, calculating $3,500-dollar-a-week, dope-free, mohair-suited cat who had played the Palace earlier. After his bust at the Gate of Horn in Chicago, where they arrested the club owner, there were very few offers for Bruce's controversial act.

He was willing to work for half his price. Rumours that he was pissing on the audience as part of his act didn't bother me; I was beginning to feel like pissing on them myself, without getting eighteen hundred a week for the privilege. My unconscious resentment at the way I'd been deserted left me feeling exactly like Lenny. He told me it meant a lot to him to get the date at the Palace; it meant a lot to me to have him back. Together, we might do something about straightening out the squares.

Picking him up at the airport this time, I nearly missed him. Instead of the mohair suit, he was dressed in a long, black, collarless jacket, looking like a young Nehru. On the drive back to my house, I got the Lenny Bruce version of constitutional law and briefings from the Supreme Court's last three decisions on the obscenity laws. Obviously, I was dealing with a lawyer who used to be a comic. My experiences in trying to fight the obscenity law with Legman were nothing compared to what Bruce was engaged in. His fight was a struggle to the death. With right on his side, he was sure to lose. Bruce seemed to have taken on some of the characteristics of Legman. He felt secure in victory because he had incontrovertible proof he was right. I didn't have the heart to tell him he was on a losing roll.

It was a new Lenny Bruce we were dealing with. On stage, his act was a strange mixture of constitutional law and some very dirty talk. He was still attracting large crowds, but of a different kind. Along with the die-hard Bruce fans, there were many in the audience who only knew of his reputation and wanted to see what all the fuss was about. They were straight sensation-seekers.

Bruce packed a lot of action into his two weeks. There was always a line of groupies who wanted to give him something to remember them by. Meanwhile, he and Fran had progressed from playing footsie under the family table to meeting down in the dressing room for something more intimate. One night, the fun turned sour when he gave her a shot of Dilauden right through her knitted skirt, straight into her ass.

About the only thing Lenny and I had in common was dancing. He would join one of the waitresses and me in the Twist room after his show, and the three of us would give exhibitions of the proper way to do the 'Madison' and other variations of the twist. Bruce was a natural dancer and we would both throw ourselves into the performance. People were used to seeing me dance, but the dancing Lenny Bruce was a sensation. It seemed to be the only thing that gave him any kicks during his engagement, yet the dark circles under his eyes were like bruises by the time he left us. His act had not gone over very well. His lectures on jurisprudence failed to captivate the audience and they left feeling cheated out of the real Lenny Bruce. There was no need for Fran to open up a sore point by asking him if he still felt that 'bread was the motivation for work'. But Bruce didn't mind. He understood Fran's 'I wanna be bad' role and played upon it every chance he had. He liked her distant look and once, from the stage, he said: 'Ah, the boss's wife is in the house tonight. I recognise that heavily sedated laugh.'

For all his crusading, Bruce was, underneath it all, an old fashioned Jewish puritan. When Fran occasionally let go of a 'fuck' or two, he'd disapprove. 'Don't use that kind of language. You sound as if you've been hanging out with hoodlums.'

It was a relief to follow Bruce with the cleanest act in show business – the Smothers Brothers. At least, that was the image everyone in America wanted to believe. Their gentile sibling rivalry was a tonic after the nasty alienation of all those Jewish New York comics. In real life, it was the Jewish comics who were chasing the shiksas and hitting the booze. With the Smothers, it was the opposite; they were the family men and more 'chicken soup' than the Jews. Their strong sense of family loyalty and rhythm fitted in perfectly with our little community. After a particularly long stretch on the road, living and working with faceless people, coming back to the Crystal Palace was like coming home. They felt a part of the Palace's success and took a great interest in the growth of Gaslight Square. They participated in all its functions, making friends with the other establishments' owners.

After twelve years of producing shows, I was creatively exhausted. Without the Palace, I didn't see any future for us in St Louis. I couldn't go back to the antique business with Cutie. I didn't want to be trapped in the real world. We began to think of places we could escape to. New York was a possibility; Fran was, by now, a recognised songwriting talent, collaborating with Alec Wilder, one of the most respected composers in the business. There was no doubt that she could promote her career if she lived in Manhattan. But what would I do? There wasn't a big demand for my talents. I revived the idea of us living in Connecticut, in the barn; Fran would work at her career, and I would become a country gentleman with no visible means of support. Fran didn't want to take the chance – her parents were still a hazard. Then I got a fantasy of going someplace exotic, like a Greek island, leaving the commercial world behind.

'All I want to do is watch the flowers grow.' I tried to make it sound romantic, but the idea of communing with nature gave Fran the horrors. 'I don't want to go any place where they don't speak English,' was the other demand she made.

When the newspapers heard we were going to London, they wrote it up as a news feature: 'Landesmans to London for talent tune-up'. A writer friend of ours, Martin Quigley, wrote an article about our leaving that presented a fairly different picture.

Now Jay and Fran Landesman are leaving town, and their going marks the end of an Era – the Era of The Crystal Palace and High Style. They are leaving with no boo-hoos, no bitterness, but with a little sadness and a touch of puzzlement. They are not leaving for a better

offer. They are leaving us to get away from us and take a look around
another town ... What are they worth to us? What did they cost that
we were not willing to pay? All of us, those who love them and those
who are saying good riddance, have been enriched by them. We become
a little more drab as we say goodbye.

'St Louis isn't a place. It isn't a city,' wrote Bob Miller, my co-pro-
ducer, to us many years later. 'St Louis is something that happens to
you once in a lifetime when you are just right for it and then it never
happens again.' I knew it was over. I would never return.

When it came to saying goodbye, Alfie dressed the children as if
they were going to another party. Fran and I had done nothing about
the house; we left it in Fred's hands to dispose of it and the contents
any way he saw fit. Saying goodbye to Cutie was going to be the hardest part of leaving.

'Well, old girl, you'll be happy to know that the psychiatrists have
given us a clean bill of health and we no longer need them.'

She looked at me with an expression of old-fashioned Jewish con-
tempt. 'So what did you learn from all those fancy doctors?'

The corners of her mouth twisted upwards, exposing her two
gold incisors.

'They told me that you loved me best of all the children.'

Her hand shot out, striking her forehead in the classic gesture of
frustration. 'Why didn't you ask me? I could have told you and saved
you all that money.'

I picked her up and waltzed her around the Galleries for the last
time.

'You're right, Cutie, but look at all the fun we would have
missed.'

2

I N February 1964 we set off for London. The only things we brought with us were all the wrong clothes, a trunk full of manu-scripts, and Peter Cook's phone number, given to us by poet Adrian Mitchell, the only Englishman we knew. Peter and his wife, Wendy, took us under their wing. They did everything within the bounds of decency to make us feel comfortable, but it was hard to function at their parties filled with famous overachievers of the Sixties. I must have met Kenneth Tynan half a dozen times in Peter's living room without exchanging a compound sentence. Fran did well with Annie Ross, who threatened to sing one of her songs one day. She did even better with Dudley Moore, who began to set some of her lyrics.

Peter was at the height of his popularity, enjoying it with a mod-esty and good humour that would have been unheard of in Ameri-ca. I warned him of the perils that lay ahead. 'Why should success change me?' he asked. 'I'll have the same wife and friends that I do now.' We wanted to believe him, but as he gained international rec-ognition we watched the cracks form in their once idyllic marriage. I told them that we were still married because neither of us had ever had a success that lasted more than fifteen seconds.

That summer I wrote a piece for the *Post-Dispatch* on the chang-ing scene in London. They liked it so much that I was made their Special Correspondent in London. It looked good on the cards I had printed; they gave us entry to every theatre and opening we cared to attend.

Only a few months were left on our lease and we couldn't find anything decent. Once again I put an advertisement in *The Times*: 'Shabby-chic lodgings required by American family...' Again a posh voice on the phone answered. 'My name is Tom Driberg. I have a lit-tle country place you might be interested in seeing.'

Bradwell Lodge, he told us, had once been the summer studio of Thomas Gainsborough. What might have been perfect for Gainsborough in the eighteenth century was too much for the Landesmans in the twentieth. Its glass-domed observatory overlooked a nuclear power station. One of its ceilings had been painted by Angelica Kauffman; the Adam brothers' handiwork was everywhere. With two frisky children and no help, keeping such a treasure trove from disintegrating would have been too big a responsibility for Fran. Reluctantly we turned it down.

On the way home Miles got car-sick, throwing up over Driberg. Far from being put off, Driberg invited us to join him the next week on a pub crawl on the Isle of Dogs. He took us to a pub whose clientele comprised lesbians, transvestites, ageing pederasts and amputees. Fran and I felt like the Odd Couple. 'This kind of place keeps me in touch with my constituents,' said Driberg. 'I'm Labour, you know.' He was the only Labour MP who sounded like Noël Coward and knew René Clair and Elsa Schiaparelli.

At a party in Guy de Roche's antique shop in Camden Passage, we met his friend Tony Flavell. Tony owned an empty house in Duncan Terrace, three doors away from us. A former industrial workshop, it was in such a distressed state that even gypsies would have turned it down. We were desperate, however, and took it when he said the rent would be £30 a month.

Neither Fran nor I had accomplished anything from a career viewpoint. So many people we had known and worked with had gone on to successful careers: Mike Nichols and Elaine May, the singer Will Holt, and Woody Allen. We began to wonder if we had any talent left to tune up. Fran's first chance came with an invitation from Ned Sherrin to discuss writing some topical lyrics for *Not So Much A Programme, More A Way Of Life* – the most talked-of television show since *That Was The Week That Was*. He turned out to be a secret fan, having heard her *Ballad of the Sad Young Men* in an H. M. Tennent revue, *On The Avenue*, some years previously. He had seen the show with Noël Coward, who had insisted on going backstage to congratulate the singer on 'doing justice to such a wonderful song'. Fran promised to rent a television set to watch his show. 'I hope you do,' he said. 'We're doing one of your songs from *The Nervous Set* this week.'

We began to think seriously about acquiring an agent. We asked around for the best, which led us to Peter Cook's agent, Peter Rawley. 'I'm a terrific lover,' he told Fran, 'but a lousy agent.' 'Oh, what a shame,' she said. 'I have a lousy lover – what I need is a terrific agent.' We compromised. Rawley became my agent, and Fran was lucky enough to get Peggy Ramsey.

We realised we weren't the only Americans over here trying to get their act together when we invited Lionel Stander to dinner. He was the gravel-voiced character in such 1930s films as *The Scoundrel*, *Mr Deeds Goes to Town*, and *A Star is Born*; later he became the lovable rogue in the television series *Hart to Hart*. His career in Hollywood ended when he was blacklisted in the Communist witch-hunts of the 1950s. He became a successful stockbroker, but eventually decided to go back into show business. He received rave reviews for his role in Brecht's *St Joan of the Stockyards* in London, but the show closed quickly and he'd done nothing since. Desperate, he asked me to ghost his autobiography to generate the cash to enable him to stay. Even though he had led an amazing life, my chance of getting an advance on someone not in the public eye was too slim.

When we heard that Fran's parents were coming for Christmas, we were prepared for the worst, but we needn't have been. Their present to us was an offer to finance the talent tune-up for another year, with the proviso that, if we didn't make it by then, we had to return to the States. On New Year's Eve we drank Israeli 'champagne', ate smoked salmon, and felt like a family for the first time since we'd left America.

The influx of Americans was changing the London scene. Many of them could be found playing baseball in Hyde Park on Sunday mornings. When an American puts on a uniform, even if it's only a baseball cap, he tends to take himself seriously. This was especially true when the players were Tony Curtis, John Cassavetes, Larry Gelbart, Marlon Brando and Charles Bronson, and the umpire was Phil Silvers. Once, when Silvers was called away, I was asked to replace him. Within ten minutes I'd made so many questionable calls and bad jokes I was asked to leave before I emptied Hyde Park.

Norman Mailer was in town promoting a new book. We went back to the mid-1950s, when he first became interested in hipsters and Beats, a piece of research that led to his famous essay on the White Hipster. Mailer confirmed that we'd left America just in time. 'Fucking has become a matter of status in America,' he told a contentious audience at the Mayfair Theatre. 'The civil rights movement will never solve anything. As long as people see themselves as a minority, there is no help for them. The matter will be decided by an increase in violence... Modern man is becoming schizophrenic, caught in a double bind, between the dream that the culture tries to sell him and the realities of life.' This was not what a predominantly leftish British audience expected from the spokesman of liberal culture.

At our party, he seemed to have cheered up. He had a nice word for everybody, including me. It was only when I became a publisher, years later, that he decided I was a devil. Yet, when I asked him for a cover blurb for *Rebel Without Applause*, he came up with a dandy: 'Jay and Fran Landesman could be accused of starting it all. By God, were they there at the beginning!'

Timothy Leary, another figure from our past, dropped in at Duncan Terrace, repaying a visit we had made to his Millbrook commune when we were trying to escape from St Louis. We had met him and Richard Alpert while they were on a speaking tour spreading the gospel of LSD. While at Millbrook, I took my first trip in their 'nose cone' – a room in the tower of their great Victorian house, specially equipped for space travelling. After hours of waiting, Leary could not account for my still being grounded. He claimed I was too 'transcendental' for LSD.

Leary was in town to touch base with R. D. Laing. 'He's very important,' he said. Arrangements were made to meet him at Kingsley Hall in the East End. At lunch with Laing's extended family of schizophrenics and staff, it was difficult for me to distinguish the one group from the other. It was when we saw the 'hopeless' cases lying uncommunicative in rooms of indescribable squalor that I realized why Leary was anxious to meet Laing. Leary thought LSD might be useful in their treatment.

Laing always seemed so unhappy when he was serious. There was another side to him that I came to know and love: Laing at home, in front of a piano, with a glass of Scotch and a joint, playing Cole Porter, Gershwin and Rodgers and Hart. If he hadn't become a doctor, he could have made a living as a jazz pianist. During his last few years, when his fame was tarnished and he was no longer practising, he acquired a new wife and new baby, gave up drink and pot, and went to live in a new country, enjoying his anonymity.

I was subjected to a tarot reading by Hanja Kochansky, who was a greater friend of Laing's than I. She was very disturbed when the Death card came up. 'It's not your card,' she said. 'Something strange is happening here.' Five minutes later the phone rang. It was Laing's ex-wife, Jutta, with the news that Ronnie had just died on a tennis court in France.

We started to see a lot of Hanja and her husband Hugh, a couple who couldn't help our careers, but who knew where the action was. The Pickwick Club in Great Newport Street was the first port of call. There, one evening, I was entertaining the American agent Irvin Arthur, while Princess Margaret and Lord Snowdon were having dinner at a table by the bar. I mentioned that Lord Snowdon looked bored, and threatened to go and cheer him up. I wove my way to the bar, ordered a drink, caught his eye and said, 'I liked your aviary.' At the time, his structure in Regent's Park was a controversial postmodern design with few defenders. He seemed quite pleased, and invited me to join their table. For ten minutes I talked aviary aesthetics with an expertise I'd never suspected I had. Words like 'organic', 'revolutionary', 'environmental compatibility' and 'spatial configurations' cascaded from my lips.

I hadn't been back at my table ten minutes before Angelo came over. 'His Lordship would like you to return to his table,' he announced. I went, but His Lordship's interest waned as I tried to tell him the story of my life, even though it was the *Reader's Digest* version.

Next door to the Pickwick was the Kismet, an afternoon drinking club which was host to a collection of Soho writers, artists, punters and former Rank starlets, whose past was their only recommendation. Jeffrey Bernard told of a stranger entering for the first time and asking, 'What's that smell?' Without looking up from his glass, actor John Bey shouted, 'Failure.'

But not everyone at the Kismet was a loser. On a good day there would be Marty Feldman, Peter Finch, Alan Lake and Sean Lynch; writers Frank Norman, James Deakin and Dan Farson; artist Francis Bacon, dancer Sue Bardolph, and Rank starlet Susan Shaw. Hugh Bebb introduced me to Christine Keeler. She was still attractive and vivacious, but suspicious of people, particularly 'curiosity seekers', whose stupid questions she parried with the skill of a seasoned street fighter. She became a friend whose presence lent a *soupçon* of mystery to our parties.

The Dublin Theatre Festival decided that they wanted to do *Dearest Dracula*. We had almost forgotten they had the manuscript. They offered $10,000 towards its production; I was required to raise the rest. A letter to fifty close friends and former business associates in St Louis brought thirty-nine cheques within two weeks. The show, which had been conceived above a garage in St Louis and rehearsed above a pub in Islington, duly arrived at Dublin's Olympia Theatre. On opening night it received a seven-minute standing ovation. The Irish critics were enthusiastic – one went over the top with superlatives: 'A production which, for visual attack, stagecraft and all-round excellence of singing, acting and dancing, surpasses anything I have seen in Dublin in the field of musical comedy.' The English critics nailed Dracula through the heart with a stake.

Then Busby Berkeley came to London to give a talk at the National Film Theatre, chaired by Philip Jenkinson. Berkeley had been one of the heroes of my youth. I made arrangements to interview him for another of my dispatches to the home front. He turned out to be a very uncomplex person; I could see that all the attention was making him restless. It occurred to me that he might like to work again. I told him about Dracula and his eyes lit up. It seemed a great idea to bring Berkeley back to Broadway with a dancing chorus of vampires.

I wrote to ask whether he would work with me on the revisions, adding, 'How would you like to stage and direct the show?' I received his reply almost immediately: 'So far, I think your suggestions well taken. I like the therapy idea – the mad doctor and the mad patient. It also might be well to lose the romance between Seward and Lucy … I like you personally, Jay, and I instinctively believe you have a potential property that can be developed into a most unusual and exciting hit!'

There was no doubt Buzz was serious, especially about 'front money', which I did not have, nor could I raise it without a commitment from Vincent Price or interest from a legitimate Broadway producer. When George Hamilton played a prancing Dracula in the hit film *Love at First Bite,* I thought of how close I had come to fulfilling two of my favourite fantasies – pumping life into something that was already dead, and working with Busby Berkeley.

1966 started out with an invitation from the Cooks to dinner with Paul McCartney. We couldn't understand why they would ask us. Pop singer turned actor Paul Jones gave us the answer: 'You two are closer to being 'niggers' than anyone they know in London.' The invitation caused a flutter around the house. Even Cosmo was impressed.

To show Paul we weren't your ordinary, middle-aged beatniks, Wendy showed him the original cast album of *The Nervous Set.* Studying Jules Feiffer's caricature on the cover, Paul groped for words. 'That's – ah – a nice drawing,' he said, handing it back to Wendy.

Word had evidently got around Hampstead that a Beatle had been caught. Before we finished the first course, the fans had caused an obstruction, like pre-French-Revolution peasants beating on the windows of the rich. The only difference was that this mob was demanding autographs.

We moved on to a disco in St James's Place. Nobody came to the table there for his autograph, Peter Cook's, or even mine. Paul and Fran began to build a pyramid of glasses while talking about the songwriting game. He confided to her that he and John Lennon wanted to write the kind of songs Bob Dylan wrote, but that their record company was being difficult. He whispered her the lines of a song he was working on, about a girl named Eleanor Rigby. The pyramid came crashing to the ground. A waiter rushed over, took a look at the wreckage, bowed, and said, 'That's quite all right, Mr McCartney. Would you like another drink?'

At closing time, we went out to our cars. It's hard to believe that a Beatle could be lonesome, but what other reason was there for Paul to ask, 'Where to now, Jay?' When I said, 'I don't know about you, but I'm going home,' Fran gave me a kick that could have seriously damaged my manhood.

Next time, when John and Cynthia Lennon were the Cooks' guests, Wendy didn't supply a background for us, which must have left Lennon with the impression that we were a couple of house guests who had to be invited. The dinner was not a relaxed affair. He was uptight about Wendy's insistence that he sample her *salade niçoise*. Christopher Logue irritated him even more by asking why the Beatles wouldn't play a *Private Eye* benefit. There was no way I could get to know him, but my heart went out to Cynthia.

'Making it' had become less important to me than it was to Fran. Success was something I only wanted a taste of, not the whole cake. 'Let's give it another try,' said Fran. 'Once we've had it, we can put it down with authority.'

In April 1966, Fran's father died. For the first time since we left the States we were financially secure, temporarily. I continued to write the occasional article of 'lasting insignificance' for my paper; the fire of the original copy had died down by now. When the

Art Destructionists invaded London for three days, your reporter watched then blowing up empty buildings, throwing acid on canvases, burning towers of books and crushing automobiles. The police charged Otto Metzger, one of the organizers, with 'offences against society'.

Artist Ralph Ortiz asked me, 'Like, man, do you have a piano around the house I could wreck?' We did have the piano on which the music to *Dearest Dracula* had been written. His mouth watered. 'Let's have a party and invite a couple of curators from the Tate.' With the help of Miles's mates, we got the piano halfway down the steps to the basement, where we had planned to stage the event. It wouldn't budge. We had to carry on with it wedged where it was.

Two gay curators arrived, clearly not expecting to be greeted by a handsome Puerto Rican American with an axe, an infectious smile, and a printed statement on the New Aesthetic. Ortiz stripped to the waist and began his descent into 'benevolent violence': 'Each axe swing unmakes this made thing called a piano. Each destruction unmakes any made relationships to it. It is no longer for playing; it is no longer beautifully designed or ugly…' Ortiz called his masterpiece *Piano Destruction Concert Number 8* and left his phone number with the awed Tate curators.

The next day, for an encore, he disembowelled a large mattress. It ended up looking like a monstrous horsehair vagina. 'Big Alice' hung over the hearth until Victor Lownes sent his art expert, Barry Miller, for a serious appraisal. The price was fixed at £500. I balked at letting him try it out on approval, but said that, if he gave me a £50 administration fee and drayage, I'd make an exception. The idea of 'Big Alice' becoming a part of the Playboy collection of erotic artefacts appealed to my sense of history.

Word came through that the Bunnies couldn't stand the competition and had asked Victor to 'shift it'. Charlie Kasher wanted to buy it, if the Tate would accept it, but it was rejected on the grounds that it might become a health hazard. I found a place for 'Big Alice' in the garden.

Swinging London was turning into Raving London. In the King's Road, it seemed that everybody was in uniform, auditioning for *The Chocolate Soldier*. Was this a nostalgia for the days of imperial glory? Interviewing a cherub-faced teeny-bopper, I was taken aback by her directness. I asked what was bugging her. 'Old folks. I'm under tension from old folks.' It was right after this interview that I bought my first pair of plastic leather trousers. I knew I had made the right decision when I wore them to meet BBC producer Julian Holland at El Vino in Fleet Street and was refused service. I was forty-seven years old but slipping back to childhood fast.

Cosmo's terror became obvious. We were proving to be an embarrassment. So sensitive was he to our behaviour that, when asked about his parents, he'd say they 'died in a plane crash'. Years later he wrote about our decline and fall in the *Literary Review*: 'The thing that upset me most was their dress and appearance. I can remember when I first thought of having them committed to the Institute for the Criminally Dressed. It was Parents' Day at school. They arrived looking like two hippies who had failed the audition for the musical *Hair*... Dad came with his long hair, mirror-lens sunglasses; the *pièce de résistance* of this visual cacophony was not the orange rudiments of a shirt, but the black plastic trousers. In those days the only people who wore them were industrial workers and the insane.'

Miles felt differently about us; he didn't mind our getting down to his age level. When he brought one of his mates home to find Fran in a bikini getting some sun, his friend told him, 'Your Mum doesn't look like a Mum. She looks like a gorgeous bird.'

Being without a project, I was open to suggestions. An American stockbroker contacted me, saying that he was starting a disco in Covent Garden based on the Underground formula of mixed media, 'only this one is going to be for grown-ups'. A quick estimate of what the Electric Garden must have cost staggered the imagination; I could see it was already dated before it was finished. I told him he should go for something that nobody else was offering. Talking to many artists who had taken part in the Art Destructionists symposium, I discovered that they were real hams whose need to perform was their motivating force. Why not take their act out of the galleries and streets into this kind of environment? Both the artists and the stockbroker agreed. The idea even appealed to me. The pay – £200 a week for the Artistic Director – was also attractive. I charged forward with annihilating press releases:

> *The Electric Garden announces a series of summer environmental entertainments on Sunday nights... Warp-In-Rites will probe areas of contemporary tensions... Rope (a study in bondage); Coloured Tape (interlocking envy problems)... Drag-It-On-Home-Baby (a psychedelic drag show); Books (a physical fitness programme for diary devotees) and Concert (visual trickery incorporating non-musical instruments).*

At Yoko Ono's debut, she sat on the platform, bound in surgical gauze, and invited people to cut little pieces off it in an attempt at 'mass communication'. Yoko made love noises for about five minutes and then screamed for another five. Most of the audience were fascinated, but some weren't. When they began to hurl abuse her way, the managers lost their cool – they demanded I stop Yoko's act. I refused. She continued to scream as the guests took sides, creating a scene out of *Metropolis*.

The electrician killed her microphone. The DJ cut in with loud music. I encouraged Yoko to continue screaming. Her husband, Tony Cox, rushed to the tape deck to cut the music. He was grabbed by the manager and bouncers, dragged to a corner and thrown on the floor, and was about to be pummelled when I arrived. I told Cox to announce to the audience what had happened. 'This club is run by gangsters,' he hollered into the mike. 'Will somebody call the fuzz.'

The audience lapped it up, thinking it was all part of the show. Yoko was still screaming, helpless in her bondage. Order was restored when she stopped. At midnight the police arrived. Tony and the manager were having a shouting match; I tried to cool the scene. Yoko's and Tony's demands for money were refused. They left.

When I confronted the owner and manager, I was fired. By 2 a.m., after a serious discussion about the future of the club, I was reinstated with complete control over artistic matters. I called Tony and Yoko, and promised to drop by with some grass to soothe their hurt nerves.

The lights went out on the Electric Garden soon after. Reconnected as Middle-Earth, without the art and the stockbroker but with a new Artistic Director, it became the new headquarters of the Underground and a big success. So far my record was one hundred per cent *projectus interruptus.*

Fran had to go to New York to be with her ill mother. It was the first time we'd been apart since our arrival in London. To our surprise, being apart gave us the opportunity to say things in letters we couldn't possibly say in person: 'I'm so homesick I can't bear it,' she wrote. 'Jay-sick really, you lovely person. Please let's try to meet each other when I'm home. It's the only real thing, at least you are for me.'

When she returned, we took advantage of the Summer of Love: picnics on Hampstead Heath, swimming in the Serpentine, flying kites on Primrose Hill with Yoko Ono and her sad-faced little girl. We travelled around to pop concerts in a customised Mini Cooper that had once belonged to the Rolling Stones' manager, Andrew Oldham. These idyllic times came to an abrupt halt after a weekend of torrential rain that seeped into our tent. 'I am now old enough never to have to go to another fucking outdoor pop concert,' Fran declared vehemently.

Often, in a volatile marriage, when one partner is up, the other is down. I had nothing to be up about. Fran had. Her collaboration with Georgie Fame resulted in *Try My World*, a single record that got the full treatment – *Top of the Pops* and *Juke Box Jury*. It sank without trace, but the collaboration survived to rise again another day.

I was invited to dinner by Cambridge lecturer Nathan Silver, author of Fran's favourite book, *Lost New York*. I expected a roomful of musty dons drinking sherry, but it was a small affair, with only phi-losopher George Steiner and poet John Hollander, their wives, and us. I was apprehensive at meeting Steiner, whose books I had bought to lend some class to my bookshelves; I even read some of them. 'Ah, Landesman,' Steiner said. 'The editor of *Neurotica*. I remember your magazine well.'

At another of Silver's events I met someone as provocative as Steiner and clearly marked for a brilliant future as an academic stand-up comic. Germaine Greer arrived late, drenched from the rain, and proceeded to strip off her wet blouse – she had obviously burned her bra. Even the women present recognized the chutzpah she was later to make her trademark. She was beautiful, she was funny, she was smart, and she knew it. After *The Female Eunuch*, the world knew it too.

One night, in the Speakeasy, I watched her challenge Jimi Hen-drix to an arm-wrestling match, and win. She was the champ, or so we thought, until we received a mayday call from her. 'May I spend the night at your place? I'm fed up with my lover. Never want to see him again.' After dinner she became restless, explaining that she was worried about his state of mind, since he'd been tripping when she left him. Would it be all right if she called him? Once connected, the Boadicea of the women's movement turned into a coy, baby-voiced little girl, offering to return if he was unwell. When she left, it was the first indication that the 'movement' was one thing, and needing a man was something else.

It seemed that Fran and I were doing what everybody else was doing by the end of the decade – non-stop partying. Our parties were mostly impromptu, but, when friends from America were in town, special rituals had to be observed. Barbra Streisand and Tom-my Smothers of the Smothers Brothers were in London at the same time. As young unknowns, they had played the Crystal Palace on the same bill. We used to hang out together after the show and talk about our futures. Tommy said he and Dickie couldn't believe they were going to be stars. Barbra had no doubt she was going to be one.

During the hot summer days, Fran and Barbra used to catch the Olive Street trolley and go shopping in the air-conditioned stores downtown. They would try on everything, but buy nothing. Both of them were dressed by Goodwill and Salvation Army charity stores; *Second Hand Rose* might have been written about them.

Now Barbra was in London to repeat her Broadway success in *Funny Girl*. She told us she wasn't going to do the show that night as she was feeling ill from her pregnancy. She accepted the invitation to our party, but on one condition. 'You've got to feed me,' she cried. 'Will there be any food left by the time I get there?' What worried me more was how all of us would react to a reunion after so many years. Last time, we had been the big shots and they the struggling artists.

We needn't have worried; the four of us picked up right where we'd left off in St Louis. Barbra arrived in a Daimler with her hairdresser and a ferocious appetite. She couldn't be expected to notice Weston Gavin's late entrance, but she heard his opening line: 'Okay, who's the Batmobile waiting for? Speak up, don't be bashful. We're little people here.' Barbra looked up from her food mountain. 'Who the fuck do you think it's waiting for?'

I found myself on a bus to Stonehenge with a group of people who were celebrating the summer solstice. On the bus were a few familiar faces, but one stood out from the rest – Jordon Reynolds. I knew him from the Underground days when he was a bouncer at UFO. 'You are what you eat,' read his T-shirt. He saw himself as a member of the Brigade of the Betrayed, an organization devoted to lost causes. 'After all the worthwhile wars are lost, you either become a religious nut or a nutritional expert. In my diet, you get to be both,' he claimed.

It was the first time I had heard the word 'macrobiotic'. Jordon kept up a steady spiel: 'The average person consumes ten times more protein than his body requires ... food manufacturers know the poor are suckers for their processed, heavily chemicalized, carcinogenic, highly sweetened food... they are engaged in genocidal devastation.'

Jordon and I got high at the sight of Stonehenge. Sitting among the stones, instead of looking at them from a distance as is required now, gave a sense of being 'at one with the universe'. We walked round in a giant circle, holding hands, waiting for what the Master Druid called 'the Great White Light'. When it was rather slow in coming, he asked us to go into reverse, an idea that struck us as hilarious.

I saw a lot of Jordon. He had pamphlets carefully placed around 'Rice House', as his squat was called. Take the one on tobacco: 'Smoking isn't the only cure for cancer.' Another on milk warned of its dangers unless, of course, you were a calf. The founder of macrobiotics, I was told, was a middle-class Japanese who spent a lifetime experimenting with oriental herbs to find a drink as satisfying as Scotch whisky. Jordon made light of the fact that he died of heart disease 'caused by extreme frustration and too much alcohol'.

I came from St Louis, a city that won the Quasimodo award for having the highest strontium-90 count in its milk, and the hottest chilli this side of Mexico. This all changed dramatically under the influence of Jordon Reynolds. At a smart meat-eater lunch at Alvaros, I stared at my steak tartare; it looked like it was daring me to make a move. The raw meat had metamorphosed into a fragment of a Hieronymus Bosch triptych – the part that can't be looked at without killing your appetite for the human race.

Fran watched the new convert throw away everything in the kitchen except the sink. Within twenty-four hours, restocked with traditional oriental and natural foods, it looked like a corner of a budding sushi bar. Fran was prepared for change, but the children were not. I insisted on preparing their lunches: a Thermos of hot miso soup, two lovingly hand-wrapped seaweed rice balls, tahini brown bread sandwiches with white pickled radish, and chopsticks wrapped in a damp napkin. Stories drifted back after the first few days: horror stories of brown rice balls being chucked around by junk-food louts. Cosmo accused me of culinary sadism.

Carried away with my new philosophy, I became a cog in a miniature macrobiotic empire started by the teenage entrepreneurs

Gregory and Craig Sams, fellow Americans. They started with a restaurant, progressed to a natural food store, and eventually ran a wholesale distribution company. Natural foods were almost unheard of in those days. I started as a waiter, rising to salesman and public relations expert. I felt a deep sense of accomplishment when I sold a cover story to *Fiesta* on the sexual advantages of the diet.

Fran's apple strudel won the coveted trophy of rosewood chopsticks in the first International Macrobiotic Bake-Off contest. John Pilger, with tongue firmly in cheek, produced a full-page analysis of the event in the *Daily Mirror*. I invited Lesley Garner of the *Sunday Times* to dinner, which resulted in a feature on our new role as the 'ideal macro family'. The accompanying photo of the smiling children at dinner, watched over by doting parents, was photo-journalism at its most creative.

Friends brave enough to accept an invitation to dinner stayed for the miso soup, but left before the lectures. Others gave up on us entirely. By now, I didn't give a damn. All my abortive projects had left me feeling I had to find God, or a substitute. Finding God would have finished me off; a diet I could handle. There were many who said I would have been better off with God. My sister was one of them. She sent me an article with the caption 'This Diet Can Kill'. It was written by an MD who was chairman of the Department of Nutrition at Harvard. To us knowing and dedicated macros, it was nothing more than propaganda subsidized by the food industry.

When we decided to take a holiday in the Dordogne, I loaded the boot of our vintage Mercedes with macrobiotic food and utensils, plus a camp stove. Our first destination was to visit my old adversary G. Legman, who lived above Nice. He still hadn't forgiven me for 'maligning' him in *The Nervous Set*. 'Did you have to make me look like a fag?' he growled. When we said we were macrobiotic, he turned nasty. 'I know about that diet. It's a crock of shit,' he hollered, and refused to let me use his stove. I cooked the rice on the camp stove, and brought it proudly to the table.

The next morning I told Fran to round up the children: we were leaving. 'What a shame that a one-time giant could become so small,' I said. The last thing we saw was a furious Legman running after the car, shaking his fist and shouting, 'Landesman, you can't run away like this. You haven't washed the dishes!'

The walled city of Carcassonne offered some temporary relief, but Fran bought a choc-ice, which was a no-no in the diet. A sense of betrayal swept over me. Fran couldn't believe anyone would be silly enough to name a choc-ice as co-respondent in a divorce, which I mentioned was a possibility.

With the arrival of the Boston Macros, London became a battle-ground – the beginning of the Great Macro Wars. They accused the Sams brothers and London's macros of 'dietary revisionism', a crime worse than the Western diet. To undermine the Sams' influence, they used every trick in the trade, including sexual entrapment. They brought with them a supremely organized chef, a woman whose main talent was renowned throughout Boston: she could get to the heart of Macro Man through her superb rice balls.

Her first target was Gregory Sams. We watched horror-stricken as she cooked delicious meals that went straight to his heart. They fell in love. For an engagement present he gave her the restaurant. The funky atmosphere that had made it so popular disappeared. Another blow came when the cultural commissars tried to impose their pronunciation of *yin* and *yang*. The Third Rice Fascists had won the war, but they were on the point of losing the Landesmans, their most dedicated soldiers.

Our friends from America, Jackie Caine and Roy Kral, and their teenage daughter Dana, moved in during their gig at Ronnie Scott's. Jackie and Roy had been the first to record Landesman/Woolf songs in the early Fifties. Their version of 'Spring Can Really Hang You Up The Most' still stands as a classic. They were Fran's most loyal boosters and they proved it again one night at Ronnie's when they introduced her to Michel Legrand, a devoted fan of theirs. Roy did everything to recommend Fran as a lyricist, short of giving Legrand her social security number.

Dana introduced us to Jason Holliday, a black, middle-aged homosexual from New York who was here for the showing of Shirley Clarke's film about him, *Portrait of Jason*. Clarke's film had given him cult status in New York, and about fifteen minutes' attention in London. We sat up for hours, night after night, entertained by his tales. I decided that the King's Head Theatre Club needed a 'Sunday Night with Jason Holliday', and that Jason needed was to show the world what he could do on his own. It was my pleasure to present him in a two-hour, one-man show. Nobody wanted the evening to end, especially me; I invited the whole audience back to our house for a party.

Jason played the room like the star he was. As the evening progressed, he grew carelessly affectionate and slipped his hand over the ass of one of the pub crowd, a gesture that turned the man hostile. Jason, ever streetwise, fled trembling to the basement for sanctuary as the victim and his buddies went on about the 'fooking fag'.

Time Out writer Jerome Burne tried to lower the temperature. 'In these days, young man, may I suggest to you that a hand on one's ass is not the most awful thing that can happen.' The Irishman thought otherwise. His punch sent Jerome's granny glasses flying. Within seconds the house looked like a scene from a John Wayne bar-room fight.

Jason's exit from London could have been conceived by film director Preston Sturges. All his fans, including children and babies, escorted him to the train to bid him farewell. As he stood on the train's steps waving goodbye, he began to sing the opening line of the hit song from his show: 'I'm the most happy fellow on the road to Portobello'. The train didn't move. Another take was called for. He kept singing and waving. The platform guard signalled again. He broke into song again. The crowd surged around him. By now it had been swollen by strangers eager to see what was going on. The signal came once again and the train slowly moved out of the station, the crowd running alongside, shouting goodbyes and promises to write.

Whether it was the boys' diet or just an adolescent phase, their behaviour became a cause for concern. Miles became an expert at bunking off from school. One of his teachers, who liked him, told us he used the school as if it were his club, 'dropping in occasionally to see if anything was happening'. Cosmo began to read Dostoyevsky, Beckett and Kafka, and to associate with Kentish Town toffs; his future as a Romantic Depressive was assured. Miles chose his friends from the council flats of Islington, which guaranteed him a future in minor crime. It didn't take a genius to realize we were a family heading for trouble.

I made an appointment with the local child guidance clinic to stop the rot. After two sessions with us as a family, they declared that Miles and Cosmo were OK, but that they'd like to see more of us. 'I love to talk about myself, but I thought this was a child guidance clinic,' Fran said. 'It was,' Robin Skynner said, 'until we met you two!' He obviously had a sense of humour even before he started his collaboration with John Cleese on their book *Families and How To Survive Them*.

We savoured the final words of Skynner and his associate: 'You're Hansel and Gretel walking into the woods, holding hands like children. You refuse to grow up.' It was the best news we'd had in ages.

After the therapy, we sank back into our hedonistic ways. I received an invitation from Jim Haynes to join a 'distinguished' group of people as a juror at the Wet Dream Festival in Amsterdam. As far as I know, it was the only festival in the world that demanded a nude photograph of each jury member.

It featured hard and soft core films, performing artists, parties, workshops, seminars and orgies. On its last night, Otto Muhl's commune of sexual revolutionaries took the stage. Their frenzied naked dancing and lewd gestures to the excruciatingly loud music of the Rolling Stones set the tone for what was to come. Muhl sat in a corner of the stage stroking a goose. Two women on their hands and knees were centre stage, each with one end of a rolling-pin up her anus. Then Muhl decided to kill the goose. Heathcote Williams rushed to the stage, grabbed the goose from Muhl, and tossed it to writer Anthony Haden-Guest, who fled the hall holding the goose above his head like the cup in a football ceremony.

The audience cheered; Muhl and his comrades had a tantrum. They shook their fists at the audience. Finally, to show their dedication to art, they crapped on the stage and made their exit.

Jim Haynes' London Arts Lab, a multi-media gallery, restaurant, bookshop and theatre, had developed into a small-scale version of the Wet Dream Festival. No matter what play was on in the theatre, it was always a full house, thanks to Jim's idea, for a while, of not putting seats in the theatre – you bought a ticket and carried in an empty beer crate for your seat. The floor of the cinema was covered in foam mattresses. If the soft porn film got boring, there was always the odd couple around to provide a live show. 'The only thing I remember about the Arts Lab cinema was the smell of dirty feet,' said one disgruntled patron.

We were there one night when Jim invited us to his private quarters, a platform approached by a rope-ladder. 'I have someone very special I want you to meet,' Jim said. On his bed was Ken Kesey, reading a comic book. We had never met him, although we had a lot of friends in common. 'Landesman... early Beats... *Neurotica*... New York ... Fifties,' Kesey said, extending a warm hand of recognition.

Kesey's practice of experimenting with drugs was no secret (read *One Flew Over The Cuckoo's Nest*). The lack of them reduced him to desperate attempts to find a substitute. He would grind up some of Fran's diet pills for a fix. If that didn't work, he'd go on to shoot up Robert Stone's gout medicine. A final assault with aspirin was a low as he went. His saving grace was that he laughed at his foolish antics.

We went down to Stonehenge with Kesey to scout the scene for a documentary he wanted to make, a sort of *Hell's Angels Meet the Druids*.

When he discovered the place was fenced in, he flipped. 'It's an outrage, man. Stonehenge is the heaviest place I know. It's a temple, man, a temple of the world.' The other cradle of civilization for Kesey was Apple. 'Every day I thank God for the Beatles. They wanted me to make 'paperback records' of my London experiences, but Apple collapsed before I got a chance to start.' Kesey was so disappointed that he liberated a professional tape recorder.

While in America I had stopped off in St Louis to see Cutie. She had recently recovered from being mugged by a gang of small boys, but was in hospital for other complications. Her health had deteriorated rapidly. I had always remembered Cutie as full of life and it was sad to see her lying so helpless. I don't suppose I had cried since I was a child; the boy in me welled up uncontrollably and I bawled like a baby. A passing nurse put her arm around me, and I wanted to tell her how much I loved Cutie and how much I missed her. I wanted to tell Cutie how I had settled down, as she would have liked me to do, and how happy the children and Fran were in London. She wouldn't have believed me.

Cutie rarely looked on the bright side. I brought Miles into the room to cheer her up, this being Miles' speciality, but Cutie refused to be comforted. She looked at him with a frown, then turned to me. 'His teeth need fixing,' she said bitterly.

Neither Fran nor I was interested in politics, but I couldn't resist getting involved when Norman Mailer decided to run for Mayor of New York on the battle cry of 'Vote The Rascals In'. He had many friends in London who felt the same way. A Friends of Mailer Committee was formed by a high-profile, eccentric hustler named Harvey Matusow. One of his ventures was a fund-raising auction. I tried to contribute a few items that might bring in some money, but Christine Keeler's bra was the best I could do.

I had obtained the services of Bill Mitchell, King of the Voice-overs.

Dangling the slightly soiled bra delicately before his audience, Mitchell opened the bidding with a request for £100. There was a gasp from the audience, which included me. I knew it was going to be painful to watch him adjust the price downwards. 'Do I hear fifty?' he asked. The silence indicated no. 'Ten?' he asked. 'Come on, we're dealing in a psychosexually historical area here in a never-to-be-repeated offer.' More silence. Desperate measures were called for. Somebody in the back bid ten shillings. I raised my hand, just to keep the bidding going, but it didn't do any good. Mitchell was forced to knock down the bra to, as he said, 'the connoisseur' in the front row, namely me.

Years later, my friend Hanja confessed it wasn't Christine's bra, but one of her own. 'Christine doesn't wear a bra,' she said sheepishly, 'but I thought the deception was justified for a good cause.'

Into our lives came the American cellist Charlotte Moorman and her partner, Nam June Paik. They looked like the usual mismatched, attractive, urban couple, but their act was from Mars. Charlotte was famous for her annual parade of *avant-garde* happenings in New York. Paik was an electronic genius, who had designed the world's first television bra – a marvel of engineering – especially for Charlotte. It featured two miniature television sets projecting from already ample breasts which could present *News at Ten* and a BBC documentary simultaneously.

A dress rehearsal was held in our living-room to a very mixed reaction from the Landesman family. Miles's tongue was hanging out; Cosmo's scepticism was showing. Fran and I worried about the fuses blowing. One of the sets short-circuited while strapped to Charlotte's breasts. However, her performance in London went off without a hitch. The caption to the *Daily Mirror*'s picture was 'A Girl with Two Points of View'.

One night we came home to find Charlotte had left the television bra in the living-room. I suggested to Fran that she slip into something uncomfortable. 'It might save the marriage,' I said. I got a cold reception. I slipped it on and turned the knobs, but I couldn't get a clear picture.

My affair with the *avant-garde* covers many gruelling years, so I should have been prepared for Charlotte's *pièce de résistance* at the Roundhouse. Bare-breasted, she performed an entire Saint-Saëns concerto on a cello made of ice, with a glass bow, until the ice melted.

At the end, she rushed backstage in a panic – an asbestos pad had slipped. 'Is there a doctor in the house?' she cried. 'I think my left tit is frost-bitten.'

We began seriously to look around for another place to settle. England was sliding into economic disaster. Friends were leaving London for Paris and points east. Then the opportunity to buy a vintage Art Deco bus for peanuts came up. Turning the bus into a mobile Hilton, with chemical toilet, fitted kitchen, refrigeration, a dynamic sound system and generous sleeping arrangements, we were ready for any contingency. Its main attraction was that Fran's bed-life was uninterrupted. The bus had large windows in the sides of the roof, enabling her to see the sunset lying on her back.

We set our sights on France. We had been there a number of times, always regretting our inability to master the language for the full flavour of the country. The time had come for us to go back to school.

We jumped in at the deep end, signing up for a term at the Lycée Français even though it was on the other side of town, in South Kensington. We needed the discipline of a classroom and a stern teacher.

The trip across town would have been a drag had we not travelled on our bus. We must have looked like two delinquent schoolkids on their way to a picnic. Overtaking cars honked and waved their approval.

Our class was small enough for us to receive the kind of special attention required by two genetically handicapped pupils. Fran never learned how to link up letters in her progressive school, and I was hopeless at everything except geography. The only thing that made us think we had a chance was our dedication. The teacher was impressed with Fran's explanation of why we were late one day: 'Le chien a mangé mon mari,' she said confidently.

Getting accredited to the Cannes Film Festival was harder than getting into Oxford. I had to ask the newspaper publisher Joseph Pulitzer to use his influence with his city editor and send me a letter saying I was going to write the best-ever column on the Festival, because I was going down there in my bus and would invite the whole Festival to tea. I received the letter, but no expenses, even for tea bags.

Cannes was the last place I ever thought I'd see Groucho Marx. I don't remember why he was there – he certainly hadn't made a film in years – but his press conference was a lively affair. Groucho was old and rather deaf by then. A black reporter asked him what he thought of the Black Power movement in America. He leaned over to a press office and asked, 'What did the *schwatza* say?' Whether that was his way of answering the question or whether he really didn't hear it, no one will ever know, but he caught a lot of flak for the remark.

Bearing a famous name has one obvious advantage: head waiters in smart restaurants do not ask you to repeat it. It also has disadvantages, as was brought home to me when I opened the door to one of its victims. He had a sheaf of foreign-looking flutes handing from his shoulder, some penny-whistles in his shirt pocket, a beard and gold-framed glasses.

'Hello. I'm John Steinbeck Junior, a friend of John Simon's. Can I crash for a couple of nights?'

'Yeah,' I said, 'if you promise never to play those flutes in the house.'

His career was not going well. The best I could do for him was to introduce him to Rosie Boycott. It was as if they had been waiting years to meet. On the next day, Rosie reports in her book *A Nice Girl Like Me*, they took some acid in a field full of cows. Steinbeck did a number with the cows, playing his flute; they gathered around him as if he were the Pied Piper. Later, at lunch, Steinbeck told her he loved her and moved into her place. I was glad to see the end of the flutes, but I missed our ridiculous daily conferences. As a parting gesture to express his thanks for our hospitality, he gave me a hug which bruised my entire ribcage.

When I heard that Cutie was near the end, I flew to St Louis to be with her. I had some unfinished business which needed sorting out. At her bedside, I adopted what I thought was a light-hearted approach.

'Well, Cutie, are you satisfied with the way life turned out for you?'

She gave me that look of hers which said, 'What a question to ask at a time like this.' With a great effort, she raised her eyebrows and a suggestion of a smile crossed her ancient lips. 'I stayed out of jail, didn't I?' I couldn't help but laugh. Did she think that to show any vulnerability was a crime?

I was just beginning to feel comfortable in the Svengali role with Fran when she accepted an invitation to tea that turned out to be an invitation to change my life – again. I went to pick her up at Jill Neville's house. While waiting, I spotted a lonely-looking manuscript among the dozens of books that Jill was reviewing for the *Sunday Times*. It was a collection of poems by Elizabeth Smart.

I had met Elizabeth the first week I came to London, and had had a crush on her ever since. I was one of the 300 people at the launch of the paperback edition of *By Grand Central Station I Sat Down and Wept* in 1966. Jill told me Elizabeth had been living in Suffolk taking care of her grandchildren and trying to cope with writer's block. 'Why don't you publish them?' said Jill. 'You did such a good job on Fran's book.'

I called Elizabeth. We met at the French Pub, then went on to Wheeler's for lunch. I discovered she knew a lot more about publishing than I did. I promised to find a contract form that would give me some idea how to arrange the foreign, American and paperback rights.

I found the perfect office in a squat in Maida Vale, and subscribed to *The Bookseller*. The first person I saw was John Hyams, buyer for W. H. Smith, who gave me a firm order for 350 copies. I hit upon the idea of dealing directly with distributors and bookshop owners. The telephone technique became my trademark. I rallied all the friends I had made in the media over the last fourteen years. The first edition of 2,500 copies sold out. In those days, a slim volume of verse which sold 500 copies was considered a best-seller.

With Tom Maschler at Jonathan Cape I made a co-publishing deal for Elizabeth's new novel, *The Assumption of the Rogues and Rascals*, but the major reviews were literary muggings. Elizabeth was very hurt – no, she was furious.

The next book I published was written by fourteen-year-old Gideon Sams – the son of Ann and Craig Sams, with whom I had worked during my macrobiotic days. His mother noticed the exercise book in a rubbish bin while she was tidying his room. 'It looks interesting,' she said to me. 'He wrote it as a school project. His teacher thought it showed promise. Would you like to see it?' It was a short account of the punk scene, which was breaking big around that time. To publish the world's first punk novel would be a coup. Most of all, it would be a lot of fun to upset the publishing trade with a well-written book on such a disgusting subject.

My reputation as an original publisher was growing. The range of subjects, the unconventional promotional drive behind them, amused and impressed other publishers, the trade and the public. For the first time I had genuine overheads and an overdraft, and I wasn't looking too well either.

I would have kept on my existing Girl Friday, Annie, if she hadn't introduced her friend Pamela into my life. Little did she suspect that the woman who showed up at the office to say hello in a tight pair of blue jeans and high boots would be my next employee. Annie was busy at the time, and she said, in her sweet, motherly way, 'You two go out and have fun.' Three hours later we returned. Annie was not pleased to see Pamela collapse in a corner, throw up in the waste bin and pass out. I thought it showed a certain amount of flair.

Most publishers would need a new book to justify a party. Pamela needed no such excuse. She organized small parties on national holidays and obscure literary anniversaries, and would often lobby for a bash just for the hell of it. They were never the cheese-and-plonk launches most publishers had, but full-scale rehearsals for *La Grande Bouffe*. Luckily I had a bent smoked salmon connection on Meard Street who knew me only by the codename Operation

Banquet. Pamela's guests were mostly my friends, chosen by her for their inability to get us any publicity.

Miles and his group, now called Miles Over Matter, were a nightly fixture in the basement of the house, blasting away for hours. Just as he was about to sign the big contract, the band broke up. Miles became unofficial roadie for the all-girl group The Slits, who made a dramatic appearance at our New Year's Day party with the professional irritant of the punk world, Johnny Rotten. He was just what I needed – somebody to get silly with. I watched him squirm as I introduced him to our friends, who must have looked to him like outpatients at St Bart's. Rotten called out to Miles: 'Hey, your old man is crazy. Get him off my back.' Fran had written a poem about Rotten; the opportunity to recite it to him was irresistible.

Fran still felt she was Mrs Someone instead of Someone. However, Tom Maschler at Cape then decided to publish her second book, *Invade My Privacy*. My grand design was to co-ordinate the launch of the book with appearances by Fran at Ronnie Scott's. There was resistance from Ronnie's partner, Pete King, but he relented under pressure from Ronnie and me. Fran opened on a bill with Dexter Gordon, and by the end of her two-week engagement the *cognoscenti* had given her their seal of approval.

'For years I sat in the dark watching other people in the spotlight doing my material. Now I ask myself why I waited so long. I just love going out there, giving of myself and receiving all that love and energy,' she told Michael Zwerin, the music critic who was covering the event for the *International Herald Tribune*.

The next time Fran played at Ronnie's, Tom Waits was in town playing at the London Palladium, We had met when he was a jazz cult singer doing gravel-voiced imitations of Jack Kerouac and Neal Cassady at Ronnie's. Fran laid her latest book on him. He told her later that he was so inspired by her poems he couldn't stop writing for the rest of his gig. What really knocked her out was to read, in an interview he gave to *Melody Maker*, that she was one of his heroes. I saw him again backstage at the Dominion Theatre. Married by this time, travelling with his wife and baby, he presented us with a picture of domestic bliss that would have been inconceivable a few years back.

When Fran appeared at the Edinburgh Festival that summer of 1978, her venue, Better Books, was off the beaten track, and it looked as though she wouldn't have a quorum for her debut. It was my job to see that she did. I stood outside on the pavement, hustling the passing crowd with some colourful commentary. By the time she was ready to go on, there were bums on seats and critics poised for either praise or poison. A review by Allan Massie appeared in *The Scotsman* proclaiming her lyrics to be 'wittier and truer than Sondheim, more rhythmical, more alert, and more sensitive'. By the end of the week she was playing to packed houses.

Returning to the mundane business of being just a housewife presented problems. Her dim view of marriage had been instilled in her by her mother and nurtured by her search for her own identity. 'I always knew,' she once wrote, 'I ought to get a divorce. I would have looked so good on the witness stand in an understated outfit. The only sticky bit would be going home without you.' Sally Vincent was doing a series of articles for *The Observer* on couples who lived unconventional lives within the framework of a conventional marriage. She chose us as a couple who stabilize each other's adventures. Her article got into the eye of the hurricane: 'Like the fabric of their home, the Landesman life is either a terrible mess in need of major repair, and a good clean-up, or it's eccentrically, humanely, bravely and infinitely generously disposed.'

By 1980 I had a collection of writers unsurpassed for eccentricity who were no strangers to failure. Jeremy Thorpe had been front-page news for the better part of a year. Dan Farson had the idea of writing the story of what really went on while the trial was in progress and having it in the book stores on the day the case went to the jury. In order to avoid libel, he'd tell it from a dog's point of view, with all the dogs based on real-life characters. Unfortunately, the jury returned a 'not guilty' verdict, but the book was well received by the critics.

I took a serious look at mainstream publishing, and my literary standards began to slip. Nothing could have pleased me more than to receive the manuscript of the world's first cookbook devoted to canine gastronomy. Author Richard Graham was a writer for *The Times* and *The Good Food Guide*, and a passionate lover of dogs. With Don Grant's clever illustrations, and cover quotes by Elaine Stritch, Robert Carrier and Jilly Cooper, the book earned that choice place next to the cash register in many a bookshop.

Frankfurt, the world's biggest book fair, was the great test. I was determined to get my share of attention. A friend who lived there came by with his huge Pyrenean mountain dog. I asked Pamela to help cook a meal for it. You would have thought I was asking her to perform an obscene act. When she saw me in a chef's hat, she said it was not her idea of how a publisher should behave, so I decided to wear the chef's cap and take the dog on a parade through the halls. I sold the rights to seven countries including Japan, whose publisher thought it was a book about how to cook dogs. When I set up the dog's bowl, soliciting contributions for a Home for Aged Gourmet Dogs, it proved all too much for Pamela. She packed up and left Frankfurt.

Graham came up with the idea of a book about cuisine for cats that would be even more popular than the dog cookbook. In the meantime he produced *The Good Dog's Guide to Better Living*.

When Pamela saw my Christmas present to her, a redundancy notice, we had a row that led to my hasty departure, narrowly avoiding injury from a pot which flew out of a window, aimed at my head.

With our careers in top gear, Fran and I saw less of each other than ever before. She wrote even more frankly about the ups and downs of her life, but now without any regrets:

> *I devote myself to making small jokes and screwing*
> *And I spend my spare time polishing my art*
> *And you ask me if I'm happy in what I'm doing*
> *I ought to be – I wrote the part.*

I was as proud of her accomplishments as she was of mine, especially when I published her third volume of verse, *More Truth than Poetry*. She was attracting the kind of adulation few poets ever receive, and was especially chuffed when it came from people she respected.

Bette Davis was in London in 1975. We couldn't get tickets to her performance, but Fenella Fielding, who was at the concert, told Fran that Miss Davis was going to record *Ballad of the Sad Young Men*. Fran sent her a copy of *Invade My Privacy*. Miss Davis wrote her a note: 'Your lyrics of *Sad Young Men* plus Mabel Mercer's record have haunted me for years. I am so thrilled to be allowed by EMI to have it part of my LP. Your book of verse is sensational. We must meet! Call me Friday. What a talented person you are. *Most* sincerely, Bette Davis.'

We were invited to have tea with her at Grosvenor House. She met us at the door in a pink-flowered housecoat which I thought any male over fifty-eight would appreciate. Once all the niceties were exchanged, she became the vinegary Bette Davis we knew and loved. She was completely open about her liaisons with the Hollywood Casanovas and her failed marriages. Even when I put my hand on her knee to ask her an intimate question, she did not seem offended. Only when I asked about Joan Crawford did she draw herself up and remove my hand delicately: 'That we will not discuss.'

By 1980 publishing was becoming more a part of show business each day. The book fairs, with their dazzling promotions of best-selling authors, left little room for the small independent publisher. I invited Cosmo to help. His first suggestion was to put Jeffrey Bernard between hard covers, but I knew Jeffrey had driven many a publisher to aphasia waiting for a manuscript. 'Let's do the best of the High Life and Low Life columns from *The Spectator*,' said Cosmo. I agreed, as did Jeffrey, but I didn't know about Taki, who wrote the High Life column. To my surprise, Taki invited me to Aspinalls to talk it over. He thought it would be fun, and accepted.

High Life, Low Life was warmly accepted by the media. Auberon Waugh, who had mugged Elizabeth Smart for making such a mess of her life, now gave me a rave quotation for two men who had made a profession of messing up their lives. Jeffrey's fortunes changed overnight. Suddenly he was in demand, doing 'A Life In The Day Of ...' profiles and putting up with BBC camera crews who followed him around Soho as he tried to explain his 'useless' life. 'By and large I've met a better class of person in the gutter than I have in the drawing-room,' he once wrote. It would have been an appropriate time to remind him of Graham Greene's dictum: 'Fame is a temporary postponement of failure.'

The list of books that Cosmo wanted to commission was a perfect formula for either a brilliant future or bankruptcy. Who could resist *The Good Guide to Joyless Sex*? Unable to find an author, Cosmo attempted to undertake the research himself, but couldn't find a partner who would put up with his basic premise. I chose instead to publish a scholarly bibliography of the collection of erotica in the British Library, which they kept locked up, unknown to the public. Scholars and collectors knew of its existence, but were seldom able to study its contents. No one had ever catalogued the whole collection until my new author, Patrick J. Kearney, decided it must be done. I produced a limited edition of 1,000 numbered copies, beautifully designed and printed on expensive paper, and bound in a special cloth which some joker claimed looked like foreskins. Thanks to a well-targeted campaign, over 450 copies were sold in the first three months. I was particularly delighted when Hull's most famous librarian, Philip Larkin, ordered a copy.

Browsing at America's largest book convention, I came across a tall, sombre-looking man playing free-form jazz on a soprano saxophone. Martin Shepard had just created a new imprint, the Second Chance Press, and was looking for an adventurous co-publisher and distributor. 'Each year many books are condemned to die, struck down by such diseases as neglect, bad timing or lack of exposure.' We published an initial list of six titles, with modest success; later I went off the idea of bringing literary orphans to Britain, but Martin and Judy Shepard went on to become successful in America, admired by writers, booksellers and reviewers.

Landesman's last stand took place at the London Book Fair. There was a lot of action, but nothing materialized. I folded up the stand, sold my lease on the Wardour Street office, bade farewell to the girls in the sex show next door, and moved the remaining stock to the basement of Duncan Terrace.

It seemed the perfect time to retrieve the manuscript of the memoirs I had started years ago. Friends divided into two camps: those who thought I was presumptuous – 'Who wants to read the memoirs of a Mr Nobody?' – and those who thought it was a good idea. I was miserable company for the next few months, but Fran didn't notice. When the first draft of *Rebel Without Applause* was finished, I couldn't wait to show it to someone other than the family. Pamela was the first guinea pig.

'You want to know what I think of it? Here's what I think of it,' she said, trying to tear the manuscript in half.

I leapt in and saved what was left. 'Why did you do that?'

'I, I, I, I and Me, Me, Me. There's too much of you in it,' she said.

Reminding her that it was, after all, an autobiography made no impression.

I sent the manuscript to Sterling Lord, a leading New York agent, whom I knew from the old days when he handled the unknown Jack Kerouac. It stayed unopened for seven weeks. Finally I received a call from Sterling while I was in Fran's room. His opening was, 'Jay, you've written a beautiful book.'

Fran gave me a big hug. 'I'm happy for you,' she said, and went back to her television viewing. I wanted to celebrate, but there was no one to celebrate with.

The problem was solved next night. Carolyn Cassady, Neal Cassady's wife and Jack Kerouac's lover, stayed over on one of her rare departures from her cottage in Winchelsea. It was an intimate evening with just the three of us. Carolyn was mellow enough to let down her hair and tell us what it was really like to be a victim of Cassady's notoriety. Since Jack's and Neal's deaths, she had been trying to correct the prevailing distortions and lies, with little success.

Miles was working as a salesman for Boy on King's Road, but still working nights at becoming a rock star. Cosmo's only accomplishment up to then had been making an art form out of mixing the perfect martini. Then he planted a time bomb in our life – its name was Julie Burchill. The affair had been going on for some time, but it was only when they showed up seeking sanctuary from her irate husband that I discovered they were serious.

Next to Cosmo, I was probably her biggest fan. I had been reading her columns in *Time Out* and the *Sunday Times*. With two professional critics on the premises, Fran and I felt like the homosexual couple in *La Cage aux Folles*. Cosmo had already warned us that Julie knew all about us. She made it plain that she intended to make Cosmo over into a real working-class hero. The first sour note was her introducing white bread into the house. Cosmo, who hadn't seen any since puberty, thought it was exotic.

The obvious affection between the two of them led me to lament the lack of it in my own life. Dinner with just the two of us was a lonesome affair. Big table, bigger silences. For the next few weeks I was seldom seen at the French without my dirty Humphrey Bogart Burberry. One night, Gaston, the owner of the pub, was drinking with the prettiest girl in the room.

'May I buy you a drink, Gaston?' I asked, looking directly at the girl.

'What a good idea,' she said. 'We only drink champagne, though.'

When she came up to collect it, she seemed even sexier. 'We've met before. I'm a friend of Ian Dunlop. He introduced you as the publisher of the Sears Roebuck catalogue. It intrigued me at the time. You looked so unlike a publisher.'

A delicious wave of irresponsibility swept over me. I was afraid she might decline my invitation to dinner, but the offer of more champagne brought her to her senses. At the end of dinner I asked what she did when she wasn't picking up dirty old men. 'If you must know, I work for the Girl Guides. Isn't it a shame?'

To keep up the illusion that we had something in common with Cosmo and Julie, I suggested that Fran and I go out on a double date – dinner at the Ritz to see our friend, cabaret artist Steve Ross. For Julie it was an evening of high embarrassment. The table setting had such a variety of silverware, it left her no alternative but to eat with her fingers. Worse, I failed to notice that Fran was miserable. Hutchinson had rejected her new book of verse. The writer's block was back. And she had lost Cosmo. Her temper flared up at the slightest provocation.

Cosmo and Julie moved out. It was sad to contemplate how things had deteriorated between us. Fran said it might be a good thing. 'He finally has something to rebel against now,' she said, hoping it would help me come to terms with the problem.

An avalanche of rejections all the way up to Christmas ensured that it wouldn't be a merry one for me. Tom Maschler returned my manuscript of *Rebel* with egg salad sandwich stains, which mysteriously stopped around the third chapter. Sterling Lord was still having marketing problems with the book. London agent Richard Gollner had the chutzpah to send me his reader's report: 'Reading it is like being chained to the stool of a bar-fly, trapped in a life with a terminal bore.'

I received a postcard from Pompeii. I couldn't read the signature, but I knew immediately it was from the Girl Guide. I had given up on ever seeing her again. Her phone call later lightened a heavy day. We drank champagne backstage with Al, an actor friend who was appearing in *Evita*. 'I like your friends,' GG said. 'I thought there was a dinner involved.'

'I lied,' I said. 'Let me take you home. You're pissed.'

A perfect parking place right outside her door left no doubt the gods were smiling. She changed into something more comfortable – a man's frayed bathrobe – and started to drink Irish whiskey straight from the bottle. 'How old are you?' she asked. Now I knew why she needed the whiskey.

'Would you believe me if I told you I was seventy-five?' I answered.

For a horrible moment she stared at me as though to analyse my chances of surviving the rest of the evening. 'You're almost as old as both my parents. How sweet.'

'Are you trying to tell me something?' I asked. 'If you are, I must tell you that it has long been my cherished hope to die in the saddle.'

Introducing a new girl to Fran was important. Fran liked to know what the competition was like. When GG asked for seconds, I knew they were going to hit it off. Fran introduced GG to her beloved Spastics Society shop, the Bloomingdales of Islington charity shops. GG turned Fran on to her latest anti-histamine pill. Fran admitted that GG was an asset when she saw her high up one of our trees, sawing away the dead branches. 'A Grade One preservation order should be put on that girl,' she said.

I saw my basement studio taking on the qualities of a slum when Miles began to use it as a storage place for his musical equipment. When our lodgers moved out of the top floor, I had second thoughts about renting it out again. It would be much simpler if I moved there instead.

Pamela had persuaded Fran to be interviewed for Robyn Wallis's television documentary on mistresses. The interview was filmed in Fran's room, with Fran sitting on the bed, looking like a young Edith Sitwell. 'I think you'd have to have a tiny, shrivelled-up heart if there was only place in it for one person for the rest of your life,' she said.

'Do you ever feel jealousy?' Robyn asked.

'Yes, I do,' Fran admitted. 'I'm not some kind of superwoman ... sometimes you get lazy or prey to those emotions, but if you kind of keep yourself in trim, you can deal with them. And if you have a choice of learning to deal with them or cutting yourself off from all the experiences that make life exciting, I suggest to you – learn to deal with them. The alternative is just too bleak.'

Most of the reviews of the programme were sympathetic. However, New Year's Day started off with the bad news that Fran's new agency had gone bust before they could get her one gig. A visit from her Norwegian collaborators, who said that her songs had been featured on television there, cheered her up a bit. When Julie heard about it, she said, 'Of course Fran's popular in Norway. They're a deeply melancholy people.'

When GG's landlord gave her thirty days' notice, we offered her temporary residence. That first night GG made a cheese soufflé, Fran made the salad, and I washed up. GG reminded me that love nests are usually places away from the lovers' homes. 'I know. That's what is going to make this one so much more fun.' Julie and Cosmo displayed a peculiar reaction to GG's presence. They denounced her for letting down the image of the mistress by integrating.

Fran and I flew to St Louis for a revival of *The Nervous Set*. From the moment we stepped off the plane we were treated like returning heroes. The two leads captured us perfectly. It was spooky to discover we were still fighting the same issues. On the first night of our cabaret, my reading from the memoirs touched an audience whose average age was about the same as mine. At the end I joined Fran in the spotlight and the two of us danced to a medley of songs from the show. The fact that this triumph failed to bring us closer together confirmed my theory that success doesn't help; we had one of the biggest fights of our marriage.

On our return to London, we heard that we were going to be grandparents. Fran was more ready for the role than I was. She toughened up. She would damn well do what she wanted to do, and she wasn't going to take any more shit from anyone.

I sent copies of *Rebel* to the two people I could count on to level with me: Robert Stone and John Clellon Holmes. Stone's novels had earned him the reputation of a 'writer's writer'. His letter came as a great relief. The response from Holmes was equally gratifying, but in another letter he disclosed that he was awaiting operation number three for a cancer-savaged jaw. We had been in correspondence for over forty years. Knowing him and Shirley had kept me creatively alive. I wrote back thanking him for the life-preserver he had thrown me.

The love nest went up in flames. Fearing that the bathroom pipes would freeze, I had left the wall heater on day and night. The thin wooden wall panels dried out and caught fire. Luckily Cosmo was there to rescue Fran. I found her sitting in the park opposite in shock. It was only later that night, in a strange hotel room, that we realized how perishable our pretty kingdom was. GG and I moved to the basement while the builders wrestled with the roof. By a strange co-incidence, on the day of the fire GG had found a flat she was ready to buy. Had I been more perceptive, I would have realized that both the fire and the impending birth of my first grandchild would affect our relationship.

At eight o'clock one night, Cosmo rang from the hospital. 'It's a boy,' he shouted. 'Thank God it's a baby,' said GG. When we arrived at the hospital, there was Jack, sleeping peacefully next to Julie, being watched over by a proud Cosmo. 'Hello, Gramps,' said Fran as we got into the car.

Jack was the best audience Fran had ever had. In effect, she had a new boyfriend who didn't criticize her. 'We've got seven or eight years before Jack dumps us,' she said. 'By that time, Miles will have some children.' Cosmo made discreet enquiries about the availability of the top floor. We were delighted.

GG thought I was carrying the concept of the extended family too far; Jack had replaced her as the focal point in our life. A few weeks later we were dining at Langan's. I looked at her over the rim of a big brandy glass. 'It's over, isn't it?' I said.

'Yes. I didn't know how to tell you.' She began to cry. The pain came from imagining that it would never happen again.

At the London Book Fair, I said hello to a dozen ghosts from the past before I found Martin and Judy Shepard's Permanent Press. I left a copy of *Rebel* with them. 'Just for laughs,' I said.

At dinner the next night, Martin said he had upset his fellow publishers. Judy explained: 'Martin started reading your manuscript and laughed so much and so loud our neighbours came around to find out what was going on. We'd like to do your book, Jay. We would consider it a great honour.'

Liz Calder, who had moved from Cape to start Bloomsbury Press, asked to have a look. She called later to tell me she loved my book and wanted to do it following its publication in the States. The dream machine went into overdrive.

G. Legman called me when he heard I was going to be published on two continents. 'Give me the name of a good lawyer,' he yelled. 'I'm going to sue your ass off.' I asked him if he was going to say terrible things about me in *his* memoirs. 'The worst thing I can say about you, Landesman, is that you were a playboy.'

I told him I'd settle for that. 'What's wrong with having some fun?'

3)

ONE DAY, RIGHT AFTER RECEIVING one of Julie's naughty faxes, we saw that someone had scratched on the seat of a bench
we usually use: 'Scary bitches are everywhere.' It made us laugh so
much we fell into each other's arms. We could have been taken for
two old-age pensioners in love. Maybe we were.

We had time to notice that the leaves were changing, or that the
roses that year were better than the previous year's. I even bought
a mechanical litter-picker to clear paths of unsightly trash as we
skipped along the sidewalks. Strangers would often stop and say nice
things: 'You look like a happy couple.'

And why shouldn't we be? I had apologised to Julie and Cosmo,
and made as many amends as possible. Fran had a new book of her
lyrics coming out with a new publisher, on her favourite subject – all
the ways love could go wrong. I had an offer to co-produce a musical
version of F. Scott Fitzgerald 's *The Great Gatsby* from a flamboyant
English producer, Peter Cranwell, who had spent the better part of
his life in Hollywood hustling. In spite of his dodgy background,
and of the fact that I hadn't produced anything for the theatre since
Dearest Dracula in 1965, I jumped at the chance of getting involved
with such a challenging project. It was a subject I knew intimately,
having patterned my lifestyle on Scott and Zelda for 60 years, and
changed my name in homage to them.

The deal with Peter Cranwell was that he would get the rights
and raise the money. In his Hollywood period he had raised over
twenty million dollars for United Artists and MGM to produce special projects. He left it to me to handle everything else. I went into
overdrive, putting together a team of accomplished people. Simon
Callow faxed his acceptance as director: 'My gonads tingled at the
suggestion of a musical Gatsby,' he wrote. Peter Cranwell was not

without a sense of humour: 'I'd like to have a recording of Callow's gonads tingling – might have a hit record there.'

Everything was going great with my side of the project; I had secured Richard Rodney Bennett for the music, Jeremy Brooks for the book, Fran for the lyrics and Ralph Koltai for the sets. We had reached the point of casting even before we had the rights. Callow thought Keith Carradine would be perfect as Jay Gatsby, having worked with him in Hollywood. Carradine was even more enthusiastic than Callow or I, and decided to come to London for further talks. The meeting with him was a great success. When Fran joined the conference wearing a pair of purple shoes with a colour-coordinated outfit from various charity shops, Carradine rose from his chair looking as if he were experiencing some kind of religious vision and kissed her hand reverently. Callow warned us: 'You mustn't mind Keith's exuberance. He's just demolished two English high teas.'

Cranwell put himself in the hands of an expensive showbusiness solicitor to negotiate the rights. I was beginning to feel we had a show until Cranwell told me he had set up offices in the Picasso coffee shop on King's Road. Within the circle of Picasso patrons was a cell of ageing entrepreneurs whose capacity for cappuccino and bullshit was legendary. He managed, however, to find an American who claimed to have recently come into a large inheritance and who was prepared to finance the whole deal. After a few meetings, I noticed he always showed up with steak and kidney pie on his ties. Cranwell didn't mind the stains but soon tired of his lame excuses. This suave fund-raiser finally leaned over the table, grabbed his lapels and shouted, 'Where's the fuckin' money?'

Trying to get the rights proved even more difficult. Although we offered the Fitzgerald estate a respectable advance, they turned us down. Their excuse was that the film rights were being contested by David Merrick, the producer of the Mia Farrow/Robert Redford film version of *Gatsby*. Callow set up a meeting with the owner of London's Duke of York Theatre who seemed very enthusiastic. 'Don't worry about money,' he said. 'We can handle that.' What a relief it was to have that kind of interest. After many, many discussions, Callow's agent pressured us for a contract and money; Cranwell told them it was against the law to give a contract (and therefore money) before the rights were secured. We had no money; nor was any forthcoming from our enthusiastic producer. It looked as though we were about to lose Callow and Bennett. They had done considerable work on *Gatsby* and deserved their agents' modest demands.

Since Cranwell had not come across with his side of the agreement, I was thrown into a dilemma. It looked as though we were about to lose the whole project because of him. In a monumental decision I managed to sack him and explained our problem to Bennett and Callow, then released them from the project with my thanks and abject apologies.

Being no stranger to raising money, I decided to have a go. I had recently read an interview in which Lord Sainsbury said *The Great Gatsby* was his favourite novel. He had a charitable trust of some thirty million pounds called The Gatsby Foundation. I wrote to him, suggesting he join us on the Appreciation of F. Scott Fitzgerald Committee, but being careful not to mention the musical. He wrote back saying that he didn't 'go in for committee activity'. I tried again when I heard that J. Paul Getty was a *Gatsby* fan. I mentioned my need for an angel. He wrote back: 'I love Fitzgerald above all other authors. He introduced me to book collecting – that doesn't mean I want to invest in a musical based on one of his masterpieces.'

Somewhat disappointed at this reaction, I tried to interest my nephew, Rocco Landesman, who had become one of the most daring and popular producers on Broadway. He too appreciated Fitzgerald as one of America's leading novelists, but vetoed turning the book into a musical. He had just produced *Angels over America*, a highly controversial play. Why not *Gatsby*? 'To produce a full-scale musical today on Broadway would cost about twelve million dollars,' he said. 'It would be difficult to raise that kind of money after looking at the record of two flop films on *Gatsby*. It's best to leave it as a novel.'

Undaunted by his conclusions, I tried the West End producers Cameron Mackintosh, Trevor Nunn, Bill Kenwright, and Andrew Lloyd Webber, all of whom, except Trevor Nunn, declined to read it or listen to the music.

With Fran's encouragement I decided on a drastic course of action to keep the project alive. First I signed up a new composer with whom Fran had collaborated on other shows. He came up with a wonderful score that gave us new hope. The composer, Jason McAulliffe, had connections with Time-Warner who were so enthusiastic about *Gatsby* that they offered Jason their theatre if he wanted to do a platform performance with full cast. McAulliffe's enthusiasm was so extraordinary that he decided to put the whole performance on for practically nothing. It was an offer we couldn't refuse (even if we had wanted to, which we didn't). Fran and I hopped on a plane to New York ready to convince the producers and potential backers we were inviting to the performance that the production would be a smashing success.

'Gatsby lives,' we chanted, toasting our luck with champagne on the night of the show. The cast turned in a very inspired performance. It was as exciting as any first night. There was real enthusiasm from the audience of friends; Rocco even said he loved Fran's lyrics and many of the songs, but still felt it wouldn't work on a Broadway stage. When the few producers who had also come began to sneak out without a word, I knew we had been, to put it mildly, unsuccessful. (It reminded me of the first night of our first Broadway show: everyone loved it except the critics.) We were as confused as Nick, Gatsby's only friend, who sings at the end of the show,

> *So what if fortune eludes us*
> *As it eluded him then?*
> *Tomorrow we'll run faster,*
> *We'll stretch our arms out further,*
> *Tomorrow we'll try again.*

The *Gatsby* debacle was thus consigned to the Landesman trunk of broken dreams. This trunk was so full by now that we moved it into the living room and used it as a platform for our growing collection of electronic equipment. At long last we had found a proper use for it.

Working on *Gatsby*, I had forgotten that the second volume of my memoirs was ready to hit the bookshops. Considering that I had only received a thousand-dollar advance from the American publisher for *Rebel Without Applause*, the ten-thousand-pound advance from my English publisher Weidenfeld seemed finally to confer on me the title of 'author'. I remember telling Fran back in 1950 that I never intended to be a writer. She was shocked. Her main excuse for marrying me was that some day I would write the great American novel.

With my background of promotional know-how, I was very keen to control the agenda for my own book. My first volume had been about the end of innocence in America. The second volume was about the swinging scene we had found in London. I had the complete co-operation of the Weidenfeld publicity department, including a personal appearance before their sales representatives to explain to them how and why I had escaped the fame game and that it was time for them to correct this flagrant 'miscarriage of justice'. They enjoyed the joke and promised to try harder. They set me up for a wide range of interviews and personal appearances. They arranged for an appearance at the Birmingham Literary Dinner, an annual event for Birmingham's cultural elite. I was to share the spotlight with Claire Rayner and other best-selling authors. My self-denigrating speech didn't get one laugh. It was obvious the audience thought I had come from another planet.

After the speeches came the humiliation. In the sales hall, where authors signed their books for queues of hungry book buyers, I sat, pen poised, before an enormous stack of copies of *Jaywalking*. The one person who came up to me apologized when he realized he was in the wrong queue. When no other customers appeared for the next hour I realized I was in the wrong place. I needed a drink badly. I asked the security officer to guard my stall, secretly hoping that someone would at least steal a copy. Needless to say I never returned.

Jaywalking fared much better in the press, receiving a few favourable reviews; even those who thrashed it used my picture. Within a week of its publication Weidenfeld's publicist managed to sell an excerpt to the *Independent*, dealing with my relationship with Burchill. It may have helped sell a few copies or it may have not, but there was no doubt that it enraged her and Cosmo.

When the excitement of the book died down, I fell into the clutches of the *Antiques Roadshow*, a television programme in which members of the public are invited to bring along their ancestors' leavings for appraisal by 'the experts'. They had come to Islington and Fran dared me to take a painting her father had given her forty years ago to find out if it was worth anything. It had hung on our wall for years without anyone ever saying a kind word about it. When I appeared on television awaiting their decision Philip Hook, their art expert, said it was worth fifty thousand pounds! I went into my Gary Cooper kicking a cowpat routine. 'Aw shucks,' I drawled.

While this performance may not have received an Oscar, it made an immediate hit with the programme's six or seven million viewers. As I was walking through Chapel Market the next day, stallholders leaped out either to congratulate me or to ask for the loan of a fiver. One or two villainous-looking traders believed in my innocent act to the extent of asking for my address. In the years since the broadcast I have been recognized at bus stops, in McDonald's, and in various salsa pubs on Upper Street. Once, a policeman on horseback asked for an autograph. Homeless beggars in doorways smiled and wished me luck. The tabloid press did features on me. It was ironic that I should have found the kind of attention I had always longed for through one small painting of three nude ladies with large necks by a Japanese impressionist.

'Success destroys your soul,' I said to Fran as we strolled on Upper Street, on the lookout for babies to admire.

'I wouldn't know,' she said. 'I've never had any.'

With all my other projects on hold, I confessed I could use a little hit about then.

'Don't change, Jayboy,' she pleaded. Later that day she wrote a flattering poem with some good advice and gave it to me, framed and hand-decorated, for my birthday:

Don't change
Stay the way you are
Don't change
You were always a star
It's wonderful the way you hold up
When others are beginning to get fat
When everybody else has sold up
You're still pulling rabbits from a hat
It's marvellous to see you coming
Arrayed in splendour cheering up the street
A Jewish prince who's done a little slumming
Like Fred Astaire, you never miss a beat
Time marches on but you're still dancing
Still trying to extend your range
Technology may keep advancing
And things and people grow more strange
But please don't go too far
Just stay the way you are
Don't change!

If she wrote my obituary, it would be worth dying for.

After the publication of Fran's new book, Howard Samuels put together a mini-musical, *Invade My Privacy*, which he called 'a celebration of the works of Fran Landesman', which successfully put bums on seats at the Riverside Studios. Fran's activities left me room for some deep shallowness, using the Groucho Club, the Colony Room, Jerry's and the French House as my headquarters. The history of these clubs and bars needs no documentation from me. As with the Stations of the Cross, one made stops at all of them, but seldom found any salvation in any of them.

But then, I wasn't looking for salvation. I was looking for good conversation, a buddy, or just to get laid, and in some cases I found all three, up to a point. Fran understood my appetite for new challenges and thought of my forays as being as good for her career as they were for mine. Our open marriage was common knowledge. Cosmo once described himself as 'son of an open marriage'. It was part of his arsenal of weapons to use against us, particularly me. Everyone thought it was I who conceived the open marriage syndrome, but from the very beginning our extramarital affairs were Fran's idea. It was her way of maintaining a certain amount of freedom of choice within marriage, something which appealed to her nature and which was necessary to her happiness. Who was I to deny her anything?

With Fran's career running smoothly, I took up an interest in neighbourhood activities. I had always been interested in getting to know my neighbours. By going through their dustbins, perhaps I could discover some of the secrets of their success. The author of *The Hitch Hiker's Guide to the Galaxy*, Douglas Adams, lived a few doors down from me. I always checked out his dustbin, only to discover empty bottles of a very good vintage wine drunk at parties to which I was never invited. There were huge heaps of computer magazines and, frequently, odds and ends of discarded equipment. A friend of mine who is a computer whiz claimed he did the same thing and collected enough discarded equipment to build a decent computer. Peter Ackroyd, who lived next door, never threw away anything, probably saving it all as archival material to be sold to some university in America. He was the ideal neighbour; once he sent over a case of champagne to thank me for allowing his builder to put up some scaffolding in my garden.

My obsession with rubbish – I once claimed my house had been decorated with rescued items from skips – led me into constant confrontation with the bin men (or garbage collection operatives). They started to toss my dustbin lids around like frisbees, forcing me to collect them from the stairwell after each visit. Once I confronted them wearing a neck brace, complaining about their lack of dustbin etiquette, but to no avail. Seized by dustbin rage, I screamed that I was going to report them to the Council, adding that they could forget about their Christmas tip in the future. It did not improve our relationship.

My relationship with Cosmo and Burchill had not improved either. By the end of 1994, we had to admit we had lost them, but we still had regular visits from their son Jack, who gave us great pleasure. Fran's career had begun to show signs of taking off – again. Her mini-musical was chosen by the Prince Edward Charitable Trust for a charity performance at the Criterion Theatre. Nothing was as gratifying as seeing the 'sold out' sign in front of the theatre. When the theatre's spotlight picked out Fran for a bow, she told me it was one of the happiest moments of her life.

More good news was to come. *The New Yorker* drama critic, John Lahr, who had seen the show, telephoned my nephew Rocco to tell him that the show was ready for New York and added that he must come and see it himself. Rocco said he would, if we could give a private performance (so that he would not be swayed by audience response), which we did. Although he had some reservations he loved the show. Negotiations progressed and it looked as though we would be returning to New York after thirty-five years. Expectation ran high until the final meeting with Rocco. It turned out he had reservations about the direction and Howard Samuels' starring role, suggesting that, for Broadway or even off-Broadway, it needed beefing up. This was unacceptable both to Howard and to us.

That was only the beginning of the incredible events of the year. My younger son Miles got divorced, I got involved in a dangerous affair, and Burchill ran off with a woman.

Cosmo wasn't the only one in shock. Her mother wasn't the only person who couldn't believe it. However, the newspapers had a field day. Burchill tried to explain: 'We are not lesbians. We just fell in love.' She left Jack with Cosmo and after a few months moved to Brighton where, by Christmas, she had become a spokesperson for the gay community. Although she re-established contact with Jack on weekends, life for Cosmo was tough no matter how philosophical he became. When he was linked to a new partner he said: 'We are not in love. We are only heterosexual.'

Fran and I tried to make it the best Christmas Jack had ever had. We overdecorated the house; the presents piled up under the tree; the atmosphere was electric. It was the first time that just the original family had been together for Christmas in years. From the first cracker Jack pulled with Cosmo, everyone was friends again. Nostalgia was rampant. Fran's face wore a permanent smile. We brought out all the old jokes and told stories of the good old days when we used to take acid together or just get high. As he was preparing to leave, I stole a hug from Cosmo. I didn't know about the rest of my family, but it was the best Christmas I'd ever had. The only person I felt a little sorry for was Burchill, who had missed a good party.

After everyone left, Fran gave me a big kiss. 'I really like my life,' she said. It was the best Christmas present I'd ever received.

By New Year's Eve I felt like doing something outrageous.

'What's the most outrageous thing we could do to usher in the new century?' I asked Fran.

'How about getting a divorce?' she suggested, showing off her famous Cheshire Cat grin.

The early summer of '97 had some compensations. I was able to wear my beloved battered Panama hat and meet up with an old drug connection, who was now selling Armani shirts and Versace jeans that had 'fallen off a truck'. Fran had enough new poems for another book and a birthday coming up in October. She was collaborating with Simon Wallace, and they took the best of their songs to make a CD featuring the singer Nicki Leighton-Thomas. With that backup there was only one thing to do - start a record company. Like all my other projects, it began with a business card and a catchy title, DOWN RECORDS. Since most of Fran's songs were downers, capitalizing on this aspect of her work appealed to our sense of irony. We called the book *Scars and Stripes,* and the CD, *Damned If I Do.*

As a gimmick we decided to attach a free CD of Fran performing some of the lyrics and songs to the back cover of her new book.

I decided to capitalise on the fact that she was seventy years old and still hungry. We landed her a slot on a new Carlton TV show, whose producer, Ms Copstick, fell under the spell of Fran's unorthodox way of life. When it was suggested she'd make a good subject for Ruby Wax's show, however, Fran put her foot down.

There was some doubt as to whether Fran would be able to fulfil the heavy schedule, as she was under attack from mysterious stomach pains, which to her meant the big C. Refusing to follow through on the tests required to determine the extent of her illness, she discovered once again that the only thing that relieved her distress was performing - the 'Doctor Footlights' syndrome. We had seen it happen so many times before with other artists. (At a charity benefit for mental health where Spike Milligan was appearing, Fran commented on how old and fragile he looked. Once on stage, however, Spike came to life, performing with the energy of a young alternative comic, only funnier.) Deciding she didn't want to do all those gigs lined up for her, she agreed to swallow whatever it was that would diagnose her condition.

While I sympathised, I tried to minimise her wild fantasies, which had been brought on by reading John Diamond's amusing horror stories in *The Sunday Times* on his fight against cancer.

Our anniversary and my birthday on July 15 brought the family together with a dinner at the restaurant in which I had a small financial interest. The place was empty and remained so for the rest of the evening, creating a Last Supper atmosphere. I tried to lighten the event by recalling the better times we'd had. Cosmo told of the embarrassment he and Miles suffered when we used to take them out to dinner while tripping on LSD. The owner of the place joined us briefly for a drink, a little depressed by his lack of success. Our grandson, Jack, speculated as to why the restaurateur was leaving so early: 'Oh, well, he probably has a date,' adding with a smile, 'to commit suicide.'

After the meal I opened up my birthday presents. Miles had given me a compilation cassette of his unreleased songs, which I had trouble recognising as music. Cosmo presented me with a rare copy of *The Rationale of the Dirty Joke*, an eight-hundred-page analysis of sexual humour by my old friend and adversary, Legman. It was Jack who got the laughs with his packet of one condom that glowed in the dark. 'Read the instructions, Grandpaw,' he cautioned.

I wrote a letter to my brother trying to bring him up to date on what had been happening, not having written to him for years. He was dying.

September 23, 1997
Dear Gene,
Postcard from Gert tells me of latest events that led back to the rehab centre. Since I don't have any idea of the damage this third stroke caused, I'm very concerned. Perhaps Ellie could write me the latest information. I've been concerned about my own health resulting in my giving up smoking and drinking. I've joined the local Y and work out two or three times a week. I really am benefiting from it all, although I've slowed down the last few years. Everything functions except the water-works but that goes with getting old.

Fran was worried about her digestive problems and finally swallowed the camera which showed there was nothing 'nasty down there'. Greatly relieved, she's much better. All she has to worry about now are whether her new songs and book of verse are going to be well received on October 21, her 70th birthday. Her brisk walks in the neighborhood keep her in condition, but don't stop her from complaining.

We're very interested in our grandson, Jack, who has turned out to be an avid student, first in his class. We wonder where he picked up that trait. Miles still lives at home, still does his music, and is still good company for all. It's hard to believe that Cosmo is 43 years old. At least he has a steady job on the London Sunday Times. He writes about the same things I was writing about in Neurotica in 1950. I sometimes think he's recycling my literary life. He doesn't seem to be having the fun I used to have. In short, he's a very serious guy. He resents my not taking life more seriously. I wish sometimes he could forget how silly I've been.

Don't know when we're coming back to the States for a visit, but am in no hurry except I'd like to see you while you can still see me. Grim thought, ain't it.

Do you think I'm too old to trade in my Porsche for a Harley Davidson?
Tell Ellie to write, we love her letters. Love, Jay.

Gene died peacefully on the morning of December 22, 1997, surrounded by his wife and all three of his children. Although we grew up together and had an active business partnership for over twenty-five years, I feel as though I never really knew him, but I liked him. For many years I thought of him as the square Landesman, but I was amused by his eccentricities: his old fashioned corn-cob pipe, his little black debit book in which he recorded his children's misdemeanours, his outlandish camping holidays in Godforsaken wildernesses, and his loyalty to the Casa Loma Dance Hall, which he attended regularly for over fifty years without ever learning how to dance. In the end he turned out to be the hippest and the most creative member of the family. He and his spiritual wife built a model ashram in the wilds of the Ozarks of Missouri and became healers and teachers to an emerging spiritual world. His wife helped wayward Catholic priests who had strayed from the path of righteousness. Gene taught advanced yoga to middle-class suburbanites.

The last time I saw him was at a celebration of their fiftieth wedding anniversary at the Missouri Botanical Gardens. He looked great and amused the crowd with his offbeat comments. His daughter summed it up to me over the phone after his death: 'I've been having crying jags in between feeling he had a good life and was loved by so many people.'

As I approached my 80th year, I still hadn't worked out what was left of my future. The only thing I was sure of was Fran's devotion. To make one woman content turned out to be the most important thing I had ever accomplished in my wayward life. Gone were the unrealistic big dreams. Now we actually got more pleasure from the smiles of babies we saw in Upper Street than we did at the first night of any of our shows. Yet it didn't stop us from working and re-working our careers. If my career had been as 'pathetic' as Burchill claimed in her series of nasty faxes, how come the muse was still on my shoulder, urging me to keep trying? A few weeks after Gene's death, Julie's memoir was serialised in *The Guardian* under the headline 'Born To Be Bad'. The contrast of her life with the life of Gene and his wife couldn't have been more obvious.

The business of recanting my early life – something Burchill never did – has almost been an obsession with me. Alistair Cooke in one of his *Letters From America* commented on my being one of the two people whom, on a recent visit to London, he was jolted to read about: 'The old incorrigible Beatnik Jay Landesman and the writer of *A Clockwork Orange*, Anthony Burgess, had recanted.' Cooke went on to say that 'Landesman deplored that the youth of today were imitating that destructive and self-destructive business of undermining the traditional values of American society in the name of self-expression and freedom.' While we were young and in a hurry the intentions were valid; but the results were disastrous.

'Somewhere in every intellectual is a dumb prick,' a Bellow character says in *Herzog*. The critic Alan Brien once called me an intellectual, 'although an ignorant one'. I couldn't blame him; my lifestyle at the time was a combination of Hellzapoppin and the Theatre of the Absurd – full of prankishness, eccentricity and maladjusted chutzpah. John Clellon Holmes summed me up thus: 'Landesman's personal preoccupations had the maddening habit of becoming cultural tendencies ten years later... He possessed, years before it was chic or marketable, what was called the Pop Imagination. Things that were counter, wry, eccentric, special and excessive stimulated him. He revelled in it, but never patronised it in the manner of camp, and his ear was always cocked for the psychic throb within it – seismographic evidences which filled the pages of *Neurotica*. But for all the barefoot crusades of those *Neurotica* days, it was the sheer excitement, the high pitch of fun, that I remembered longest.'

My New Year's resolution was to try to win back Cosmo. He accepted my invitation to have a cuppa at my place. I outlined the depth of my depression and the possible reasons. He refused to accept my assumption that I had failed to further Fran's career over the years, my sense of a useless life, etc. 'There's a limit to what you can do with a clever poet in today's market. You've done a fantastic job,' he said. 'Now, about you. You've lived a fantastic life, Jay boy, but it's a mistake to seek outside validation for it.

'You need to write a new interior scenario. You're rudderless. You don't know what to do with yourself. You're stuck with a bunch of worn-out concepts that no longer work for you.' I had to agree with him. It was time I did some housekeeping.

Since I wasn't famous enough for a kiss-and-tell book, my little affairs would not have made a bestseller. They had a certain amount of honesty; but none of those affairs altered my love for Fran and the life we led for almost fifty years while pursuing romantic adventures.

'Isn't there a time when old rakes like me give it up?' I asked her.

'I hope not, for your sake,' she said. 'You know how much I hate it when you think change. You're not changing when you try new things, you're just trying to broaden your perspective.'

My brother Gene had pointed this out to me after not seeing me for about thirty years. 'The one thing about you is that you're still the same.'

There were signs that my rapprochement with Cosmo had made some room for the new scenario he talked about. Self-denigration was no longer so attractive. I didn't care about success; all I wanted was the challenge to break even, which happened with every change of careers.

Not being used to such a positive outlook, I found it invigorating. It helped me to unload a doomed affair – for the first time I noticed how much it had distanced me from Fran. When I complained to Cosmo that Fran wasn't as adventurous as I would have liked, he laughed. 'What do you expect from a seventy-year-old woman you've lived with for almost a half-century?' he said.

Fran and I still walked through the Angel Park, arms around each other, frequently stealing kisses; she was one happy grandmother. At times she looked as beautiful as my departed friend. 'I really love you,' I would say. 'Moi?' she would exclaim, as though she was hearing it for the first time. But she knew I meant it. It was definitely the start of a new era, which included plans for a weekend in Bilbao to see the new museum.

Carolyn Cassady had been one of the first to subscribe to *Neurotica* in 1948, but I didn't meet her until 1970, when she decided to move to London. The world knew about the affair she had with Kerouac while still married to Neal Cassady, but few knew that Jack and Neal really had a desire to lead a bourgeois life with Carolyn when off the road.

She exposed their basic squareness in her memoir, which told the world that both her lovers were really homebodies, anxious to lead a normal life. Nobody wanted to believe her. She subsequently began to try to straighten out the public's image of the Beats. Chandler Brossard wrote the first critique in his ground-breaking essay *Reflections on My Beat Generation*:

> *There's a Beat Generation manufactured by brazen academic hustlers who write about it, third hand, and give courses on it to somnambulistic college students. There's another fabricated Beat Generation with which the European remnants of the Children's Crusade, mainly the French and German divisions, have passionately identified; their own cultures are not capable of providing them with a viable mythology with which to live in the current European abyss. The BG seems to be playing all the circuits involving a troupe of grinning, nudging, bisexual scamps who juiced and doped heavily, bummed, slummed, gummed, and thumbed rides to Nirvana, and who created poetic epiphanies by the thousand. In point of historical fact they got their act together several years after a far less romantic, perhaps less huggable, and certainly less publicized group of pioneers had agreed that The New Yorker was hardly the last word, and that Ernest Hemingway was a catatonic dreamer with an affected and unfortunate Castilian lisp.*

I did not escape a certain amount of embarrassment; Cosmo and Miles were suspicious when books came out on the Beats, as there would seldom be any mention of the Landesman name – although once in a while someone would write that Landesman was an antique dealer who had started *Neurotica* magazine. Brossard gave me a plug in his article: 'Landesman was always very insightful, very ahead of everybody on the culture scene, and very encouraging.'

I had a fear of success. I had met so many successful people who had been made unhappy by it. Yet, because I never wanted to die anonymously, I did everything I could to establish myself. Cosmo used to torture me about all the press releases relating to our various activities I asked him to edit; after thirty years he refused to read any more, claiming they were, like cigarettes, dangerous to his health.

After Fran's all-clear from cancer, she confessed: 'I really enjoy my life. I love doing everything throughout the day.' Her routine consisted of the morning walk with me, shopping at the market, a visit to Baby Park, coming home refreshed from watching the babies at play, preparing her lunch, having it on her bed, then napping; back into the kitchen to chop the vegetables for dinner while listening to Radio Four; another walk to the market; then back on her bed, rolling a joint for the evening, writing some long-overdue letters, watching *Star Trek*, and joining me for dinner at eight. After fifty years of angst-ridden existence, it was amazing how those little routines gave her such pleasure.

I was certainly enjoying my life. I had my private quarters in the granny flat basement completely furnished, and lined with old panelling. There was room enough for my office, my library, and the Ralph Ortiz art destructions. The walls were covered with memorabilia from unimportant periods of my life, and - the best thing about the place - it had its private entrance.

Out for a stroll with Fran one day, talking about how well things were going for us, I suddenly got so dizzy I had to sit down. Several angina attacks followed. A visit to our local GP for an ECG and some other tests suggested something was wrong.

I wouldn't have paid it much attention but for the fact that my father and brother had died of strokes. The attacks became more frequent; when the medicine refused to work, I asked for advice from my GP, and called the ambulance to take me to the hospital. Fortunately I was taken to the University College emergency department, which was the best place possible for heart cases. I breezed through test after test, convinced I was wasting their time, but the attacks continued. A week later I was back in the hospital full-time.

Although in a ward full of bypass-scarred veterans, I managed to isolate myself in an ideal cubicle where I could entertain my visitors without disturbing anyone, including the nurses. Cosmo, much to my surprise, was unusually attentive, bringing me a TV, cassettes, books, and the most welcome treat of all – Jack. One day they caught me completely wired up for a new test; I looked like Frankenstein's monster. Cosmo explained to Jack that it was a life-support machine. Jack enjoyed seeing his favourite monster tied up, so to speak. When they came to leave, Cosmo turned to Jack and said: 'Don't forget to turn off that machine.'

The week in the hospital acted as a morale booster. I never realised I had so many friends left. Friends who cared more than I did whether I lived or died. (A friend of Miles, actor Perry Benson, brought me a copy of the *SAS Survival Handbook*.) Even the NHS was concerned about my condition. They sent their top cardiac specialist to discuss my future; he turned out to be a closet poet who, when he discovered I was a publisher/writer, sought my advice on what to do with his 300-page verse about wooden ships and pirates and smugglers around Wembury Beach.

It was good and I told him so. He told me I had a damn bad case of angina and he didn't like it. I put myself in his capable hands and his manuscript in circulation. He whisked me into the operating room, and assigned me to a woman specialist with nerves of steel who had a balloon up my groin before I knew what was happening. She handed me a mirror and I saw the progress of the operation on colour TV. I was a success. I hoped to be able to tell the poet he was a success too.

In November '98, Fran accidentally discovered she was simultaneously an 'old lady' and a 'born again child'. Walking past the school as it was letting out, she was having a little trouble navigating her way through the mothers and children. One boy of about seven or eight noticed her problem: 'Hey, let the old lady through,' he shouted to his friends. It stung, she told me later. She had just been telling me that she was regressing into childhood by enjoying watching *Sesame Street* and the *Teletubbies* every morning.

Although Fran was 70, she still looked (and acted) youngish. I kept looking at her face trying to find the wrinkles she was supposed to have. All I ever saw were the smile lines. I once described Fran as having a beautiful smile, with a perfect gumline; she still has them today.

Just ten days after my 79th birthday, Cosmo wrote an article about Fran and me in *The Sunday Times*, demanding that we stop shagging our way through London society. Of course he was referring to our open marriage and the effect it had on him way back in the 70s. 'For most teenagers, the idea of one's parents having sex is pretty disgusting,' he wrote, 'Particularly when they talked about it openly to the press, on the radio, and on one occasion even appeared in a television documentary on the subject.'

Cosmo thought we were using our open marriage to keep ourselves in the media spotlight and further our careers. He hated the fact that we were so honest about our sex lives. 'If only my parents had been more hypocritical and less honest, I would have been far happier. I longed for a drab dad who pottered in his shed and a sweet, fat mum who baked cakes. Asking them to be more discreet was like asking a flasher to please put on some underwear before opening his raincoat.'

We were not unaware of Cosmo's plight. 'Hey, relax. Lighten up. The trouble with you is that you take everything too seriously,' I would suggest. My other answer was that he shouldn't undertake to raise two rebellious parents at the tender age of 16. 'You can't spend your life always worrying about what people will say. We're going to live our lives the way we want, and if you don't like it then that's too bad!' Fran told him. He said he couldn't understand how we could be so indifferent to his feelings. 'He's just pissed off at you for marrying Fran,' said one of my psychoanalytical buddies.

My fear that the tabloids would have a field day with the subject matter was unfounded. Instead, it was the quality dailies that picked up on what was turning into some kind of family feud. *The Daily Telegraph* assigned their ace feature writer, Michael Sheldon, who is really an English professor at Indiana State University, to get our side of the story. His caption over the story quoted Fran: 'I was bad, but I wish I was worse.' Then *The Independent* did a telephone interview by Emma Cook that summed up what an open marriage meant to Fran: 'I think it's hopeless to expect everything from one person. Certainly for the first four to five years I wouldn't recommend an open relationship. But after that period of time, it doesn't last; that frisson that everyone gets at first when it's more exciting. Someone once said everyone needs a little strange, and I believe that. Once I fantasized about running off with this composer but then I thought, 'I wonder if I can take Jay with us?''

I appeared on a religious programme (it was not *Songs of Praise*) defending my position against a devilish attack by saying Cosmo was a journalist who had to present a sensational point of view. Cosmo said: 'Soon my voice could be heard from the mud huts of the Amazon (when I appeared on the World Service) to the homes of middle England when I appeared on the guest slot on the *Richard and Judy* TV show.' He was in danger of becoming an Embarrassing Parents correspondent. 'In the spirit of discovery, I contacted the agony aunts of a string of teenage magazines - and swiftly discovered that my theories were wrong. All of them agreed that teenagers want their parents to be square just as I did.'

Then Cosmo went to Jack's Class Day. 'I made every effort to appear as straight and conventional as I can be. I spoke softly. I smiled a lot. I did not greet his headmaster, as my father once did, with the cry of: 'Hey, man, what's happening? This is a groovy place you got here.' And yet I can see by the shy and silent do-I-know-you nod he gives me when I enter his classroom that he is just another boy, deeply embarrassed by his dad.'

By the end of the summer, with the big eight-o on next year's horizon, I could spare a little time to sum up a decade of yearning for recognition, fame, and satisfaction inspired by one of Julie Burchill's insightful columns in *The Guardian*. Her period of fame was like a nightmare; she had left it behind her and thrown out a lifeline to those poor 'hot couples, those social dynamos and networking nonces who spend more time having their picture taken by gossip columns than having each other. It's a dog's life, really. So if at first you don't succeed – give it another half-hearted bash, and then give up. And get down to actually ENJOYING your one and only life.'

Of all my lives, the only one I took seriously was my marriage. All the other lives were just careers; time spent in trying to find out the best way to enjoy life; how to get rid of the contradictions in my own character. I was too restless, too inquisitive. Perhaps I had inherited an artistic nature from my father, but I was without an art. It gave me the opportunity to test myself instead of accepting the roles other people wanted me to play. Behind every mask was another mask, which successfully hid the fact I was a nice Jewish boy whose theatricality and decadence gave a lot of pleasure to a very small group of people. It was an act that could never play globally in spite of the fact that a radical notion of sex was behind most of my projects.

Of all the careers I've had, doing nothing was the best one and the most profitable. I learned more about life walking to the corner shop than I ever did at college. The extravagant exchanges I've had with strangers as well as acquaintances, whether personal or private, were often inspirational as well as informative. Workmen in an empty store were always eager to share the mysteries of their toil. 'What's the story, Jay?' Fran would ask as I stopped to talk or stare at blank walls. Curiosity has been an ally throughout my life. All that and delicious gossip to feed my gross appetite. A better career I can't imagine.

I overheard one of the most engaging conversations of the year while walking with Carolyn Cassady and Fran. The two of them were discussing what literature they really liked. The doyennes of the Beat Generation confessed they really didn't like any list of books that didn't include A.A. Milne. The two of them ignored the traffic as they crossed the street quoting excerpts from *Winnie the Pooh*.

As Christmas closed in on us, the end of the 98th year of the century, we had regained our health and focusing facility. It had been a big year for us in many ways. The opportunity to relax loomed large, so naturally I embarked on a project that would achieve the opposite. Like most worthwhile projects, this one originated in the French House. Drinking with a charming man I hardly knew, but remembering he was in the film business, I asked him how many copies of a film script I should have printed up if I wanted to send copies around to producers. 'You know that producers don't read scripts anymore,' he said. 'I'm probably the last of a dying breed of producers who do.'

I had just finished my second martini, ordered another and asked what he was drinking. 'That's very good of you,' he said. 'A Guinness, please.' What the hell, I thought, and asked him if he'd read mine if only to save me some money on the printing. I honestly never thought of him in a producer's role, but I knew he'd been in the business a long time and knew the score. After all, he only made documentaries and none of them were about my generation.

'Tell you what. Send me a copy. I have two very professional readers on the payroll. They're not very busy. It won't cost you a thing.'

It was an offer I couldn't refuse. We parted, shook hands, and I finished my martini with a feeling that maybe it would really be a big year.

A week after I sent him my script, I called him. He had given it to his partner who had left it, along with some valuable properties, on the bus. He was terribly sorry, but he was in touch with the lost and found department where he hoped it would turn up. I sent him my last remaining copy.

Two weeks later he called saying he had an interesting report and we should meet for lunch. He was an hour and a half late. As I was leaving the French, he called to say he was on his way. It did not please Fran whom I was to meet later in the afternoon. It would hardly be enough time for Aubrey Weller, the producer, to tell me he was ready to take a year's option on my script. Before we left Kettners he gave me the report his two readers gave him. I read it in the taxi home: 'Finally, as I am sure will be understood, the appraisal and analysis of screenplays over a period of years can lead to a certain condition which is a mixture of blasé and cynicism. It is a dangerous condition and we attempt to fight it. With this screenplay we did not have to. A sure sign is when one 'takes it home' in the head; we did.'

After dinner that evening, Jack asked if he could read aloud a few scenes. Cosmo stood up and said, 'Nice one, Jay. It's really good.' Nothing like that ever happened before and it will never happen again.

I could feel the unrealistic expectations rising over the next few days. I wrote to my old friend Irvin Arthur, alias the Prince of Darkness, who had been the official booker for the Crystal Palace and whose penchant for off-beat talent matched mine. Fran liked him because he would be enthusiastic about a new act who would be perfect for us, 'if only I could remember his name'. (He once booked a singer who had died but was still on his books.) He opened a smart little cabaret room to keep his acts working until he got a booking for them. He then went through a tough period and lost the club; most of his clients had outgrown him. I heard nothing from him for years until I saw his name in *Variety* as the one of the agents for a new actor on the scene, called Jim Carrey. He had moved to Los Angeles and worked his magic on some of the most hardened agents in the industry. Last I heard of him he had gotten twenty million for Carrey's work in *The Truman Show*.

I sent Arthur a fax asking if he'd like to see my screenplay about a New York he once loved. In the middle of the night he called: 'Send me the script.' Needless to say, I didn't get back to sleep. I visualised his getting Jim Carrey to play me ('Arthur, he even looks like me'). The script was with a friend of mine, an actress, whom I asked to deliver it to Arthur in person. He was in touch the next day: 'I'm a slow reader. You'll hear from me in a couple of days.'

I decided the script needed more than just 'fine tuning'. Quite by chance, having my usual martini at the French, I met a film producer who knew about – and was in love with – the period in which it was set. Phone numbers were exchanged, the script was dropped off, and, from all indications, he read and loved it. His wife was an agent for Helmut Newton, my favourite photographer. If nothing happened with the script, at least I would have an introduction to Newton.

The most important character in the script was based on Gershon Legman, my deputy editor on *Neurotica,* who had died; I had written his obituary for *The Independent.* When I first met him he was putting together a massive collection of erotic limericks, and translating de Sade's *120 Days of Sodom*; his scholarly works included *The Rationale of the Dirty Joke* and *No Laughing Matter.* Our relationship had lasted almost fifty years.

Another echo of the past was the arrival of my friend Paul Mazursky's memoirs of life as a Hollywood director. He had been part of a circle of talented out-of-work actors, editors, comedians, architects, poets, artists and writers who were destined to become famous, but who spent the Fifties sharpening their act in living rooms in New York. Mazursky did impersonations of Marlon Brando which always pleased the crowds. The book was the best Hollywood memoir I had read. Mazursky described my own memoir as 'The most neurotic book I've read' - a blurb I was not crazy about, but my American publisher thought it was very funny.

In spite of daily walks for morning coffee, we were falling apart together. Fran had a series of complaints that would win a prize in any hypochondriac's contest. My depression was more serious; it was called 'getting old'.

Cosmo was still secure at *The Sunday Times*. Miles's career as a musician and lyricist had not been such a success as his mother's, but it was certainly more colourful. At fifteen he became a messenger boy in the City: 'Stock market and Lloyds are on my list/Up and down I'll take the risk/as long as I'm there my feet burnt rare'. It gave him enough material for two plays, *The Lost Messenger Boy* and *The Final Circumcision, A Jewish Rock Horror Musical.* Resuming his musical career he formed his first band, Renoir, with his mates. This included actors Phil Daniels and Peter Hugo Daly, who were graduates of Anna Sher's renowned acting school. Renoir wrote a collection of songs for the film *The Class of Miss McMichael,* starring Glenda Jackson. While it didn't do much to further Miles's career, it helped Daniels and Daly, who had roles in the film, to move up the ladder of success while Miles moved underneath the ladder as a roadie for various groups.

Miles continued to write songs and play lead guitar, yet his main asset was his good looks. He became a model for Boy's catalogue of punk products from safety pins to whips, which influenced him considerably. Cosmo told me that he and Julie had seen his act in one of the sado-masochistic clubs in Soho, although Miles claimed he was only trying to liven up the place.

It wasn't until he became associated with Agent Provocateur, a firm specialising in highly erotic knickers, that his career became respectable. He had finally found a profession that combined all of his previous jobs and obsessions. He worked his way up from delivering ladies' exotic undergarments to becoming head of their special promotions, which included everything but modelling the knickers. The owner of the company was a flamboyant promoter whose dream was to have an all-girl rock group perform dressed in knickers and bras from Agent Provocateur. It was Miles's job to find girls who could sing as well as model the knickers; he did not consider it so much a job as a dream come true. When I cautioned Miles about the direction his career was taking, he took great pleasure in recalling my own attempts at pioneering the sexual revolution of the 60s. At 42 years of age, he still had big dreams, just like his old Mum and Dad.

Alarmed at the discovery that I was pissing blood, I called the hospital and they put me under observation. After innumerable tests they decided I probably had cancer of the bladder and suggested an immediate operation, which they assured me was only routine. Unfortunately the doctor described what would happen if things went wrong – an explanation that scared the shit out of me. I decided to postpone the operation until I knew more about the hazards or until I could find a doctor who had a more cheerful bedside manner.

The songwriting team of Simon Wallace and Fran Landesman was beginning to attract attention on both sides of the Atlantic thanks to the recordings of singers such as Nicki Leighton-Thomas, Ian Shaw, Sarah Moule, Susannah McCorkle and Imelda Staunton. There were productions of their musical *Forbidden Games* at the Young Vic (RSC), the Theatre Royal in Bath, The Pleasance at the 1998 Edinburgh Festival and the 1999 Gdansk Shakespeare Festival. Their songs were included in shows and revues in London and New York. My nephew, Rocco, presented a retrospective of Fran's work (*The Decline of the Middle West*) at the Smart Supper Club off-Broadway. English National Opera star Sally Burgess highlighted her concert with *The Ballad Of The Sad Young Men*. Four more of their songs were included in the Songbook Concert at the Wigmore Hall, and a complete evening of their work was presented by the National Theatre. Their collaboration was beginning to mean something. Someone asked me if I was jealous of Fran's success. I said, 'No – not until I am referred to as Mr Fran Landesman.'

On 4 July, Independence Day, Cosmo had a piece in *The Sunday Times* which made me sad. It was titled, 'How I lost a wife and gained a loving son'. And what a fight it had been. His attitude towards Fran and me changed significantly. His readjustment to us was all-embracing, including weekly dinners together with Jack. His sense of humour returned. He was like a person who had come out of the fog and was seeing us now as allies instead of enemies.

Since 15 July, my birthday, was the same day as our fiftieth wedding anniversary, why not hold a celebration? We invited our fifty closest friends to help make it memorable. Jack came with his film camera and crew (his Iranian school chum) to record the event. The guests were unprepared to be approached by two 14-year-old kids, with a hand-held camera, to answer such serious questions as 'What do you think of Jay and Fran's marriage?' While all of the interviewees agreed we had an excellent marriage, Cosmo's publicly testifying to that effect was a welcome surprise. One guest whom Jack questioned, a French transvestite, replied, 'Let me see your dick.' Jack told me later it was the best offer he had ever had.

A week before our departure for a holiday, Fran had an accident. The first time I met Fran, I discovered she didn't know how to cross a street. I saved her that day from being run over by a motorcycle. I'd been doing it ever since. Nothing could stop her challenging the traffic.

This time she was hit by a motorcycle a block from our house. Called to the scene by a witness, I rushed over to see her sitting in the ambulance, blood all over a face that suggested she was shocked rather than seriously hurt. She had a loss of memory, a split lip, and a bruised kneecap. I decided she would be better off in her own bed than going to the hospital. She agreed, once she established she could walk home. I reminded her she had a show to do that night. When she looked at herself in the mirror, it was obvious her split lip would seriously hinder her performance.

Fran decided she would fulfil her gig at the Groucho's annual talent show, due in a couple of days. She bravely went on to give a show that had a packed audience crying for more, according to my associate Terence Doyle. When she concluded her act with a recent composition, 'Scary Bitches', the audience broke up. It was the kind of piece that Dorothy Parker might have done with her sharp claws at the Round Table. It fitted the Groucho clientele perfectly.

In New York we visited my brother Fred's apartment, in which we had stayed on past visits. Fred and Paula had died in their bedroom and I saw them every time I entered the room. The ghost followed me around, but unlike me, didn't bump its head on the oversized

Tiffany lampshade in the kitchen. There were other surprises: a large stuffed raven lurking on the top rung of a winding staircase, as if warning the climber not to go any further; a glass birdcage stretching from floor to ceiling, empty of birds; a painting of a wooden arm with a tattoo. I suspected that those little touches were there not as pure decoration, but for psychological reasons.

We still have friends in New York whom we shall probably never see again, even though we love them. We're getting too old to travel. Every time we have to go there for professional reasons, we're really going to see the people we miss. However, this time our visit really was career-related. Fran had been told by her agent, Irvin Arthur, that her songs were being sung in cabarets all over the city. Susannah McCorkle was singing three new Landesman /Wallace songs at the prestigious Oak Room of the Algonquin Hotel and she had covered them on her new CD *Hearts and Minds.* Fran enjoyed meeting her and told how much she loved her interpretations.

On our last night in New York, the playwright Arnold Weinstein gave us a farewell party attended by all our friends, which was pure magic. Jackie Caine and Roy Kral premiered Roy's and Fran's latest song. Even the tough critic Rex Reed and writer James Gavin were visibly moved. Jackie's rendition was so moving, Fran's lyric so timely, and Roy's music so melodious that the small group of people privileged to hear the song realised we were coming close to fulfilling our dreams. Would we be around much longer? Roy had had open-heart surgery, Arnold had cancer, and Fran and I had suspicious symptoms.

Back in London, Fran found a play that I had written before we left St Louis. She felt it would be perfect for Diana Rigg, who had shown an interest in working with Fran. Diana loved a song of Fran's and Simon's titled *There's One Good Scandal Left in Me.* We both re-read the script and decided that it was perfect for Diana.

A friend of mine complimented me by saying he really liked my second volume of memoirs. 'I have it on my nightstand. Every time I can't get to sleep, I pick it up, read a few pages and zap, I fall asleep.' I had a biography of Saul Bellow on my night stand and felt the same way about it. I remember when Bellow's first novel *Dangling Man* was featured in the window of the village bookshop, Four Seasons, in St Louis. I gather that didn't seem to get any satisfaction from being featured in the window, nor did he appreciate the complimentary reviews. Naturally he blamed the publishers for not pushing the book and eventually broke with them. It led me to believe that he was disappointed with everything in his creative career, except the nookie he got as a result of his good looks and his name.

He had numerous wives, all of whom he expected to leave him alone so he could get on with his work. As I read more about those early days I couldn't help feeling that he took himself too seriously, although he had a comic touch that saved many of his novels.

Bellow lived his life as if there had been no Beat Generation. There was a misunderstanding among writers as to what we wanted to accomplish with *Neurotica*. We wanted needle-nose analysis of a culture that was clearly going insane. Furthermore, we wanted to put the blame on those who were responsible. *Neurotica* was designated in *Life* magazine as one of the four most highbrow magazines in America. According to Marshall McLuhan, Henry Luce wanted a monthly for the literary gourmet: 'He wanted to reduce the then role of arts and letters to a simple pattern which could be reproduced monthly without disturbing the existing affinities between his other magazines.'

It's uncanny to look back and see how the Henry Luce episode changed my life. I had just met Fran and had fallen quickly in love with her. I had become disillusioned with the reaction I was getting from *Neurotica*. Legman was difficult to work with. He was on a crusade to nail, among others, the United States Government. The Luce offer was rejected by Legman, who was determined to fight the censorship laws. He deliberately began to toughen up *Neurotica*. (In those days the use of the word 'prick' was forbidden.) I was so in love with Fran I had to decide whether to join Legman and possibly go to jail. I chose Fran, gave *Neurotica* to Legman, and never looked back.

With a broken leg, he went to Washington D.C. for his appearance at his hearing on charges of obscenity. He defended himself brilliantly but lost the case. They cancelled his mailing privilege. Legman, forced out of America, fled to France after publishing the last issue of *Neurotica,* which was entirely devoted to the castration complex.

In 1982, I was planning on publishing my book *The Bedside Book of Erotica*. Although I had had little communication with Legman for about thirty years, he was the world's leading authority on erotica and I wanted his advice on what to avoid. I sent him a sample of the text and a sample of the kind of pictures I planned to use. I knew I'd get some abuse along with useful advice. I also sent him a manuscript I had written at the time we were working together on *Neurotica*. It had remained unpublished for fifty years. He dismissed the book I had asked his advice on, but was fanatically interested in the novel.

My dear Jay,
The real harm I did you - and I see that I really did you harm - was in somehow so intimidating you at the time that you overlooked to show me this gem-like period piece you have written when it would have been so easy to encourage you to have it published, and when all the allusions and caricatures (McCullers, Baldwin (?) etc., would have been amusing to identify. Whoever you showed it to then, such as Felix Giovanelli and Holmes, certainly did not do right by you in allowing it to stay in the drawer until now! What do I have to do to make you see that it is still the moment, still publishable, and still very much worth publishing, not for its scintillating and over-scintillating dialogue (always a sin of young writers) but for its perfect portrait of the period, which I do not believe has ever been portrayed at all let alone so well. You write as the perfect insider, wholly disabused and heartbrokenly mocking, and with a competence I never suspected you of, you bastard! The description of the woman with her face too repressed to uncrack at the cocktail/tea party, was a jewel, and there are many such things all through. I am absolutely intent on getting you to print this NOW! As the titles like The Idle Rich (in your psych translation of this as The Nervous Set) are no longer hip I will give you a title that should do - since Erich Segal went and used up Love Story - call it RETRO. Just that. I have a friend who goes around with Diane Keaton: she will play

Fran. But even if the movie is long in coming this is a very short book and will not cost much to put into type. A thousand or two thousand copies are essential to get into the libraries of the world, as a document, even if you never make a dime out of it. If you are ashamed to put your imprint on your own book, use 'Alfred Towne' or we will use my imprint for you (and you for me!) as above. I am not kidding about this. Of course, the parts about me are bad and unfair, but I won't sue, and it doesn't matter. Where you are great is not in your closing up on the intellectual life of your times, but in the coleoptera and jitteroptera of the worthless set you dipped into there. You could have been the Michael Arlen of your time, not to say the Roland Firbank (minus the homosexual varnish, of course) or a lesser Fitzgerald. It was a terrible failure of communication that you did not put me in a position to encourage you to do it then; let us do it now. As you can't spell I will even offer to edit (very lightly) if you wish, for auld lang syne and a small fee, but you don't need it. The printer will know how to correct the spelling errors - what do they matter? Do it! R.E.T.R.O. This is not a mad, foolish, flattering notion. It is a cultural duty. You realise it won't make a dime but that does not matter. We will give away a copy free with every issue of the Complete NEUROTICA, in which historically it should have been serialised at the time. What a blunder not to. Let us rectify this now with a few hundred pages of printer's type, so I won't have to retype the whole thing myself, and a pirated photocopy edition for the Library of Congress and my favorite twenty other repository libraries in America and abroad. This won't be the first time I did this. Or we could reissue it that way under my imprint, if you have it typed up.

I took his letter as some sort of apology – something I'd never heard coming from him.

Four of Fran's lyrics had been published in a book that celebrated the 'best American and English lyrics of the twentieth century'. We sang her praises and so did she. Fran was enjoying every moment.

By Christmas 2000 we were in close harmony. An unexpected present came from the Middlesex Hospital; it had to be the best present I'd ever received. The cancer problem had all cleared up. I could now return to my normal regime. Fran and the rest of my family were very relieved. Cosmo gave me a copy of *The Assassin's Cloak*, an anthology of the world's greatest diarists; from Miles came a tape, *The Best of Miles's Recordings.*

Fran was working on a book of verse for children, and Simon Wallace's wife Sarah Moule had recorded a new CD of songs by Fran and Simon. Fran couldn't resist the combination of food and jazz; she chose the local organic cabaret and restaurant as the launch pad.

Jack rewrote a sci-fi musical on which Miles had been working for ten years. Miles had written some great songs, but it lacked the sort of narrative required by Hollywood. Miles offered Jack a deal: 'Add a few laughs to the script and the job of directing is yours.' He said he'd think about it.

'This is the best part of my day,' Fran said as she sat drinking her latte in Al's Diner and listening to the new CD by Sarah Moule. 'I must be the luckiest girl in the world.'

'Is it enough?' I asked.

'Yes,' she said. 'I don't think I could handle any more attention than I have right now.'

'You once wrote a haiku : *I got everything I wanted, it was more than I expected, it wasn't enough.*'

'I know what's important now.'

We would read amusing snippets to each other from the newspapers. However, there were many other things to do at Al's. Sometimes, as we entered the place, the music would grab us and we would go into a dance, ending with a kiss or applause from the ancient Indian dishwasher. Our coffee and pastry were always ready for us and we would take our places like children in kindergarten. Sometimes the boss would hand us a note from other customers, who just wanted us to know they enjoyed our little antics, or liked Fran's and Simon's songs. There weren't many people in the place, just as there weren't many people at Fran's gigs, but we didn't complain.

Tom told us that customers frequently asked about us. He would tell them that we used to be King and Queen in America. Or he'd say we were a retired show business couple who were making a comeback.

At weekends we would go to La Patisserie because Al's opened too late. It was a completely different ball game. We behaved ourselves at La Patisserie because of Frank Johnson, a respected columnist for the *Daily Telegraph.* He sat in the same seat each day with a stack of the morning newspapers, scanning them for ideas he could write about in his political sketches.

He had the look of a man who didn't want to be disturbed, which always encouraged me to distract him with quasi-serious questions. I was never in his class, although we used to meet at the local sleazy salsa bar at night, where he would let himself go, especially when we were with a certain stunning blonde. She had a crush on him, which led to an exciting exchange. It was amusing to see him dancing the night away. It developed into a few dates at the Garrick Club, where it was rumoured they discussed the indiscretions of the last ten Prime Ministers of England.

Frank disappeared from La Patisserie during the cold spell over Xmas, driving Fran and me to Starbucks, where we had enjoyed our special iced tea all summer. No nonsense at Starbucks, though. There was little to distract us except the many well-behaved babies who seemed to enjoy Starbucks as much as we enjoyed them.

I had a bad post-Christmas patch: bitter cold weather, expensive repairs on Miles's caravan, Fran's teeth, Cosmo's wanting me to bail him out of a request for sixty thousand pounds so that he could settle his flat purchase, plus a bear market. My way of handling it was to suggest we go to the Bahamas to sit in the sun. 'And get cancer,' Fran replied.

It led to a full-scale confrontation. She accused me of failing to appreciate all the things she did for me. When she threatened to take her dinner to her room to escape further discussion, I indicated that was okay with me as I didn't want any dinner anyway. The next morning we walked to Al's in silence; she was in no mood to forgive me.

A week earlier, she'd told me she was deeply unhappy with her work. Now she was unhappy about the way the world was going. I suggested that the world had been in terrible shape for thousands of years, yet it always survived. Since we didn't have a lot of time left, why not make the most of our life?

The next day she had her friend, the jazz singer Nicki Leighton-Thomas ,and her new baby round for lunch. Fran, with the help of a little talking pink pig, was a big hit with Matilda; she gave Nicki a period see-through silk dress and started to snap out of her depression.

She was ecstatic when she heard from Ned Sherrin that he was planning to have Simon and Sarah on *Loose Ends* for the launch of her CD, and there was a phone call from BBC's drama director, Ned Chaillet, giving the go-ahead for a radio project she had submitted previously. 'A double-Nedder,' Simon said when she told him.

I had been examining all our projects and coming to the conclusion that none of them was going anywhere. That idea would never have occurred to me when I was younger. It didn't matter that many of them were destined for the scrap heap; it was enough that I was engaged, full of excitement and anticipation, not taking them seriously, but having a bit of fun. I was creating a new lifestyle - putting the fun back into failure. Now, at the age of eighty-one, was I becoming serious about my wasted life? Was it too late to have an epiphany? I had a vision of a life that was free of projects. I would succumb to the gentrification of my life. I would re-design my living quarters to include a live-in mistress, a new fridge, and cable television. I would discontinue my vendettas on all celebrities, indulge in e-mail, and improve my spelling. I would finish my memoirs.

Our park is full of diversions in the winter. We watch our favourite trees change into something more comfortable; we kick the golden leaves; we criticise the inept cutting of some favourite bushes. The dog owners treat me like a long-lost friend. I have a beautiful white spitz who's nuts about me, a couple of Jack Russells straining at the leash to kiss me; some ugly bulldogs give me the eye. We comment on the fickleness of pigeons as they ignore us since we don't feed them their favourite buns. The beautiful bronze lady of the First

World War memorial still attracts them, however.

While waiting for Spring to hang us up the most, we had a rollicking round of parties enlivened by our personal aromatherapist and long-time friend Hanja Kochansky. Fran had found a miracle cure for her aches and pains by keeping the company of babies. She never missed an opportunity to introduce herself to the new babies we encountered; smiles were exchanged and, like photographs, they last forever.

Whenever I complimented Fran on an old lyric or a new dish, she would say, 'I didn't do such a bad job raising our kids either.' She still felt she was not appreciated by me or, in darker moments, by the world in general. I could usually convince her about the musical world, yet whenever I said how much I appreciated her she would say, 'That may be so, but it's not chic to be complimented by your husband.'

We were both brought up by parents who didn't believe in complimenting children for fear of spoiling them. When Fran's mother heard her songs for our shows, she seriously asked Fran if she had really written the lyrics. I cannot recall my mother ever complimenting me on anything but having stayed out of jail.

With Cosmo and Miles we didn't expect anything in the way of achievements. If they failed any subject in school, we would compliment them for being different. If they were able to bunk into rock concerts without being caught, it was cause for a drink. We sent them to the worst schools yet Miles learned how to swim there. When Cosmo's teacher began to take an interest in his writing, we tried to get him to change schools. We were awful.

You might say we trained them to be underachievers, but the brats outwitted us. Cosmo became a critic for the *Sunday Times*. On our golden wedding anniversary, Cosmo took style guru Peter York on a tour of Miles's premises which included a room full of the kind of memorabilia that wins Turner prizes. York, reeling from the profusion of accumulated junk, commented to Cosmo, 'Your parents gave the kid everything.'

As we were figuring what it would cost us to accept my nephew Knight's invitation to a dessert dinner, tickets to *The Producers*, a hotel suite with twin toilets, pastrami sandwiches, two first class air tickets, I received the following Fedex: 'Dear Mr Landesman. You have been named one of the beneficiaries of Mr. M. Hubert Macklin's estate. The settlement process must be completed before we will be able to give you an idea of the amount of your inheritance.'

Herb (to his friends) was the ticket-taker and head usher for the Crystal Palace's theatrical events. In his spare time he bred prize pigeons. As a former actor, he couldn't stay away from anything to do with show business. He even brought drama to tearing up the cloakroom tickets. When the Crystal Palace production of *Dearest Dracula* opened the Dublin Theatre Festival of 1965, Herb was there at the door keeping an eye on things.

On a visit back to St Louis, Fran and I accepted his invitation to meet his pigeons. It was a real treat to see this kindly man interact with his favorites. When we returned to London, I took a photograph of Miles - then only four years old - feeding the pigeons in Trafalgar Square and sent it to Herb. For the next thirty-five years Herb sent us articles and photos of events going on in St Louis which he thought would interest us. He gave us a love for pigeons that would have otherwise been unimaginable. We play with them every day on our walks, marveling at their good humour, their ability to communicate. The only mystery that eludes us is, why have we not ever seen a baby pigeon?

I had no idea of how much he left me, but it was rumoured he had left a hundred and fifty grand to a pigeon organization. In any case we decided we'd have a holiday on Herb no matter what the cost.

Rocco always gave us Annie Oakleys for all his shows when we hit New York, but there was some doubt he'd pick up the tab for Broadway's sensational show *The Producers*. We had heard that tickets were being sold by scalpers for five hundred dollars on the day we arrived in New York. We needn't have worried; the tickets were waiting for us on the night, fifth row centre.

Dammit, I wanted to like the show, as I had liked the film. Fran had said I couldn't like anything that was a hit. I had always denied the charge. While the musical version was beautifully crafted, the actors superb, the music catchy, the total effect was smartass. That a talent like Mel Brooks should have to rely on such old burlesque standby situations to get laughs was a disappointment. There were enough genuine comic situations to make you cry from laughter without the need to stoop to stupid camp.

Mel and his wife came to the party but I was too pissed by the time they arrived. I was told I had annoyed his wife, Anne Bancroft. I reminded her I had sent my play *Nobody Knows The Trouble I've Been,* about an ageing jazz singer making a comeback, to her agent, who told me she had read it on the plane. She didn't remember.

Neither Fran nor I had brought anything we could plug or promote. We saw a number of people already there that we would have liked to promote, but they were doing such a brilliant job of plugging themselves there was no need to gild the lily. God, it felt good not to be selling anything.

Fran had been uncomfortable since returning from New York. Very few gigs, very many complaints. Sciatica was rampant. It forced Fran to revive her scenario for her dream suicide. The original plan was to relax in the Bentley, garaged in a council building, eating pastrami sandwiches or drinking a martini with the hose in the back seat.

'Don't like the garage being in a council building,' Fran said.

'We'll have to think of a better way. What about your pills?' I asked.

'Don't think I have enough for the two of us.'

'Couldn't we go someplace where there's a beautiful view, overlooking something memorable? What about Stonehenge? It's got a new parking lot. We could meet some nice people.'

I thought of writing a play about a suicidal couple who talk two strangers they meet in the parking lot of Stonehenge into joining them. However, instead of doing all the work of writing the damned thing, I was satisfied I had scored some points with the idea alone.

The older we become, the nicer Fran and I are to each other. We have so little time left; why waste it on meaningless rages? We have very few friends who agree with us – possibly because our friends get younger as the older ones die. By the middle of the year four or five of our most valued friends had disappeared so quickly, we didn't have time to say goodbye.

It always comes as a shock when the phone rings announcing the death of a loved one. Only recently we had gone to New York to hear Susannah perform at the Algonquin. After the show Fran complimented her on her interpretation of *Scars*; Simon Wallace's setting was perfect for a singer who could spin a lyric from romance to sorrow by bending a single note.

McCorkle was an inspired singer of her generation. After a five-year stint in London, she moved back to Schenectady, a provincial town in upstate New York. Its main attraction was its large mall and small gossip that could turn a headache into despair. She told Fran the only way to leave Schenectady would be through suicide. After the Algonquin engagement, when it seemed that she was a hit, her record company, Concord Jazz, went into bankruptcy, which released her from her contract. No jobs materialized. They found Susannah dead on the sidewalk outside her apartment building.

Fran and Simon came up with a brilliant idea for a show: small cast of three, low budget, producer available, original director, no pre-production expenses. All we really needed was Julie Burchill's permission, Liz Hurley to lisp Julie's words, Madonna to sing Fran's & Simon's songs, and the choreographers from my nephew Rocco's *The Producers*. I would produce, Simon would play the piano, and Ned Sherrin would direct. We would open in La Scala Opera House at union rates and offer free pizzas at the intermission.

The only reason I didn't give the idea an airing was that I didn't like the way it ended for Fran and me. On our sixtieth anniversary we would get divorced. The grounds? Incompatibility.

I really should write the novel. My Chinese fortune cookie said, 'Don't take yourself so seriously. Spring doesn't last for ever.'

So many old friends have died recently, death is always on my mind. I picked up a copy of Henry Miller's *On Turning Eighty* which I've had around the house since I was seventy. I discovered I had read it completely, even underlined significant sentences. Miller is one of those writers you appreciate when you become old. When young and ambitious you only appreciate him for his sexual encounters and the freshness of his erotica.

I realised how much he had influenced my lifestyle when I was young and adventurous, editing *Neurotica*. In fact he wrote me a letter which I printed in the second issue: 'Thank you for sending me the number of 'Erotica'. The lead article by Friedmann is quite something altogether remarkable. Send me issue 2. P.S. Many friends of mine have expressed their amazement and joy over Friedmann's fragment. Sincerely yours, Henry Miller, Big Sur, Cal.'

Henry Miller said, like the fortune cookie, don't take yourself too seriously. It's the little things that are most rewarding; stay away from formal education; the poor are more fun than the rich.

I could find no logical answer to Fran's health problems. A new doctor at her surgery read Fran's medical history and, finding nothing to say about her current complaints, suggested a psychiatrist. Fran mentioned that she had been through that trip many times, and she didn't want to waste any more time going to their offices. The doctor, sensing a little resistance, mentioned there was a very good psychiatrist who made house calls. Fran's eyes lit up. She had never heard of such a thing being available on the NHS. The idea highly amused her. She said, 'Now I feel like the girl who has everything.'

The young psychiatrist arrived on time with a pad and pencil and proceeded to take notes on Fran's outpourings. If he had looked around at the pictures on her walls, the bric-a-brac on the mantelpiece, and the general disorder and dust, he'd have done better to advise to sell the house and move to a nunnery. But he took it all in, suggesting he'd try to find a clinical psychologist. Although the woman he found for Fran didn't make house calls, she did have a course of exercises for difficult cases.

Fran abhorred exercises, having successfully avoided them all her life, but she was pleased that so many people were paying her attention. In the weeks that followed she showed significant signs of recovering.

An invitation from Craig and Jo Sams to spend the Bank Holiday weekend at their new house in Hastings contributed to Fran's improvement. To be free from London's drillings, smells, and supermarkets, had a profound effect on both of us. For a moment we even talked of moving to East Dulwich for some peace and play with Simon's and Sarah's baby James, with whom Fran had fallen in love.

The illusion of wanderlust didn't last long. It was impossible to make such a radical move at 82 and 74 respectfully. But there were compensations; Michael Horovitz called to ask Fran to liven up London's Poetry Week by appearing at the Queen's Theatre in Shaftesbury Avenue, with Paul McCartney and the steadfast collection of poets who regularly contribute to Michael's Poetry Olympics.

After a serious misunderstanding with Terence Doyle about the film we'd been working on for three years, I was prepared, in spite of the fun we had had working together, to throw it in the Landesman archive of lost causes. But we were getting such a good reaction to Terence's script that we booked a cheap flight to Cannes to try to get a producer interested. One of Terence's friends was also trying to find a producer. His company had a yacht, which he let us use for press conferences and as a meeting place; he even threw a party on the boat and invited a hundred or so graduates in mobile phonology. As a party piece I gave an elaborate sketch on how to make the perfect martini, which was televised by Polish educational TV.

The trip was worth making if only because we met the European editor of *Variety*. He knew all about me and *Neurotica* and did not mind sharing with the reporters at his table the secret that I was one of the terrorists responsible for setting off the biggest cultural explosion in the Western Hemisphere.

Other kinds of terrorism were on people's minds, of course. Three weeks after the September 11 attacks on New York, Fran and I found ourselves in agreement that fun was out and that people weren't going to be buying £25,000 Rolex watches. I actually called one version of my film script *The Death Of Fun*. I had begun to question the wisdom of making fun the focus of life.

Fran's performance for Michael Horovitz's poetry day was a real hit. Her combination of humour and insight was well received by a full house. The only thing that spoiled the show for me was the theatre management's placement of the poets' books in the sweets section where Mars bars ruled. Paul McCartney's contribution was enthusiastically received. He has a marvellously ironic sense of humour when he tells tales of the crazy things that happen to him on tours. Poetry certainly suits Paul, and Paul is the better for it.

I have the widest collection of repairmen you could imagine, and possibly the weirdest. My plumber is also a fancy car dealer – I bought a 924 Porsche coupé from him, and it gave me much pleasure. He was once a boxer, but retired to spend his time repairing other boxers between rounds. The real reason I still see him is not because the ancient plumbing needs fixing but because he's crazy about Fran's poetry and jazz and comes to all her gigs. His phone number is one of the treasures I'm leaving to the boys.

Fran decided to play it safe by getting a series of tests for Alzheimer's, but her memory loss was no worse than mine. I had decided that old age is not for sissies. It's tough to get laid when you're eighty-one. What can you do with all the unwanted advice you have to give that no one wants to hear? If you give up envy, what do you have to replace it with? Do you wonder what it all means when your Number One son kicks your walking stick out from under you to get a laugh?

Francis Bacon was still making news from the grave; his heir, a very hip cockney bartender, had settled his legal fight with the Marlborough Galleries, and returned to London. In the old days, I frequently ran into Bacon at the Colony Room indulging his afternoon champagne habit; an innocent 'hello' could lead to a confrontation with either Bacon or his minder/friend, John. We would talk about the poet Gregory Corso and the antics he indulged in while Bacon was a guest with him. For many years Bacon confused me with Bill Burroughs; I never corrected him.

One afternoon Bacon and I met quite by accident, in the Groucho. He was feeling particularly mean that dead afternoon. I asked him what he'd done before he became a painter. I had heard he was at various times a butler, a dresser, an interior decorator, and a house painter. 'I was once a tailor, too,' he confessed, and for some reason he grabbed me by the lapels of my jacket, tearing a button off in the process.

'Prove it,' I challenged him, dropping the button in his hand. 'Let's see you sew this fucking button back.' He looked up and down the empty bar expecting to find a needle and thread next to the glass of naked celery. He finally asked the waiter for the equipment, ordered another bottle of champagne, and went to work on my jacket. He made a complete mess of the operation, blaming his failing eyes for not being to thread the needle. 'And you call yourself a tailor,' I sneered. He was quite sweet about his failure.

I never mentioned it again, but Stephen Fotheringall must have witnessed the scene because he wrote a completely different version in his own book, a memoir of his life as the last lamplighter in Soho.

During our early-morning coffee I noticed a man wearing a jacket that demanded recognition. It was bespoke, by an artist of the gusset sleeve and triple-vented back. It was 1950, my favourite year. He was a cappuccino aficionado, and from our morning greetings we discovered we had much more in common than tailoring and coffee. I gave him the first volume of my memoir. The next day he gave me an eight-by-ten photo of himself as a matinee idol. He had been the boy in *The Winslow Boy,* but in David Mamet's version, years later, he became a witness for the prosecution. I gave him my book and I warned him it was about America's nervous breakdown and how I had caused it. He said he had a hand in the breakdown too, as he had lived and worked in America for many years.

Once he'd started the book, he couldn't resist giving me examples of where our lives crossed. He had bought a car from my first mistress, had frequented P. J. Clark's (my second office), and had had affairs with half of New York's acting fraternity, but he challenged the story of my Cardinal Richelieu bed with four carved dwarves holding it together and the consequence some years later, when my then wife divorced me, claiming I had forced her to sleep in a bed that had no safety features. He proceeded to tell me the bed he slept in had been the star witness in a famous murder that fascinated New York society. The man's excuse for murdering his wife was that she had bitten his cock while giving him a blow job in the bed.

Fran says she's nuts about me. I have tried to tell her for the last fifty years not to fall in love with me, because I'm no damn good. She was so impressed by my honesty that she wrote a lyric that captivated a small crowd of well-wishers.

Don't fall in love with me
It wouldn't do
I couldn't ever be
Faithful to you
Don't fall in love with me
I'm no damn good
You'd only lose your way
In my neighbourhood
I'm not your destiny
Kiss me and run
Don't fall in love with me
Don't spoil the fun

I had the perfect producer, Peter Bach, and director, Nick Parrish, for the film, and a new scriptwriting collaborator, Dickon Levinge. They were all young and technically knowledgeable, and none of them was a 'bread head'. Once again I was putting together

a production company, which I called Humbug International Pictures –its logo spelled H-I-P. Peter and Dickon were hoping to make
the picture (not counting post-production) for an initial £100,000.
Fran warned me against financing the film myself; my plan was to
raise the funds from people who thought it would be a success. I
hoped they had a sense of humour.

At the same time, Fran and Simon were working on a show for a
very accomplished producer who planned to open in London and
eventually take the show to New York. It was a lot less complicated
than ours, but sounded like more fun. Fran and Simon had written a
smashing score to their collaborator's very sexy book.

At our weekly family dinner Cosmo outlined his programme for
the security of 8 Duncan Terrace after my death. He claimed he had
been negotiating with the local taxidermist to stuff me and put me in
the dentist's chair by the window with a martini in one outstretched
hand. As there is a standing art deco lamp kept on through the night,
the stuffed me would deter any potential burglar from attempted
entry. Luckily for me, he has to get Home Office approval for the
stuffing.

A block from our house, a black beggar had taken up residency
in front of an empty Tube station. He worked incredibly long hours,
stopping only occasionally for his roll- up fag, or when someone engaged him in heated Biblical arguments. A repulsive looking chap,
he held a crushed Dixie cup for donations. His smile was awesome,
his beard frightening, his teeth a nightmare. I asked one day how
he knew so much about the Bible. He told me he had learned it
when he had been at boarding school. I asked him in a jocular vein
if it was Eton. He laughed and said, 'Yes – it was in West Virginia,
though.'

One day, as he was absent from his post, I decided to take over his
spot. When I took off my hat and put it in front of me, Fran flipped.
She demanded to know if I was going to accompany her home. I
told her I had to help out my pal, who showed up like a ghost, just
in time. He congratulated her loudly on her love of babies. I tried to

explain to him that she could not see their faces any more because she had macular degeneration.

Fran retreated quickly when I asked if I could bring him home. Over her shoulder, she shouted that I was crazy. 'You wrote a lyric about me, warning me not to change, remember?' I said. 'Besides, how often do you meet a beggar who's been to Eton?'

The person who handled the creation of my website not only made me an attractive and informative one, but introduced me to his internet publishing company. He happened to be the brother of a former mistress of mine so I knew he was the right man to do business with. His operation as a publisher bore the strange name Tiger of the Stripe, and its products were probably the most eclectic in publishing history; they included such classics as *The Bibliomania or Book-Madness, Containing Some Account of the History, Symptoms, and Cure of This Fatal Disease in a Epistle to Richard Heber, Esq., by the Reverend Thomas Frognall Dibdin, Fellow of the Society of Antiquaries.* Peter Danckwerts wrote an introduction to the masterpiece: 'This edition will be of particular interest to historians of printing and the book, to librarians and book-collectors; it should also appeal to anyone with an interest in human nature or the cultural history of England seen from a distinctive Regency perspective. Dibdin's *Bibliomania*, first published in 1809, is an anthem to the printed book, a warning to the unwary about the perils of obsessive book-collecting, and the confessions of a rabid book-collector.'

Danckwerts's forthcoming books include *English Bards and Scotch Reviewers,* and *Hebrew Melodies,* both by Lord Byron, as well as *The Architectural History of Canterbury Cathedral* and other potential bestsellers. His choosing a book about the lifestyle of a fellow publisher/writer who was unsullied by convention, embellished with the single word *LANDESMANIA* and a huge exclamation point in red on a black cover, convinced me he was my kind of publisher.

The author of *Landesmania!* is Philip Trevena, born in Chile, educated in America, refined in London. He lived with my ex-mistress Pam Hardyment for long enough to discover who Jay Landesman was and find out if the twentieth century owed him a favour. Over a period of six years we would meet at the Groucho Club and at my house on Duncan Terrace. I don't know if it was my battered Panama hat, my crooked grin, or my Grey Goose vodka martinis that made him propose the idea of a book about my life. When he told me I was the last cultural interpreter of my time we made a deal. He mentions in the foreword to *Landesmania* that he was impressed 'by the old bird and his cocky cheerfulness and was intrigued at what he must have been like as a young man'.

The book came out on schedule, receiving a rave review in *The Spectator* by, of all people, Julie Burchill: 'I grew to love talented Fran and stylish Jay - Scott and Zelda crossed with Ma and Pa Kettle - their warmth, outrageousness and artiness. The Landesmans are genuinely original and accomplished people, and far more worthy of a biography than 75% of the jokers who are the subject of such studies.'

I sent a copy to Lorraine Treanor, who had been in touch with Scott Miller, the producer of the 2004 revival of *The Nervous Set* in St Louis. He produced stunning promotional material that showed the background to *The Nervous Set*.

Lorraine seemed to be devoting her life to getting the musical revived. She contacted her agent, who had a solid connection with the Nederlanders – big Broadway producers. I thought the plan was crazy, but when I sent them the two versions of the show, along with all the publicity, a CD of the original score, and the reviews of its Broadway debut, they became very serious about an option. The contract was very long and very demanding. I hesitated about signing. My secretary Mary Rose insisted: 'It's not going to cost you anything to sign. They sound serious to me.' I signed.

Lorraine made up a terrific package and sent it off. After a couple of weeks. she heard from Joe Nederlander who said it looked interesting and he would look into it. I remembered all the scripts I have sent to producers who said the same thing, although some also added the word 'unique'. That became a nice way of saying, 'No, thanks.'

Diane Nine, the agent, sent Lorraine an e-mail saying she had spent all of Christmas Day with Joe Nederlander, who had played the music and talked things over. I passed the word to Lorraine that I wanted Mike Nichols to direct. I know he gets more than the $75 a week I paid him when he worked for me in the Compass Players in 1961, but he's so talented these days, I'm willing to pay him $125.

I'm still on hold, yet I don't know how much longer I can stop myself telling everyone the show is going to Broadway.

Miles's girl gave me three pounds for the one copy of *Landesmania!* she had displayed in the window of the bookshop in which she works. It was bought, she said, by a one-eyed collector who returned the next day to tell her what an enjoyable and well-written book it was. Somehow that sale meant more to me than the order I got for two copies of *Landesmania!* at my local Waterstones. I wondered if my nephew Rocco got the same thrill when he sold three of his Broadway theatres for millions. Like me, Rocco likes to gamble on his projects and always makes money.

Cosmo asked to see the third and last section of my memoirs. I'm always glad when he asks to see something of mine, even though he never comments on what I give him. He's definitely including the family in his first book; he even asked for an interview with his mother.

Re-reading this third volume I suddenly realised I've lived my life in paragraphs. There have been chapters of life which were more important, but it was the paragraphs of life that made it exciting. Little excursions to far away places, experiments with the highs of life and analysing the lows kept me in shape for the surprises therein.

I hope I live long enough to read Cosmo's book, see Miles settled and dance the last dance with Fran.

THE END

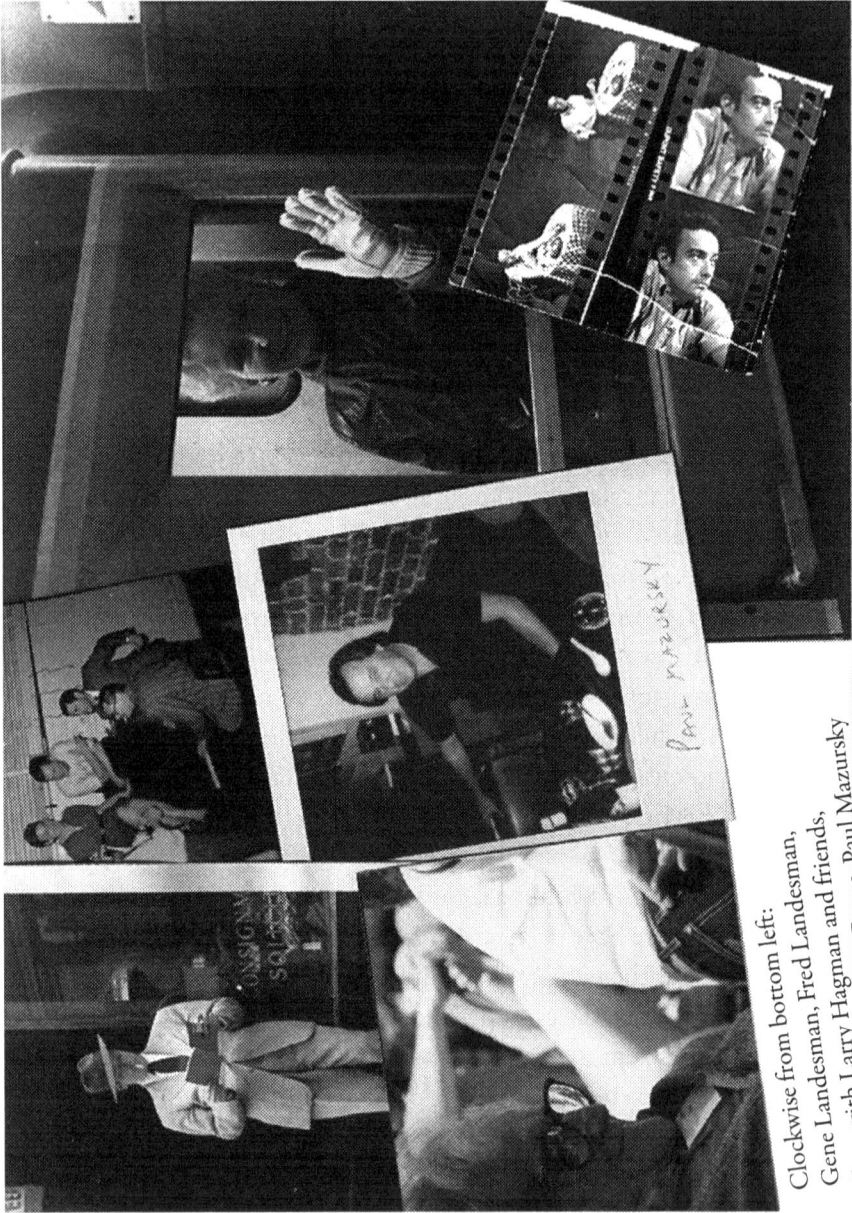

Clockwise from bottom left:
Gene Landesman, Fred Landesman,
Fran with Larry Hagman and friends,
Carolyn Cassady, Lenny Bruce, Paul Mazursky

Jay and Fran Landesman and cars.

The

Nervous Set

JAY LANDESMAN

Author's Notes

I wrote this novel in 1952 from the point of view of a disen-chanted young man. *The Nervous Set* is a poignant reminder of the pain of growing up in a society bent on repression. A bunch of cool guys hanging around the bars, playing hand tennis, flirting with high society, drinking bourbon and smoking the weed is just the back-ground to what was really going on in New York at the time.

Like the hero of my novel, America was going through its own identity crisis. The Beat Generation started out with my magazine *Neurotica* in St Louis, 1948, and within a few years its ideas had spread from coast to coast. *Harper's* magazine called *Neurotica* one of the four highbrow magazines in America.

In this lost novel, which was turned down by publishers nervous of obscenity charges, I wrote about the early heartbeat of a genera-tion that didn't want to play it by America's rules, and paid a some-times terrible price for not propping up the American Dream.

In the '60s, after a final showdown with my co-writer, Gershon Legman, I sent him this novel. Legman was generous in his praise, 'It is a cultural duty to print it! It's a perfect portrait of the period which I do not believe has ever been portrayed at all let alone so well. You write as the perfect insider, wholly disabused and heart-brokenly mocking and with a competence I never suspected of you, you bastard!'

1
New York 1950

YOU CAN'T STAY MARRIED if you want to make it in New York. It's
as simple as that. This brilliant analysis came to me as I was driving
along the Merrit Parkway in a new Mercury station wagon. I wasn't
even driving the car. Henry and Elizabeth, the coloured couple, were
in the front and Jan's father and mother in the second row while Jan
and I were sitting bored in the rear. We looked forward to the weekend about as much as Saturday's children do when they meet the old
man at the other end of the line. On top of it all the old lady was a
lousy bridge partner and it looked like rain. It was a depressing start,
one of many lately. Spring was being nervous in Fairfield County.

The weekends were never restful but the food was good. I had
little chores to do around the place. I'd light the fire, help Henry
in with the food and bring out the half gallon of Gilbey's Gin. Jan
and I when we arrived were really wound up tight; our only hope of
survival was to get tighter. Was there another way? I'd been fighting
all week, so much so that we almost didn't want to make it. Bummy's
pathetic call at noon had made me wish I'd had a job somewhere in
a Highway 40 hamburger stand. That sorry lonesome voice pleading for a telephone number, anything, anyone, somebody that would
help him share a stupid feeling. Not today, Josephine, I thought. So
when Jan came home that night from work I was numb and willing
to forget that writers existed in this lousy town.

Dinner was drag, but as I said, the food was remarkable. Shad fish
and very tasty it was. There was the usual silence during the meal like
it always is when nervous cooks get together. Jan looked up whenever we were called upon to pass the pepper grinder, a big one, really like an overstated phallus. Her father was a very small volatile

man. We silently hoped that they wouldn't get into conversation. I sensed disaster at the end of the meal, and it came. He asked me about some bonds he had given to Jan. Did we still have them? A ragged question. Very crude. It was going to be a long weekend, one of the longest. I told him we had cashed them in and invested the money with some Texan friend of mine in a wild-cat operation. He was disappointed; didn't like it one bit. Screw him, I thought. They were our bonds.

Progressive parents are always disappointed in their progressive children. They give them everything but love. They get hung up in making money, cultivating important people and collecting tasteful things for the home. Progressive parents are very disappointing. At sixteen, Jan was given her freedom. Liberty is wild. At first it was the brainy refugees from C.C.N.Y. who paid homage to her precocious maturity and the soft Rubenesque body. But homage was a bore and wrestling so tiring. It didn't take long to discover humiliation. It begins below Twelfth Street and fans out to smart addresses all over town. There are regular safaris, exciting, dangerous, interesting, with a chance of bringing home some prize and saying, 'Look what I found'. It's usually some breed of neurotic, off-beat, often off color. The reward for the catch is a twitch, a pang, a hangover, perhaps a black and blue mark. If you were lucky, a scar. Or the grand prize: the Jersey abortion.

Jan tried to find something rotten, really worked quite hard at it. She wanted these citizenship papers to nowhere. Her luck was bad, for she always ended up with some square who wanted to give her Levittown. She chose instead a friendly little art school in Pennsylvania, where it was nice to work with her hands and mind again. Besides, it did wonders for her figure. At twenty-one, beautiful and talented, a little embarrassed, she came back to the city, strangely aloof, slightly bored with experiments.

It was brisk in Washington Square's sympathetic circle that April morning when I first met Jan. She had perfect teeth, an excellent gum line, and she looked like an easy lay. She was easy to pick up;

all I had to do was touch her and I did. She was one of that peculiar group that was born in Manhattan and escaped without an accent which was another thing I liked about her. She lived in a great ornate apartment house of marble and friezes that Sanford White designed about the turn of the century. It overlooked Central Park at its prettiest.

I remember the first time she took me home. It was early morning and we caught the sun over those Fifth Avenue apartments across the park. We didn't say much but I was thinking of that skyline and that tasteful apartment and I began to like the whole set up. She fixed me some boiled eggs (I had a very nervous stomach) and even opened them without breaking the yellows. Her folks were in the country so I stayed the weekend. It was pretty much settled. We were married at her parents' place in Connecticut in July on my birthday. Jan was a little tight and I fluffed my lines. The food at the reception was excellent. We went back to our apartment that night but we were very sophisticated – we slept in separate beds.

The weekend in the country turned out to have a few memorable hours. Sunday afternoon we went to a cocktail party at Christopher's. Chris was a Russian whose tight anal drawings appeared weekly on one of those news magazines, but he was crazy good fun. He had read several of my articles and like a proud father on confirmation, was showing off his son who had just become a fountain pen, introduced me to all the debris that was loitering in his home. I was pleased when we got round to meeting Sidney Jerrod, the neat editor from Horetense, Cudely. I had seen him once or twice with Bummy whose editor he was. What a prick! I had read Bummy's final draft of 'Roomful of Losers' and read it again when it came out under the title of 'Once Around the Heart Pit'. It was the greatest job of de-balling a novel I had ever seen. 'Well, what are you going to do? I wanted it published,' Bummy told me the day it was published. 'Hang around latrines I guess until you get the kind of material Jerrod really wants,' I said at the time. But it wasn't fair and I was sorry about it later. There was a guy who worked about five years on a book and put in a lot of fresh stuff about love, good stuff, and it ended up on Jerrod's apartment floor along with the endless empty bottles and painful memoirs of countless late night conferences.

Jerrod was with a mid-western piece of trade, one of the score of literary finds he was famous for discovering and 'exploring' every six months. This one was particularly crude. His Levis were so tight, well, you know how it goes. He looked like a filling station attendant who was caught reading Tiffany Thayer one night by a Southern talent scout and was brought to the city 'as is'. He wasn't my weight but Sidney was, and I decided to send it in. After Chris left us together I sparred a little with him – he was fairly good at sparring.

'Sidney', I said, 'how does it feel to cut the balls out of a good novel? Do you go half mad with joy or is it a mild scrotum tickle? What plays?'

He counterpunched.

'You sound like one of your cheap articles, sport. Worse than that you sound doggedly young and ambitious. Keep it up and some day you''ll have my job.'

I thought it was a pretty punch but of course I ducked.

'Listen, Sidney', I said, 'there's only one job in this world that you're any good at and that's staying out of Special Municipal night court and not being charged with loitering in public places. Frankly, it's not my type of work.'

'Pity', he said. 'It's so much fun.'

Suddenly I lost interest in the whole affair. I should have know nbetter. Never fight with them because the rougher you are the better they like it and if you slug them, they're in heaven! You're an automatic loser. I left him standing in the middle of the room looking like the Times Square Camel sign, only the lips were white around the edges and every bit as round.

I went over to the bar and spotted Jan talking to the original flight from femininity, Joan Beardsley, girl fashion editor, old friend of Jan's from work. Sickeningly fashionable in her Brooks Brothers shirt, collar pin and tie – short it was of course – she was waxing smartly about an exciting new fashion photographer who flew some models to King Tut's tomb for background.

'Very sick', I said, 'who's your tailor, Joan? Abercrombie, Nerves?'

It got a phoney laugh.

I was getting drunk. Air was what I needed. Out on the terrace it was refreshing and I felt like taking a swim only I knew it was too early for the pool to be filled. I walked around the empty pool a couple of times anyway and it looked so inviting I backed down the ladder. I walked all over its wonderful blue bottom and rested where it said, VERY DEEP. I began to feel very much at home and would have dozed off, lost to the world till summer, if a Margaret Sullivan voice hadn't broken through my fantasy. It was the only voice that could have.

'How is it in that other world?' it said, and I loved immediately whoever it was that said it. I focussed on a skirt and blouse and pretty face just above where it said WADING DEPTH. It was a very literary pool.

'The water's fine', I said. 'Come on in.'

'Promise you won't duck me?'

'Listen. I'm only human'.

'OK,' she said and jumped in and started walking downhill to VERY DEEP where I had assumed the attitude of surrender.

'Well,' she said, 'you look like a handsome rotter I must say.'

'Be my guest. Sit down but any more familiarity and the duck is off.'

'What are you drinking?' she asked.

'Pernod. Rocks.'

'Why do you drink that?'

'It eats away the brain faster than anything else.'

'What do you do in New York?' I asked. I suspected she was an actress, or TV, or script girl; I couldn't tell any more.

'I'm Nora Drake's neurotic child and Amanda's best girl friend and lots more. Radio.'

'Steady, lots of money. Any boyfriends?'

'A few.'

'Actor's Lab, serious, not working. Blue jeans constantly.'

'Very good. I'm impressed. My turn.'

'Not yet. Headshrinker twice a week. You're thinking of breaking off. East thirties, small but cheerful place. Good cook. Simple fare. Broadway a must...'

'How much do I owe you?' she broke in.

'An exciting spring,' I claimed.

'Married?'

'Of course.'

'Now, let's see.' She was a picture of whimsy. 'You're the funniest man I have ever met. You're out of some 1928 novel but cute. Sports car, a must, as you say. You're probably very good in bed. Are you a bartender?'

'About that spring?' I asked

'Spring, spring,' she sang, 'spring can hang you up the most.'

'A great name for the kid. Let's get back to the party. This is too much.'

'Don't you want to know my name?' she asked.

'Naw,' I said. 'You keep it. I'll see you around.'

When I got back Chris was gesticulating wildly about abstract artists. I could see his tears running down his two thousand dollar per cover neurosis. Over by the bar was a frightening little man with a wooden leg who was trying to explain the intricacies of helicopter flight to a model (last year's). It was going over big because as I picked up Jan to leave I looked over and the girl was stroking his good leg with her spiked heel pump. It killed a Sunday.

Jan and I didn't talk much on the way back. I mentioned the swimming pool bit and she thought it was pretty funny. I told her again how I felt about Joan Beardsley and how deeply that girl dragged me. I told her I didn't like her hair cut so short, and I'd like her to pay more attention to me. If she found it difficult I suggested she do something about it. She didn't like my attitude either and I suggested again that if she wanted justice in a marriage she should have married a judge. I told her firmly that I didn't believe in justice. We tried a little bridge with the folks that night but it broke up after two rubbers. I was tired and sank into a deep funk. We barely kissed goodnight.

We drove back to the city early Monday morning. The parkway was full of expensive cars leisurely rolling into the city. They had a fine weekend; they got washed, polished, had travelled new roads and were now heading for rest in friendly garages all over midtown Manhattan. The folks dropped us off at our apartment and I unloaded our loot: bag of clean laundry, fresh fruit and country flowers wrapped in the financial section of the *Times*. It was nine o'clock and Jan rushed to work, leaving me to tote the mad array up the stairs. Everything was dusty and looked out of place. I was suddenly aware of harboring last year's Eames chair. I felt like kicking it. I puttered around the apartment aimlessly tidying up, arranging the damn flowers and spending a great deal of time looking at myself in the mirror. It was comforting to know that I still had a few years to go as boy-editor. I got all the empties together and was headed for the friendly corner delicatessen for my morning show money.

Morning movies are the privilege of the elite, the unemployed and the lonely. I have experienced beautiful moments undreamed of with an evening movie. Rise with the high-kicking Rockettes at the Music Hall before noon and you will have experienced something as satisfying and beautiful as anything in American culture! I don't care for a 100-piece band at that hour though so I seldom go to the Music Hall. It's 42nd Street, East and West, both ways, fifteen to twenty-five cents before noon, George Raft, Randolph Scott, Alan Ladd, lots of Victor Mature; Gary Cooper, Tyrone Power, Betty Grable, Shelley Winters, Dame May Whitty, all the greats, pals, friends of the morning.

2

BIRDS WERE SINGING SOMEWHERE that spring but we didn't hear them. For a while Jan and I tried to communicate with each other. It had begun to be a chore and no amount of Martinis brightened prospects for the evening. In the end it was always some friends over to help us with our drinking and share the wake for feeling. Or we moved in wolf packs to pathological parties uptown and downtown where the talented untalented threw dummy darts at cork minds and never got laid. The parties, the drinking, Jan found too much and she began to beg off after a third or fourth round and I began to feel like a gentleman alone, not lonely after midnight.

Jan didn't have to work, and I rather disliked her job; she was a lowly sketcher for a high powered Seventh Avenue manufacturer and it brought her into contact with that whole lousy syndrome. In the beginning neither of us believed in careers and I never believed in jobs. If a wife loathed housework I always recommended jobs at Doubleday book shops, Junior League Exchanges or Interior Design salons. Anything else was a career and career women were hard to take outside the home and unbearable inside.

At times it seemed my days would be pointless for weeks and I would wander through doors of fellow conspirators whose luck was worse than mine. I would watch cats copulating on smart mid-town fire escapes with a boredom that was frightening. I'd look out of windows and see giant Hieronymus Bosch murals of untouchable transients. I even saw unconquerable Dagmar hurrying down 45th Street alone and proud, headed for the sterile caress of the beauty salon.

Gossip became a fine art. Our salons were the saloons of Third Avenue. When Clark's went grey flannel we moved to Glennons where

sackcloth and ashes permeated the pin strip flavor of the neighbourhood regulars and the bartender knew Helen Twelvetrees. There was
always someone desperate in Glennons and verbal battles charged
the air. I remember one night a fight was going on outside Glennons
and I overheard a wild-eyed habitué shout warnings to passing Sa-
maritans: 'Don't stop it. This has been brewing at CBS for months.'
It calmed the air remarkably.

A wave of anti-intellectualism hit the more serious people that
spring. Vitality was reserved for exhausting sidewalk tennis games
and Indian wrestling, and some went on health kicks. Insights and
pronouncements were lavished on up and coming fighters, obscure
bongo players from Harlem, Cholly Knickenbocker and Hedda
Hopper. Sports pages were devoured like the little magazines of yesterday and the New York Giants loomed larger than the triple think-
ers – Freud, Darwin, Marx. Searching questions were asked of old
time movie bit players and evenings were devoted to re-enacting favorite scenes from film classics. Anthologists were busy recording for
posterity those cheap boots for poor cats. In the twilight of anxiety
the scene looked sick but there were laughs mixed with superiority
and it gave us a feeling of being contemptuous as well as contemporary. If you weren't contemporary in New York, you were nothing.

Jan and I were seeing too many highly nervous people and I was
beginning to twitch a little, but only in one eye. We witnessed a
beautiful mass of floating ganglia the next weekend. It was decided
not to go to the country so we were home when a spear carrier friend
invited us to join a shock troop of intellectuals who were gathered
in Uptown Bohemia to celebrate the publication of a lightweight
apology for Downtown Bohemia. Since the affair was being held at
Fritz Segal's apartment on 53rd Street, East (naturally), Jan suggested
we walk over. I put on a pair of dark glasses to soothe the persistent
twitch and girded myself for the night. Walking past the Stork Club,
lingering for but a moment to smell the Sortilege, I was attacked by
a couple of cute autograph hounds.

'Say, excuse me, Mister,' one of them said, 'but you look like

SOMEBODY. Say, who are you?'

Her friend was rather cynical.

'Aw, June, he isn't anybody. I'm sure now that I got a good look. He didn't even come out of the Stork.'

'But I tell you he is,' June repeated.

With her pleading eyes she bluntly demanded to know who the hell I was. I hemmed and hawed and did a little shit-kicking Gary Cooper bit. It was all over the next moment and I realized the great gulf in our entertainment age. I confessed rather shyly that I was Ishcabibal.

'You see, June,' the hard ruthless one said, 'I told you he was a nobody.'

I was lucky she didn't kick me. I grabbed Jan and ran.

I had been to several crucifixions at Fritz's over the years and everybody always ended up nailed or stoned, particularly the latter. Fritz was a good boy from Long Island, making quite a name for himself as a portrait painter with an aristocratic neurosis. The last time I was there everyone was pouring out their most painful recollection of youthful rejections. It was the greatest mess of mass pimples, obesity, piles, cross-eyes, bird-legs, flat chests and stuttering any generation suffered through. I remember thinking what a fashionable article it would have been for *Flair*. With a slight sobering touch I speculated on the *New York Times* magazine approach: 'The bright young men of yesterday were concerned with who shall sabotage the machines of production, once they had established who owned them. Today's young intellectuals take pride in cheap tales of spectacular rejection in their childhood, etc, etc...' I even fancied myself becoming rich if I could be the first editor of a pocket book anthology of *The World's Greatest Rejection Stories*. Simon and Schuster, of course. Nothing came of it, though.

Fritz's apartment was in extremely good taste – none of his paintings were to be seen. The floor was outstanding, with colorful paint drippings à la Pollock. Very little of it was visible by the time we got there. It was crowded with tired feet, itchy faces, Harris tweeds and

Capezio's on trim legs. Jan and I went over to say hello to the author of the book, the guy the shindig was supposed to be for. Nobody seemed to be paying any attention to him.

'Well, Johnny,' I said, 'how do you feel? How do you love it, boy?'

'Fine. Somebody is going to come over and talk to me any minute.'

'Nobody ever talks to anyone at Fritz's parties. They're too superior,' I said.

'I feel like a lowly Christian about to be stoned by my Roman betters.'

'Look over there at my pal Danny if you want to see somebody stoned. He should get the award as the most hung up poet of the year.' Danny Schwartz was fashionably entangled in a well designed diaphragm chair. He had the goofiest look in his sad, sad eyes.

Various assaults on sanity were going on all over the place. Our uniformed spear carrier friend was telling a bewildered rebel from Sarah Lawrence that 'all the beauty and brains of New York intellectual life are gathered in this room'. I was touched. I cased the place again to check my sanity. I knew almost everyone there but our friend's sharp appraisal threw me off. Across the room I spotted the soap opera chick of the literary swimming pool. She was still definitely appealing. Unfortunately she was hanging on the arm of a tall, good looking, serious slob in Murray space shoes. It looked like a closed relationship so I ignored the whole thing. Loved her, loathed him.

A delightful looking girl was trying to engage Danny in spirited conversation. Danny was charming, witty, very out-going when high. Off the weed he was a snarling, sinister, ugly little man who never forgot he was a major poet at fifteen. (He had won the title but lost the race.) Danny was softly stroking the girl's hair muttering, 'Kitten, kitten, everything's gonna be all right.'

'Hiya, Lennie, what's up?' Danny looked at me for a second.

'Brilliant, man, brilliant,' without missing a stroke.

'Danny' I said, 'don't you remember me, I'm your pal?'

'Go away, Doctor,' Danny urged. 'This girl is too tender and sacred for your harsh voyeurism. Go away.'

'You're evil, Danny,' I said, 'which way do I flee to score the sacred grass?' Danny thumbed towards the kitchen and I fled. The girl was exceedingly tender.

I noticed there wasn't much lushing going on. The bomber squadron was really rolling. I caught up with mission somewhere between the toilet and the kitchen. It hit the target almost immediately. I floated towards Jan, shared what was left and we climbed beautifully together. My flight was temporarily intercepted by New York's other boy-editor, Rick Davis. I noticed he was a little light on his feet and when he started to talk, his voice took on a lightly higher register, something like Alan Ladd being uppity but still masculine.

'Nothing's happening,' Rick warned me. 'It's frightful,' he added. Rick was going into his eleventh year as a boy-editor. He had worked on the top magazines in the country since he was twenty, always as the protege of some ageing editor who would see in the beautiful Rick the fire and talent they once thought they had. Nothing had changed about him since he'd left the campus. He was still thoroughly disillusioned, salty, impeccably dressed by J.Press. The coat he was wearing last night had so many buttons up the front he looked like a Keystone Cop.

'That's the greatest coat I have ever seen. One more button and you won't need to wear a necktie,' I said.

'Much more amazing than Kafka,' he agreed.

Rick was one of my friends from the other world. His magazine was legitimate; it had circulation but nobody paid any attention to it any more. It had been choked years ago by its reader's mediocre lust and it was now like a fast-stepping whore who had been hounded into respectability and couldn't decide which way to turn. Rick as managing editor was trying to make the magazine a cross between the *Partisan Review* and the *Daily News* but confessed to me it was really an assignation house for the big *Digest* magazine in spite of all his efforts to keep the crap out.

'How do you love all the super duper, upper upper minds here?'

'Nothing's happening,' he repeated, 'it's a vast inner Sahara and I'm slowly dying of thirst.'

'No communication all the way down the line,' I said. A faint suggestion of a smile crossed those parched lips for only a second.

'I hear you,' he answered, 'will you be serious for a moment? Now listen, I want you to write that article on homosexuality in our culture, the one you're always talking about.'

'Can you be serious?' I asked.

'Why not. You'll be paid big dough and you'll have a big audience. What more do you want?'

'I want to live in New York a little longer if you don't mind,' I said. 'If you published what I'd want to write we'd be the two most lonesome men in town.'

'Let's have lunch and discuss it sometime,' he said as his eye caught a dark, Bitter Rice stunner across the room. It was the end of the 'interview'. I sat back and watched him move in on the girl and caught his opening line.

'Tell me, are you as stupid as you look?' It seemed to work; she fell into his arms.

I was coming down a little faster than usual and a great wave of hunger came over me. Jan was talking to a group of youngsters and seemed satisfied so I wandered over to say hello to the Mermaid. She remembered me right off.

'Hello, laugh riot,' she said.

'How you doing?' I asked.

'Do you know all these people here?'

'Most of them. Creepy bunch, n'est-ce pas, but a lot of laughs. Who's your friend, the serious one?'

'My friend, and very serious,' she agreed.

'What about? Is he dangerous? Where d'you pick him up?'

'Here he comes. Why don't you ask him?'

'I think I'll catch him later. Something's happening in the other room.'

'And you don't like the looks of my friend, n'est-ce pas?'

'He's pure science fiction. See you later.'

Great peals of laughter and excited shouts of 'go' shot through the apartment. It electrified the most hung up minds. Even Danny stopped his stroking and floated towards the scene. It was a fantastic one. All that 'beauty and brain' was gathered into an even smaller room going wild watching a dazzling performance by Bummy Carwell on a pogo stick! I had to admit it was an imaginative job of crowd pleasing. The very boldness of Bummy in the choosing of his weapon! I sensed a soothing wave of liberation from the collected psyches watching this act. For there on a F.A.O. Schwartz, all aluminium, red tipped, fiercely contemporary pogo stick was Bummy giving his great big valentine to the night. The crowd felt him; they seemed to be going half mad with joy. The dear boy was speaking for everyone there.

Somebody grabbed some pots from the kitchen and started a great tattoo of rhythm that added immeasurably to the fanciful jumps. I kept my eye on Danny who was really digging the bit. I felt he was going to jump into the frame any minute, so excited was he. Bunny made a startling leap but missed coming down; Danny jumped from the herd and grappled with him for possession of the stick. The mob suddenly became very quiet as though they were watching a great struggle for life. Nothing could stop Danny; he was approaching his one great frenzy. In a sudden push he toppled Bummy and jumped triumphantly into the air, waving the stick madly. The crowd was delighted to see a winner and egged him on with shouts of 'Ride, Danny. Go, man, go. Make it, Danny boy!' He seemed momentarily confused by the sudden acquisition of so much potency. The cries of the people finally got through to him and he attacked the stick brutally, clumsily, slipping, losing balance – the boy had forgotten his childhood. The dispossessed Bummy broke through and helped him up on the twin pedals and, like a swimming instructor, held on to him while he made a few dry runs. In a minute Danny remembered the streets of his Brooklyn childhood and regained a wonderful control.

Soon he was making spectacular leaps just like Bummy. Danny was even more reckless with his leaps into the crowd. He'd fall, they'd lift him back, shouting more crazy encouragements. Danny was mastering it now. He shouted to the crowd, 'Back, you fools! I've got it! I can make it to the end of the night. No, no, no, don't stop me; it's the first time I've had it up in years!'

There was something frightening in those hilarious shouts. His grotesque leaps rivalled Nijinsky; for moments he seemed to be miraculously suspended in mid-air. I thought he was going to go through the ceiling on his next jump and he almost did. But as he landed, second later, the rubber tipped end of the weapon crashed through the floor, spilling that wild cargo of nerves. He was all over the place. The symbolic act was complete. Like a nineteenth century Russian tragedy, the crowd accepted the inevitable and Danny collected his shattered fantasies and moved through the night's oblivion.

Jan came over to me and said she wanted to cry. I felt pretty good about it myself. Danny had puked for me.

3

I WAS SURPRISED TO HEAR from Danny so soon after his midnight ride. He dropped by the office to invite Jan and me to have a fancy dinner with him and his millionaire poet that night. His friend was a choice legend around new York and I was anxious to get in on it. It was said he was a ruthless financier who wrote shameless poetry on the back of his lunch tabs at the Chambord – images that had been tutor-bought at fifty dollars an hour from shaky poets of avant-garde stature. Danny had been his tutor for over a year and shrewdly saved enough money to start his analysis, a necessity brought on by the relationship. His present mentor – there had been a succession of them after Danny – was a very bright boy who was under analysis before the job and only took the job so he could continue.

We were to meet at Max's apartment on Fifth Avenue and I passed it along to Jan. Surprisingly she refused, begging off with exhaustion in her voice and a slight overtone of bitterness thrown in. It took a certain kick out of the evening for me and made me a little jumpy during the afternoon. I knocked off early and asked Danny to join me at Nob Hill. We had some mammoth martinis and tiny talk with an ersatz bartender who had a literary noodle. He was plugging *From Here to Eternity* (who wasn't that year?) and trying to convince us what a regular fellow the author was.

'A good customer too, when he's in town. Practically lives here,' Phil said. He showed us his autographed copy with its friendly inscription: 'To Phil, the Goddamnest bartender in there here parts and he makes the Goddamnest martinis. A swell guy and great editor.' Danny shot me a look of amused disbelief and I agreed with Phil that Jones must be a regular guy.

'He's tops in my book,' Danny said to no-one in particular.

'You fellow writers?' Phil asked. 'I've seen you in before,' he said pointing to me.

'We're just a couple of regular guys, Phil. Not too big, not little. Just regular guys, Phil. We don't know all the answers, we're searching a little here and there, little fellows, Phil, not winners yet.'

'I can tell writers a mile off,' Phil said. 'A guy comes in from *Time* magazine the other day and I spotted him right off as their book man. Nice guy, doubles drinker, says nothing to nobody, good tip, good man. I got the knack.'

'You do much writing, Phil?' Danny asked.

'I hear a lot of stuff over this bar, real literary shockers. A lot of inside stuff that would really make a book but I'm not interested in writing. I want to be a critic. That's the ticket.'

'Phil, you amaze me', I said. 'You got a good head on your shoulders. Use it. You could write the chronicle of all times. Critics can't do it. It's up to us, Phil. Little fellows, but stout.'

'Hey, you guys are nuts. Drink is spoiling your copy.'

'That's a good one,' Danny answered. 'Very good. I'll have a drink on that and give my friend one, and one for yourself and give him one, and him, and get that hunch back in the back room, get him a drink.'

It was nice to see Danny lush again, I thought. He was really having a good time jerking off the bartender. We left after a couple of rounds, very pleased with the whole set-up. We were in great shape for meeting the millionaire. The door was open and we walked in. Danny gave me the quiet signal. In the living room the millionaire was reading poetry to his house boy. We tiptoed in and the millionaire looked up briefly as he motioned us to sit down and went right on with his reading. The house boy was a fine picture, standing at attention probably wondering if there was anything in his union contract that said he had to put up with this lunatic.

'Their grasshopper legs curved at the knees, tied at the toes, they spring to a dance, a family of Jackals...' The phone rang and

the 'poet' picked it up and shouted, 'Max here' into the mouth-
piece. 'Yeah, yeah, I understand all that.' Max went on. 'What? No,
no more time for the bastard. Sell him out, move the machinery
if necessary. Yes, move it and do it fast.' He slammed the receiver.
'Where was I? Oh, I see. 'A family of Jackal's legs; the family lady
in the dance corner, whose curled tongue bites brightness, who
teaches a small-bellied boy: Father runs up from behind, slower
by his hands, with starfish fingers, a figure dressed as a coward in
nothing!'

'Danny, how did you like it?' He dismissed the house boy and
in an aside to me: 'Glad to know you. Danny's told me a lot about
you.'

'Likewise, I'm sure,' I said, very softly, catching the mood.

'Danny. It's been a terrible day. I had to see you. Where shall we
dine? That line, Danny, that last line with the starfish, did you like
it?'

'Max, that was a strong line, a four level image.' Danny turned to
me and said, 'Fine life isn't it?' No answer was required.

'Clarice is going to join us but she'll be a little late.' He rasped
on and I noticed he was suffering from asthma. 'She's rehearsing a
Shakespeare production; he's very big this year.'

'How about Quo Vadis,' I suggested. 'Top snails.'

'All right with me. How about you, Danny?' he asked.

'De-vine,' he replied, giving his accent the Canarsie twist.

'Danny, I've just bought a ball-bearing plant in Worcester, Mass,
you'd love it. It's beautiful in Worcester.'

'What, poetry in ball bearings in Worcester,' I said. 'Max, are you
always so serious? It's two worlds for you, nicht wahr, Max?'

'Two worlds, two worlds,' Max repeated. 'Oh, I see, you mean
how do I reconcile poetry with reality, is that it? It's hard, it's the
hardest thing I've ever done. It's a terrible world, both of them,
and I don't do too well in either but I try, I try. Don't I try hard,
Danny?'

'You sure do, Max,' Danny assured him.

'Is it going to be a very thin volume, Max?' I tenderly asked. Max was pleased.

'Yes, it is. Which reminds me, Danny, can you get Wallace Stevens to do the introduction? Stevens is a business man who travels the two worlds. I once wrote him a letter but he never answered me. I've got to get more symbolic; I'm too weak. My hands are stone, my chisel is dulled. Christ!' he shouted. 'Where is that stupid dame?' He reached for a drink and we joined him. I had to laugh. Max was more than a legend; he was a perfect ass.

'Max,' Danny asked. 'When are we going out on the yacht again?Let's look over the Fire Island syndrome. There's some fine images there.'

'I hate that place, Danny. I had a terrible experience there last summer when I went out there. Why, I've spent thousands with my analyst trying to forget a lousy lay that time. It's the only island in the world that's completely flat-chested. Not a knocker in sight. Late one night I was shacked up with a beautiful bustless model, which was difficult enough, but when she excused herself for a moment and came back from the can, she had painted a lipstick tattoo of a piglet suckering at that suggestion of a nipple. Boy, I wanted to die! It took me months to get over it. Why'd she do it to me, Danny? Why'd she do it?' I felt for Max for a moment and I almost wanted to sober up.

'Max,' Danny said, 'It was nothing personal. Tribal markings of a strange unrecorded breed of women. You should have taken a broad social and anthropological view of their customers. We'll take Malinowski with us next time to help us avoid those irritating pitfalls.'

'You know what I did when I came back that week-end?' Max asked, ignoring Danny's bright analysis. 'I bought a plastic curtain business. I couldn't explain it. It's a good business, one of my best money-makers. I still own it.' Max was rather proud of his unconscious behaviour.

'Max,' I said, 'Put it to music; it's clean and beautiful, just as you told it.'

'I did,' Max replied. 'But it didn't go over with me. I couldn't understand why I bought that curtain business. My symbol was weak again.'

'I'll have to come back and straighten out your images, Max,' Danny said.

'I wish you would, Danny. You were my best teacher, even my best friend. I loved you like a son.' There were tears in Max's eyes for a minute. 'If that bitch doesn't show up in five minutes we're leaving. Right, boys?'

'Right,' we said. I poured another drink all round. In a moment we were ready to bump bellies and make for Toots Shores.

Clarice's entrance saved us. It was kisses and 'darling' all round and the accent was ferociously blended. I disliked the dame immediately. Where do these yokels from Utah, Scranton, and Michigan, and Washington and Delaware get those outrageous accents? It was as if they had been born in Middlesex and made their debut at the Court of St James with Lunt and Fontaine. Danny mixed her a drink.

'How's it going, Baby?' he asked.

'Thanks,' she said. 'I'm starved.'

'What delivery, Clarice,' Danny replied. 'You ought to be in pictures.'

'Max!' she yelled. 'Max, your boy is starting in again. Tell him to lay off.' Max was preparing to read again and paid her slight attention.

'How do you like this?' Max asked. She didn't give him a chance.

'I don't like anything, Max,' she said, 'and if you liked me you wouldn't subject me tonight to this surly Dead End poet. I'm hungry. Let's eat.'

'Danny,' Max said, 'she doesn't understand anything that's not written down for her. I'm sorry.'

'A very astute observation, Max. Peace, Clarice?'

'You two bards slay me. Wait a minute till I put on a face.' She left the room.

'I want you two to like each other tonight, Danny. It gave me pleasure to be with you all and I want it to be a happy time, like it used to be.'

'She bugs me, Max,' Danny said, 'but I'll do my best for you and the snails.'

'The champagne too,' I added, 'Bollinger; something very rare that will help us to love each other.'

'I think I know what you mean,' Max replied. 'I've got a great line here, it's very strong.' He started to read again.

'Save it, Max,' Danny interrupted. 'Wait a minute. Give me that piece of paper that had the great line.' Danny grabbed it.

'Here, I'll fold it into a paper glider and we'll stick it in your hat for the rakish touch. There now. Reckless, Max, eh? The way a poet should look going into Quo Vadis. When we down magnum after magnum, we shall set sail to this little plane and laugh as it soars over heads of anxious diners.'

Clarice came back to a much more relaxed room. Max was showing her what Danny had done with his poem and filled her in on the plane bit. We were ready to roll. Max was very pleased. He felt he was getting his money's worth. Quo Vadis was swell. A bald continental fat little zither player in the background was pleasant. All the waiters looked like playwrights and the wine steward had all the keys to Baldpate around his neck. After snails came a great course of sentiment, highly seasoned with garlic breath and fresh tears. The tears were Max's. He was suddenly overcome by the closeness and intimacy of the scene.

'Love, love,' Max slobbered. 'What good friends I have here tonight.' Clarice was getting quite annoyed at Max's fondling Danny and shot me one of those 'who-is-he-kidding' looks. It was a little embarrassing especially with Max slobbering over Danny, and Clarice going into a cruising operation of her own. I kept the wine steward busy bringing more buckets of champagne. I had a terrible feeling for a moment Max was going to stand up and make a big emotional pitch. Instead, Danny rose unsteadily from his chair.

'Max,' he began, pointing a huge asparagus tip under his nose.

'Max, I've had a beautiful revelation just now. I've decided I love money. Yes, I love money! Max, your money has made you a real poet, a major poet. It's bought dinners like this where you can wipe your feet on head waiters and goose wine stewards at will. It's bought you beautiful and talented women like Clarice here. You have suits of sheer poetry sewn on Bond Street and shoes carved in Turin. Byzantine splendor is yours. Oils, unguents, and scrotum massages, every day a Turkish bath, Max. Why, *Fortune* magazine is better written and more exciting and terrifying than all the world's little magazines that died to make free verse. Factories, oil wells, Willow runs, your new ball bearing plant in Worcester, great paintings, Max. When you said, "get that straight, sell the bastard out and move the machinery if you have to, but do it now," you were writing real poetry. That was one huge terrifying image with meaning much deeper than all the "grasshopper legs" in the world. Me? Well, tonight ladies, I confess, I'm sick of the academy of sterility, bored with the ugly faces of gangling poets, and disgusted with the effete critics of culture. I love money, and I want some. I want to move out of cold water flats and get out of these corny suits. I want food like this and heady nights like this. I want to be contemporary again. It looks like a beautiful life to me, Max. All I want is a stake.' Danny gingerly collapsed back in his chair and tossed the now limp asparagus tip into a nearby finger bowl.

Clarice yawned and I sobered up quick. Max, filled with rare wine and the now stale tears, could contain himself no longer. He burst into a great sobbing mess, threw his arm around Danny and slobbered kisses on his cheek. The *Third Man* Theme was playing in the background and Clarice looked most annoyed, like odd man out. The captain brought the check and Max scribbled across its face. The waiters lined up as we helped Max to the door and he sobbed lightly as he crossed each palm with a five spot. His limousine pulled up and Danny and I made our thanks and tucked him in. Clarice got around the other side. Max waved a kiss as the car pulled away.

The next day I wandered up to the penthouse of the Museum of Modern Art and sipped some insipid wine and noticed for the first time the dreadful modern furniture among the bric-a-brac of yesterday's enfant terrible. I fled to the screening room downstairs to watch Stroheim's *Greed* for the third time. It was a trifle tedious the third time; Zasu Pitts began to pall. I ducked out for a smoke half-way through. There was an exhibit of theatrical posters and memorabilia strung around the downstairs lobby and I paid mild homage to yesterday's charmers. Across the room, in front of a poster of Clive Brooks, somebody looked familiar.

I recognised her from the back; she looked, that moment, like a rear view of Charlotte Henry in the old *Alice in Wonderland* film. There she was, long, dishwater blonde hair in a pony tail, wearing a pleated blue linen skirt a little longer than they were wearing them that year, a blouse with sanitary white cuffs and a Buster Brown collar. With a Groucho Marx leer I put my arm through hers and said, 'Alone, I hope?' She half jumped out of her skin.

'Did I frighten you, little girl?'

Her tense little face relaxed. Her eyebrows, dark and thick, shielded the blaze from her brown eyes. She wore no make up. It was a lovely face but there was a suggestion of a nose-job somewhere along the line. I tried to picture the old nose, strongly aquiline probably, less like a mannikin's. Pity.

'What are you doing here?' the Mermaid asked.

'I had to flee from an old friend,' I replied, pointing upstairs.

'Anybody I know?'

'Yes. Picasso.'

'I don't understand. Don't you like Picasso?'

'Squaresville, you know, New Babbitville with framed reproduction of Pablo in every toilet.'

'I don't think I like you.' She gave her head a sideways twist which could have meant anything.

'Don't take it seriously, ' I warned her. 'I can't be funny all the time. We were funny at the ole swimming hole, weren't we?'

'Yes, very funny.' I took her by the arm and stepped up the pace around the exhibit. I wanted very much to have a drink with her.

'Are you working this afternoon?' I asked.

'No.' She stopped in front of a giant poster of Douglas Fairbanks Sr. as Zorro. 'I knew him when I was a little girl.' She touched his fabulous smile with her little finger.

'He was very nice to me. He got me my first picture chore. Did you know I was a child star at the age of four?'

'I'm impressed. Did you know any of my day dream friends? Jackie Searle, Freddy Bartholomew, Baby Rose Marie, Jackie Cooper, Dickie Moore and that crowd? Beautiful children.'

'Frankly, no. I wasn't allowed to associate with them.' She threw her nose in the air. I edged her towards the exit.

'Tell me about your life with the stars. Over Pernod of course.' She smiled slightly and for a moment I thought she was going to pass it up.

'Alright, but just one. I've got homework to do tonight.'

'Great. I know the only bar on Sixth Avenue that has Pernod.'

As we hurried out of the upstairs lobby I swung her around and pointed over at the crowded frame and print department and asked her if she would like to pick out a little Utrillo for the powder room before we left. She gave me another look of hopelessness. She had a soft walk along West Fifty-Third Street; no pigeon toes, no masculine stride. It was soft shoe all the way and matched my style beautifully.

'I found out a lot about you recently,' she said.

'Now why would you want to do a thing like that?' I complained.

'Don't get excited. You came out all right. I didn't find out anything too incriminating. I found out you are a rotter, as I suspected.'

'Jesus,' I sighed. 'What a relief. What's your name by the way?'

'It's funny you never asked me before.'

'You were too busy,' I explained.

'Or you. It's Sari Shaw.'

'Sari? Now come on, what's your real name?' She laughed.

'Alright, smarty. It's Sarah. Go ahead. Probe a little.'

'Sarah? Ugh. I don't blame you for changing it.'

We tiptoed into Butler's Bar and Grill which was around the corner on Sixth. I lived just up the street near Seventh. Jan used to meet me at Butler's once in a while after work. There were a couple of people at the bar and an undistinguished couple drinking draught beer at a table. The bartender greeted me and I gave him the order.

'Put it in an old-fashioned glass, straight up.' He shrugged a little; it probably broke his monotonous dime beer routine.

Sari and I sat down. She threw a packet of Viceroys on the table. The bartender brought over the drinks. I thought I saw him smile; I wasn't sure.

'Just like Paris,' I said.

'Do you do this often?'

'What do you mean?' She made a gesture which included herself, the Pernod and me. I got it.

'Not often, but once in a while. How about you?' She ignored the question completely.

'Chris told me you're brilliant. Are you?' Chris was Jan's friend who owned that empty swimming pool.

'Yeah, I suppose. At least I'm out of work.'

'What would your wife think about all this?'

'What 'this' do you mean?' She repeated the gesture of a moment ago.

'I imagine she'd be quite impressed.'

'I saw her that night at the party for Fritz. She's very lovely.' She took a sip of her drink. 'But there was something so detached about her manner. I kept looking at her all night.' It sounded to me like a sly put-down.

'She was probably stoned.'

'What do you mean?'

'She's not exactly a party gal. Parties scare her; she freezes up.' I didn't want to tell her any more.

'She reminds me very much of Zelda Fitzgerald, you know.' I told her the observations were beginning to annoy me.

'You know, Zelda's not one of my favourite characters in fiction and certainly not an encouraging one in fact.'

'I'm sorry.'

I wanted to change the subject. 'Who was the guy in the space shoes that night I saw you? Was that your homework?'

'Yes, that's right.' She seemed a little embarrassed. 'He treats me nicely,' she quickly added.

'That's good to hear these days, somebody treating somebody nice. Thank you,' I said, giving her a wry smile. 'My wife wants to thank you too.' She let out a laugh that picked me right up from the floor. 'You have a wonderful uncontemporary laugh, Sari.'

'It's a spring laugh.'

'So it is.' I sipped a little of the drink. 'Do you have time for a spring romance right now?' I said it as lightly as I could but it didn't come out sounding lightly this time.

'Perhaps,' she said looking into her drink. I hadn't expected that. Neither of us said anything for a while. I finished my drink.

'Want another drink?' I asked.

'Yes, I do.' I went up to the bar and got two more. On the way back I stuck a couple of nickels in the juke box and picked up some pistachio nuts. I threw them on the table and gave her the drink.

'Help yourself,' I said, pointing to the nuts. Instead, she took a cigarette. I lit it for her and she touched my hand for just a second.

'Thanks.' The music started and I looked over at her wondering whether I should ask her to dance.

'You have a lovely face,' I said instead. 'How come you don't wear make-up?'

'That is what I'm paying my head-shrinker to tell me,' she replied rather challengingly.

'Oops. I should have asked you to dance.'

'Why don't you?'

'O.K. Let's dance.' We got up and I took her hand. Nobody paid any attention to us as we danced. I could have stolen a million kisses. I decided to settle for one right along the ear. She ever so slightly acknowledged it, but it was there. The juke box played out and I skipped to the booth feeling young and foolish.

'It was a tender dance, Sari. Thanks.'

'That was it. It's getting late. I think I better go.'

'Let's finish the drink first.' I wanted to hold her hand again.

'Sari, do you like me?' It caught her with her glass to her mouth and she nodded her head a couple of times with her eyes half closed. I was glad she said it that way. She out her drink down, drained.

'Is your wife talented?'

'No. She's just precocious.'

'You dog. Finish your drink. I have to go.'

'Right. Where to?'

'A cab.' I hailed one and opened the door as she swung in.

'Call me,' she said. That's what I'd been waiting to hear all along.

4

I SCOOTED AROUND THE CORNER and made it home in about three minutes. I was feeling pretty good. The Pernod had set everything right. On the way upstairs I noticed an auction sign on the Greek restaurant below our apartment. I stopped a second and looked up at the neon sign that had flashed 'Grecian Garden' on and off into our living room every night of the week. The Greek music, weird strings at three in the morning, would serenade us no more. It occurred to me it would be quieter now in the apartment if a little more colorless than before.

I walked into the apartment and saw Jan's friend, Joan Beardsley, mixing a batch of martinis in my favourite herring jar. What the hell was she doing here, I thought. Jan knew how I felt about her. I didn't see Jan around. Joan looked too much at home.

'Where's Jan?' I asked.

'Is that you, honey?' Jan called from the other room. 'Joan's going to have dinner with us. We're doing some work on a big promotion the firm is staging. How'd it go today?'

'You talking to me?' I asked.

'Of course, silly,' she hollered back.

'O.K.' I shouted back, 'it was a beautiful day for a silent watcher.' I turned to Joan. 'Hello there,' she said, 'good to see you. Will you join us for a drink?'

What nerve, I thought. 'Hope I'm not interrupting anything here.'

Joan laughed, a little brittle laugh.

'Now you sit back and enjoy yourself and we'll give you a stiff drink and feed you.'

'Whose date will I be, Joan?' I didn't try very hard to keep the edge out of my voice.

'How civilized,' Joan laughed back. Here it comes, I thought, the professional chatter of the capable career girl.

'You'd better give me one of those civilized martinis if we are to survive. What's keeping Jan?'

'She's changing into something more comfortable.'

'How civilized.' Jan came out in slacks and an old shirt of mine. It was most disappointing to see her at the moment like that; it irritated me. She came over and kissed me lightly. I held my breath.

'What are you in such a bad mood about, honey?'

'The Greek joint downstairs is folding and I'm missing it already. Did you notice the windows all soaped up?'

'No, I didn't,' she said turning to Jan with a nostalgic laugh. 'When this doll first took me to this apartment that blinking sign threw fantastic patterns against that wall over there. I thought it was the most romantic thing.'

'It was like a cheap Warner Brothers movie,' I said.

'You told me I looked like Ida Lupino. I loved it.'

'Well, you look like Roddy McDowell at this moment.'

'Thank you,' Jan said coldly.

'You look cute, Jan,' Joan said. 'Pay no attention to him. Here's your drink, hon. I think this herring jar is divine for mixing martinis.' Jan was becoming uncomfortable.

'Come on. What really put you in such a foul humor?' she finally asked.

'Art. I was over at that mouldy Museum of Modern Art. Depressing display of Picassos.'

'I heard the exhibit was divine. Miles was just thrilled with it,' Joan threw in. I looked over at Joan and she seemed ridiculously out of place in my scheme of things.

'Listen, Joan,' I began. 'Fix me another martini in that divine jar before you go.' Jan was upset. I sat back and drained my old drink, wondering how I got into this mess.

'Darling,' Jan said, 'why can't you be nice to my friends once in a while? I put up with all kinds of nonsense from that crazy, inconsiderate gang of neurotics who show up here all hours of the day and night!'

I didn't answer. She went on. 'Furthermore, I work all day while you sit around on your ass moaning about 'the end of feeling.' Well, I'd like to feel something once in a while. I want to feel calm in this apartment, but you never let me forget that this apartment is a great battleground of sexuality. Why don't you lay off those snide remarks about sex, and your constant insinuations about me and my friends. I'm sick of it!'

'I knew you would get around to that working bit, Baby,' I answered. 'Now let me tell you something. When I start using your miserable little paycheck to support this place you can start complaining. You've never contributed one cent to this setup and don't you forget it. I'll call it until that time comes, understand?'

'My, you're a nasty man,' Joan said. Jan started to cry and walk over to Joan and put her head on her shoulder. I was furious.

'Take your hands off that girl and get the hell out of this apartment, right now.' I started to get up and Joan grabbed her mammoth purse and made for the door.

'I'll call you, sweetie,' she said as she was halfway out the door.

Jan was shaking her head, sobbing unbelievably sad sobs. I went over and put my arms around her.

'I'm sorry I was so mean. Look, Jan, people like Joan incense me. I don't like to see you with them. They are no good for you or me. As for my crazy friends, I thought you were beginning to like them. Wasn't it laughs and lots of fun? Why didn't you tell me before how you felt?' Jan stopped crying for a moment.

'You never gave me a chance. I've never been alone with you. They seem to be always here, drinking your booze, eating our food and killing our love. When did I even have a chance? Even at night after we were in bed, they would phone or throw pebbles at the window. Honestly, I haven't had you to myself since we've been married.'

'It hasn't been that bad, has it Baby?'

'Pretty bad,' she replied. 'Honestly, I am so sick and tired of those intellectual heavyweights constantly complaining about everything and everyone. They put down everything – art, books, even sex. All they can talk about with authority is how they haven't been able to get it up in years. How feminine do you think that makes me feel, hearing that over and over again? How many laughs can you get with that line? I'd love to go away for a while, some place alone with you and very far away.'

Although I couldn't think of any place to go, I knew what she meant. There was a great deal of truth in her picture of the scene. She came over and sat next to me on the couch.

'Let's try and get away from this nervous set. I have a vacation coming, maybe then?'

'Maybe. Let's think about it.' I knew we had to go some place. She fell on the couch, took my face in her hands down with her. I tasted a few left-over tears and kissed her open mouth.

'You smell like licorice. Have you been drinking Pernod today?'

'A little,' I said. She didn't say a word. I turned out the light and moved in quickly and closely and said hello for the first time in a long time.

I woke the next morning in time to have breakfast with her before she went off to work. She was in the kitchen fixing something special. I was in a damn good mood and it must have been infectious; she was actually enjoying the role of girl-cook. She was even humming a silly little tune. It sounded fine that morning. Jan's face looked fresh and pretty even without make-up and in the daylight her hair had a pleasing natural blonde tone and was neatly combed for a change. She brought in a plate of eggs and bacon that looked good enough to eat. I gave her an affectionate kiss. She pulled up a chair and started chopping up her boiled egg.

'You know, I've been thinking of places to go all night in my sleep.'

'A thirty day all expenses paid Caribbean cruise?'

'Be serious,' she chided me. 'I've dreamed up something that might be kicks. Let's go visit that mysterious brother of yours in St. Louis. You're always telling weird stories about Ned and Sunny. How about it?'

The idea appealed to me at once. I hadn't seen them in a couple of years, and they'd never met Jan. She'd hit it off pretty good with them. I thought of the similarity of Jan and Sunny. Sunny had tried to make it in New York, career and all, before she met Ned. Very unhappy in that role. Now she had two delightful kids, a great big house and was pretty much into making it as a wife.

'Why not,' I said. 'It might be amusing to see how the other half loves. Non-nervously,' I added. She was still chopping up her egg. Usually the noise made me uncomfortable, but that morning it didn't disturb me at all.

'Didn't you tell me Sunny was some sort of wild character in her college days?' she asked, sprinkling a huge dose of pepper on the egg.

'Wild?' I questioned. 'Sunny didn't give a damn about anything in those days. She was girl-rebel. Thrown out of Wellesley, ricocheting into Briarcliff and ending up in a select group of diaphragm-carrying political science majors at Wisconsin U.'

'Wasn't Wisconsin more famous for its card-carrying Commies?'

'Oh, yeah. There was an awful lot of AYD and American Student Union rallies. Come to think of it, she was going there during the Front Populaire. She still reads the *New Republic,*' I answered. She asked me about Ned. 'He's probably the only retired artist that's never painted a picture.' A very mysterious guy, but very funny, was the way I summed him up to Jan.

'Well then, what do you say?' she asked hopefully. 'Is it a deal?' She scooped up the plastic dishes, threw them in the sink and came back to give me a great big hug. 'We're going to make it too,' she said very quietly, lingering in my arms. I hope so, I thought.

The long goodbye kiss and the plans to roll got me so excited I skipped my usual morning movie. I called the station to get the dope on trains and costs. It was expensive even by coach. I needed some dough. I went into action. I called Rick Davis and made an appointment for lunch that day. Those articles were going to be our train tickets.

5

WE MET AT VILLA CAMILLO and had a drink at the bar. Camillo gave orders for a set-up at a quiet table and would call us. Meanwhile, we sat at the bar.

'How's it going with the magazine, Rick?'

'Nowhere, but I've been thinking.'

'What do you have in mind?'

'I take it that you're ready to expose yourself and write that series for me. Perfect timing, I might add. They have been after me for something sensational for weeks. They want a fresh audience. What optimists publishers are! They don't know there is no new White fresh audience any more. The Negro is the fresh audience in America. Negro publishers are going to clean up in the next ten years with their secret formula for taking the kinks out of their audience's mind as well as their hair.

'To the New Order, the wave of the future and the decline of the West,' I said. 'Let's drink on it, Massa Rick.' We drained the glasses. Rick ordered two more.

'Rick, I have a title that will get you a whole new audience: Boy Scouts Who Have Gotten the Electric Chair. A personal, intimate account of the criminal mind or organized youth. What do you think?'

'I like it,' Rick said. 'Maybe the *Digest* will pick it up.'

'Or how about: Can You Slap Your Mother: A Semantic Problem.'

'Extremely high class and provocative. Seriously, they are really on my back for something to pep up their raison d'etre. The word is out and agents are flooding us with all the stuff they usually send to

the *International Journal of Sexology,* or, if you please, to your magazine. We got an article in the other day, Confessions of a Coprophile.
Can you beat that?'

'How was it?'

'Limited appeal, I dare say.'

'Wasn't a plant of the *Reader's Digest* by any chance?'

'No, but they have an exciting one coming up in the September
issue: The Appendix: A Re-Evaluation. A crazy organ,' Rick concluded.

Camillo gave us the sign and we settled down to some serious talk
at the table he had prepared for us. Rick told him to bring a couple
more drinks over.

'Rick, do you honestly want an article that names names and really puts the finger on the whole queer set-up in the arts?'

'Yes, and more.' He was very serious.

'What makes you think you won't be sued, jailed or crucified?'

'I know this much.' He sounded very solemn. 'Nobody has sued
for being called a queer since Wilde. It just doesn't pay, boy. They've
got a better way. The queers in powerful places give you the silent
treatment. They completely ignore you for the rest of your life. They
know who to pressure to keep your play off Broadway, your songs
off the air. You could be God himself, but if they have you marked,
you're through. It's the first time in history a minority dictates to the
majority. Of course, if you get around to buying their taste, they are
forgiving just as they are forgiving with ex-communists.'

'You sound like my associate editor Yogi. If what you say is true,
why commit suicide? I don't care about myself because they have my
number in Dayglo. I don't need them. But you, you're going to be
writing novels some day; as you say, they never forget a straight.'

'By the time I get around to writing a novel, homosexuality will
be old hat. Strapping young men will become chic masochists and
women will whip our culture into shape. I've always gotten along
with women, so you see, I have nothing to worry about. I think we're
both getting a little drunk.'

'I'll write you the greatest inside culture feature since Max Nordau's Degeneration, Rick,' I said.

'Max Nordau?' he repeated. 'I haven't heard that name in twenty years. Is he chic again? Is there a revival going on in some little magazine I don't know about? Max Nordau,' he repeated, turning his head from side to side in awe. 'That's wonderful.'

'Will you give me an advance?'

'Drop by my office this afternoon and I will have a check for five hundred dollars waiting for you.'

'Five hundred dollars!' I screamed. 'Why, I'd call my mother queer for that kind of money. Come to think of it, she probably is.'

'You're doing it for the money, aren't you?' he asked.

'Doesn't everybody do it for the money?' I kidded back. 'Don't the geeks who sweep out latrines really hate that work and only do it for the money? Come off it, Rick. Doesn't the guy who plays house with the dead in dimly lit mortuaries do it for the money? Who are you parlor analysing? That's the second time this week I've been called queer?'

'Just kidding, old sport.' His brows went back into a neat knot.

'Don't try to kid the old kidder. Besides, it ain't my year to turn. I'll see you in Capri in '65.'

The food didn't taste so good all of a sudden and I wished I had ordered soft boiled eggs.

'Actually, I do need some quick dough. Jan and I are going to visit my hometown. I haven't been back in two years and she's getting very strung-out here. Can I do the articles when I come back? We'll only be a couple of weeks.'

'Sure.' We got up slightly tipsy and he paid the check.

'Arrivederci,' he said as we parted.

I spent the rest of the day sleeping off the glow in Central Park. On the way home I tried to work up a picture of what it was going to be like visiting St. Louis again. I completely forgot to drop by Rick's office to pick up the check. Funny how that much dough can slip your mind.

6

We coached it to St. Louis and got caught up in a cage of frolicsome end-of-semester students headed West. It was rather fun. After dinner, Jan and I had a couple of drinks in the lounge car. Soon it was filled to capacity with good-looking fresh kids, drinking very smartly. I got to reminiscing with Jan about all the miserable, lonely, train trips I had staggered through the last ten or fifteen years, never getting laid once. All my life I wanted to get laid on a coach – never made it. I've known guys who have laid All-American Airline hostesses 70,000 feet up cross country; athletes who have made it on canoes on lagoons all over the world: in bridges, coal mines, barns, basements, closets, toilets, even MGs; and I could never make it in a miserable coach. Perplexing!

In my early days of travel I paid attention to the kind of reading matter I carried, thinking that might help. I never made it with the *New Republic, Harpers, Consumer's Union*, the *New Yorker* or even the *Partisan Review*! All it got me was dirty, sneering looks. I switched to *Variety* and *Billboard* to attract a racier, looser crowd and was completely ignored. 'Low character' they thought. After the war I started carrying books by Karen Horney and the *Journal of Clinical Psychopathology* that got me a few inquiries of a timid sort from school teachers, but nothing I could sink my teeth into. I gave it all up in the fifties and concentrated on luggage. Of course, with alligator bags and diplomatic brief cases from Brooks Brothers, you could hardly expect me to talk to anyone less than Lucius Beebe, and that son-of-a-bitch only traveled by in his private coach.

I discovered that Jan was the best prop of all. Ordinarily her eyes never stopped asking for acceptance, but that night they never seemed to stop teasing. I looked at her very carefully and slowly realized she had turned on somewhere, probably in the toilet. I didn't like it but for some reason I hadn't forbidden it. She had got some pot from somewhere on her own. Once, when I was cleaning up around the apartment. I ran across some pot that she had stashed. I didn't say anything at the time.

I started to get into *Railroad Age,* compliments of the Penn R.R. When a couple of college punks struck up a conversation with Jan. At the beginning they were very polite about it, introduced themselves and even asked me if I minded. I was a little suspicious of all the poison Ivy League crap but I O.K.'d it and sat back to listen to their arias.

'What does your husband do?' the tall one asked.

'He's an editor.'

'What does he edit?' He was crew cut and fraternity-pinned and probably on the debating team.

'Children's books,' Jan said, sensing the beginning of a leg pull. She whispered to me, 'No future in these boys.' I agreed.

'Oh, I see. That's very interesting. A child's formative years are spent with books. Yes, very important.' He was the original egghead. Jan couldn't say anything but managed a strained smile.

'What do you do?' the Crew Cut tried again.

'Nothing, really nothing,' she said in a very discouraging way. She was trying to pull out. I kept on listening.

He pressed her hard. 'I mean, what are you really interested in?'

'I'm only interested in popular songs of the late 30's and early 40's.' I whispered to Jan that I thought I ought to kill the conversation. He looked like he was thinking over this profundity, wondering if it deserved special interpretation. He looked over at his friend, nodding some secret signal. I felt something was going to happen.

'Very good.' He turned to his mind-mate and I caught the wink.

'Songs do reflect on a popular level the dynamic aspects of a people's culture, wouldn't you say, John?'

Ordinarily that would have gotten a big laugh out of Jan and me, but there was something obscene about the wink and the delivery. I had to step in. I reached over and grabbed the tall one, wrinkling his school coloured blazer into a knot in my hand and whispered in his ear to knock it off. He made some slight attempt to get out from under the pressure and I added the word 'now'. His friend nudged him and motioned to leave it. He wisely accepted the advice, brushing his jacket smooth. After they'd left the coach car, Jan said, Ohhh, what idiots.'

I asked her whether I could get her a drink; I certainly needed one. She agreed it was a good idea. Jan got up to get a magazine and I ordered two more drinks. She came back with a dog-eared copy of Photoplay. I quickly discarded my Railroad Age. I looked over her shoulder and we smiled through pages of intimate scenes from film-land. I even put my arm around her. It was very pleasant.

7

I DIDN'T SEE ANY WELCOME SIGNS or a horseshoe of flowers but I did spot my brother Irving at the gate. I couldn't imagine why this particular member of the family was appointed delegate at large for our reception; I hadn't been en rapport with Irving since 1932. He appeared friendly enough however, and I managed a gracious introduction and healthy small talk. He sped us through the city, pointing out old landmarks to Jan and the new wrinkles to me. It was the regular guided tour and I almost wanted to tip him as we pulled up to his ranch-style house in the suburbs. The house was something new since I'd left town. Once we had all lived together in a big, old-fashioned Victorian mansion, each on separate floors. Irving was the first to break away; my brother Ned had written, 'I can forgive him for moving out but I can never forgive him for being happy about it.'

Irving was proud of his modest home; I tried to avoid thinking about the tall lamp in their modest picture window, with the cellophane still around the lampshade. I should have been embarrassed for Jan to meet this wholesome member of the family first, but I wasn't. It would be such a startling contrast when she'd met Ned and Sunny. I silently applauded the wisdom of Ned's choosing Irving to welcome Jan to the city.

We had lunch and sat around catching up on local gossip, which was about as stimulating as their décor. I played with the children a bit – they didn't remember me, but were nice about that. Marsha talked with Jan excitedly about our 'fascinating' life in New York, but it came to nothing. I caught Jan fighting an occasional yawn. She wasn't skilful at it but we hadn't gotten much sleep on the train. After a while, Irving suggested he drive us back to town so we could

173

get settled. It had been arranged we were to stay at the old house with Ned and Sunny.

On the drive back to town, Irving tried to make things peppy with simple conversation.

'We're glad to see you back. How long do you plan to stay?'

'Just long enough to rest our nerves. About two weeks.'

'Everybody sure missed you.'

'Likewise,' I answered. 'Nice little house you have. Do you like it out there, away from temptation?'

'Yep, the kids have a good school and Marsha's mother lives a couple of blocks away. Makes it very convenient. She was never happy living with Ned and Sunny.'

'I hate to see the family breaking up,' I said.

'Maybe we were too close for comfort.'

'How you talk,' I teased.

'Don't give Jan here the wrong impression.'

We pulled into the driveway and he got out to help us with the bags. I asked him if he wanted to come in for a minute.

'No. I've got to get back to work. See you all later. I hope we'll see something of you before you leave.' He smiled again and gave Jan an affectionate goose as he side-swiped his way back to the car. She liked it.

'So long,' I said, 'I see you haven't lost your touch.' He gave a little embarrassed wave and smiled again. His smile always made it difficult for me to communicate with him, but he was an affectionate chap and I hoped someday I'd get to know him.

From the outside, Ned's house looked like a dungeon that had been recently whitewashed. It had a great turret rising three storeys high. Wrought iron gates, falling off at the hinges, enclosed an intimate scene of elks etched in frosted glass front doors. The street, like most of the city, was preparing for decay. I rang the bell without much success.

'A typical family welcome?' Jan asked. 'You did write them you were arriving?'

'Wait a minute. I'll get Joseph to let us in.'

'Who's Joseph?'

'He's a toothless colored man who does his best to give the impression of a family retainer. He dodders around trying to make himself useful, but he's really a charity of Sunny's.'

I went round the back and called out to Joseph. He was in the basement. When he saw me, he burst into a magnificent toothless grin which spelled 'welcome home' for real. He had his pants on and his white long-sleeved underwear glistened against his worn-out black skin. An overscale crucifix hung mystically at crotch level. He looked genuinely excited. He excused his appearance, escorted me to the side door, through to the front and we let Jan in. He took the bags, after a friendly introduction.

'Nobody home, I guess,' I said. 'Sunny's probably out with the kids.'

'Mista Ned's home. Uh... I think he's in his studio.'

I wondered what Ned was doing these days. The house hadn't changed much. The rooms were made up of odds and ends of wrecking yards. There were slabs of marble over wrought iron stands and brass and onyx tables held lead glass Tiffany-style lamps. Interesting bric-a-brac from the turn of the century gave a flavor of disorganised, easy-going charm and excellent taste. We walked through the house trying to find Ned.

'What's over there?' Jan asked, pointing to closed sliding doors.

'It's the old ballroom, a legendary place. The guy that built this house was a Midwest version of Charles Schwab, the New York steel magnate. He tried to emulate the Eastern tycoon's way of life, even to putting in an organ. Schwab had a full time organist and this guy got an electric one, a bit of practical Midwestern originality.'

'Is it still there?'

'No, Ned gave it to some church. It was shot and needed a complete overhaul which would have cost a fortune.' I opened the doors and we curiously peeked in.

'They'll never dance the minuet here again,' I said. It was an amazing sight. Miles of flaking Wagnerian murals climbed Gothic niches two storeys high; towering stalagmites composed of mouldy books, periodicals and prints rose up from the floor obscuring lower portions of the murals.

There was a silver inlaid Boulle piano, slightly burned, with a stack of piano rolls on its top. Broken musical instruments of two centuries jutted madly from a twenty-foot wall; I saw an unstrung harp alone in a corner. There was a worm-eaten, washed-out sleigh in the middle of the room which might have crossed Siberia. It was richly carved with cherubs doing silly capers. An Emperor's chair kept company with Venetian brass lanterns and striped marble torches, stolen I'm sure on a frolicsome night along some Venetian canals. Towering blackamoors harbored plants in sturdy, upraised arms; I spied a magnificent, bejewelled motorcyclist's belt hanging crazily from the arm of one of the blackamoors. Jan screamed when she saw a Vernay Martin decorated Sedan chair, blasphemously facing a French provincial confession box, its door slightly off the hinge. They were prizes from Ned's forays into the auction rooms and occasional visits to the Salvation Army stores.

'Shhh,' I cautioned. A door opened and from where the guts of the organ once rested, Ned strode out brushing his hair with a pair of military brushes.

'Voices, voices, do I hear voices?' he asked, dodging around a displaced merry-go-round horse. Ned was tall and thin and he looked remarkably suave, but I noticed his fly was open.

'Jan, I'd like you to meet my brother, Dr. Caligari. Doctor,' I turned to Ned, 'doctor, this is Jan, my new assistant.' Jan acknowledged the meeting with a smile of appreciative bewilderment.

'I'm speechless,' she finally said.

'Say hello,' Ned suggested, languidly extending his long, bony hand to her. Jan hesitated.

'Go on, shake it,' I said. 'It's not wax.'

'I don't know,' she said. 'Are you sure?' She gave Ned a timid hand along with a friendly smile.

'What did you do with the torture chamber, Ned? That will make her talk. Where are the whips and wheels, the iron maidens of yesteryear? Look here, you've turned this place into a Santa Claus workshop of Christian curios. Come now, Ned, bring out the falcons!'

'A great little kidder,' Ned said to Jan. 'Well, gee, it's good to see you all. Where's Sunny? Have you met her yet?'

'No. Joseph let us in.'

'She must be picking up the kids from school.' He looked at his watch. I noticed it had a radium dial. It looked as though it might have been bought with cigarette coupons when he was a kid.

'Come on in the living room and have a welcome home drink.' He put his arm around Jan and turned her gently towards the door. We single-filed down a narrow aisle; as he passed the confession box he stopped a second. 'Anything you have to say?' he asked, nodding to the box.

'Well, not right now,' Jan replied. 'But I'm sure it does.'

'Mighty handy, Ned,' I said.

'Any time,' he replied. As we moved out of the room, I tapped Ned on the shoulder. 'Nice little place you got back there.' He smiled.

Jan said, 'I think I know what he means. Tomorrow, the torture chamber, uh Ned?'

'Of course, my dear. Tomorrow – the works.'

Ned had enough Dixie Peach pommade on his black hair to make it sound convincing. He hadn't changed much since I last saw him. He parted his hair a little more to the center which gave his looks a strange combination of the goodness of Herbert Marshall and the evil of Vincent Price. He was still in his thirties. I remembered letters of Sunny's mentioning an illness. Whatever it was, it had left him looking at least ten years my senior instead of four. His color was more striking than I remembered, a heat lamp tan over gray, but his brown eyes still danced bravely above abused bags.

Ned's style of dress had changed from time to time, but always four or five years behind fashion. He was just getting over his double breasted drape period; the coat he was sporting that moment was single breasted, three buttoned, albeit ventless. His pants broke off at the cuff over his Tom McAnn shoes, harboring socks with a hole or two, I suspected. But he moved like an aristocrat with security in every step. One had to be terribly secure to wear pants that broke at the cuff; I for one thought he was courageous.

'What are you doing these days?' I asked. He was pouring some White Horse scotch into tall glasses. I shuddered, but didn't say anything. He had forgotten I drink it on the rocks.

'It's sure swell seeing you two. Things have been mighty dull recently. Do you have any plans?' he asked.

'No. I just told Irving we were resting. How come you let him buy a corny house like that? I almost died from embarrassment.' Ned shrugged helplessly and gave us each our drink. 'He may turn out to be the real rebel in the family yet.' I secretly agreed.

There was a commotion in the hall and we heard the shouting of the children. 'That must be Sunny,' Ned said, rising from his wire-back ice cream parlor chair. 'Look who's here,' we heard him say from the hall. The kids came running in first; they stopped abruptly when they saw Jan, little frozen smiles on their faces.

'Hey Cunningham, hey Wabash. Come over here and give me a hug,' I said. They sort of tip-toed past Jan giving her big eyes and polite lips and spilled over me with affection. 'Jesus, you boys have grown up. I want you to meet my wife. Jan, this is Cunningham and Wabash, a couple of crazy kids.' They clutched me, nodding a dignified acknowledgement to Jan. Ned came into the room with his arms around Sunny. 'Here she is,' Ned said proudly. They looked like Red Riding Hood and the Wolf. She went over to Jan and gave her an affectionate hug; she was smaller than Jan.

'Look who's home,' Cunningham shouted.

'I see, I see,' Sunny answered, coming over and giving me an affectionate peck on the cheek. 'How in the hell are you?'

'How do you like her?' I whispered in her ear.

'Cute, very cute,' Sunny replied, looking at Jan smiling. The kids tackled her and we were one big daisy chain in a moment. 'I'm trapped,' Sunny cried. 'Get me out of here darling.' Ned went over to solve the traffic jam of spontaneous affection.

'Oke doke, kids, no rough house now. Go in and say hello to Joseph, he's probably got something for you,' Ned said.

'May we watch television too?' Wabash asked. He was the little one with blond hair, blue eyes and a ramrod back.

'Yes. Hurry, hurry now,' she said, patting their little behinds. I gave Cunningham an extra pat. 'See you guys later.'

'So long,' they said, filing out of the room neatly.

'They're going to be in crowd control when they grow up, aren't they, Ned?'

'Like you and me used to be,' Ned agreed.

'What about a drink?' Sunny asked Ned. 'I can't tell you how delighted I am seeing you both. It's a real treat.'

'Ned's been telling us things have been pretty quiet around here ,Sunny. Any truth to the dirty rumor? Who's around?'

'Around?' she repeated. 'Why, the circle is so small now we'll strangle to death if it gets any smaller.' Jan let out a small laugh. 'Seriously,' she continued, 'it's been rough. We have a few new faces, but nothing to make your heart beat faster. We're waiting for you to liven things up.' She took Jan's glass and I gave her mine and she went over to the scotch.

Sunny moved around a room like Ned – secure, free to swing little hips and solid, shapely legs ending in trim Oxford walking shoes. Her wide leather belt looked secure as AT&T stock, and her face paid off the same kind of dividends: wholesome and regular. A long bona fide head of red hair pinned into a sturdy pony tail. She wore a tan tweed skirt and a yellow sleeveless blouse with a loose turtle neck. A fetching picture of happiness, I thought at the time.

'How long have you two been married?' I suddenly asked. Sunny stopped a minute, put the drinks down and started counting on her little fingers. They stopped at eight.

'Very impressive,' I said.

'You never have to worry except for the first, third and fourth year,' Ned said, doing a little finger figuring of his own. Sunny gave him a wise guy look and said, 'that is, if you get over the second, fifth and seventh, right darling?'

'What about the eighth?' Jan asked.

'You usually die of boredom if it lasts that long,' Ned said. 'I'm only kidding, Honey,' he quickly added, looking at Sunny sheepishly. She brought over our drinks.

'A toast to the ninth,' Ned said. 'I'm picking up her option.'

'I'm going to cry,' Sunny replied. 'I'm no longer a starlet.'

'You'll always look like Norma Shearer to me, Sunny, ' I said, 'But get rid of this Niles Aster character before silent films come back.'

Sunny had an infectious laugh; it seemed louder than Jan's whose laugh was always an even, cool one which seemed to say: point. Sunny's laugh was scattered and wild, the kind that spelled victory. Ned had a confusing laugh; it always got lost somewhere, usually around his collar. His laugh wires crossed and you had to watch his legs or hands for accurate results. The legs tapped out the acceptance or literally crossed each other with rejection. I had to keep an eye on Ned's laughs.

We settled back comfortably, except Ned who retained his stiff high chair. Jan was lying in a mountain of Victorian down and Sunny curled up in an old wing chair, partly hidden from view. I had stretched out on a threadbare Recamier sofa. I felt like a young spoiled Regency duke coming home from a prolonged sojourn of debauchery in Paris, pleased with himself for bringing back an unspoiled flower from a convent and throwing her before the family as proof of his basic goodness. It was nice to be home again.

8

DINNER WAS A RELAXED AFFAIR, especially since Cunningham and Wabash ate and talked politely and, I might add, more intelligently than most grown-ups. I asked Cunningham what he wanted to be when he grew up. He said he was going to be an artist like his daddy, which made me grin and wince at the same time. His daddy hadn't touched a brush since the poster contest for Fire Prevention Week in 1931. Wabash was more realistic in his choosing a profession. 'I'm going to be a cowboy,' he grinned like a chipmunk, as he reached for his pot metal gun. He was fast on the draw as he picked us off one by one without moving from his high chair.

Jan looked warm curled up on a pile of velvet cushions in a window seat. A purple eventide light filtered through the art glass window behind her. I sat under a Waterford wall sconce that bathed me in its complimentary glow; I was sure I looked ten years younger than when I arrived. I studied my reflection in the enormous Empire mirror across the room: I did look years younger! Ned was upright on a stiff Italian carved settee, contemplating. The children played with a scrabble set on a worn out oval Aubusson rug. The room seemed to be still talking about last decade's party.

We waltzed through classic family memorabilia, touching here and there on bits of childhood rejection, ending up tired from laughter over a rising hot chocolate soufflé. Coffee was served in a more formal living room. As I looked around, waiting for Sunny to pour, I wondered if Ned would bring out cigars and call for the lutes and dancing girls.

'Alright now kids, settle down. Why don't you watch some television?' Sunny asked the children.

When they marched out of the room, quite happily, I said to Sunny I didn't think she approved of television.

'I didn't until my family gave me a set. I look at everything now, I'm a TV fiend, hooked, you might say. The kids too.'

'Why fight it,' Jan said. 'I'm so tired of people putting down everything to show that they're superior. I like lots of things that aren't supposed to be good taste, only I don't dare admit it in New York.'

'What's the latest thing they're putting down there?' asked Ned.

'You old Chinaman!' I said laughing at Ned's attempt at naivety.

'No kidding, what's being put down this season? I want to be hip.'

'Don't get sucked in, Jan,' I warned. 'How about movies?' Sunny asked. 'Is that popular to put down?' She poured the coffee.

'That's all we talked about in New York. Movies. Good and bad. B-movies and C-movies. Arty foreign films have become corny. All the uptown squares rush to them now. They'll be running them at Radio City soon.'

'Oh, I get it. The minute something becomes acceptable to the masses, it's no longer *de rigueur*.'

'That's it, Sunny. It's all over when it filters down and becomes respectable. That's how it is with Art or Music or Literature. Picasso was a great painter, but people have been told in *Life* color spreads and *Time* cover stories and *House Beautiful* that Picasso is great. "He's tops, boys and girls – a little eccentric perhaps, but pick up on him" read the captions. You can buy him framed and silk screened, cheap; hang him around the house, be a step ahead of your cornier friends. "Be daring this year in the Harlequin Period: from R.H.Macy's, Lord and Taylor, the Museum of Modern Art." When Picasso becomes a household word and Pepsi-Cola mobiles hang from corner confectioneries, it's time to say, "You've done a nice job, Picasso and Calder, and you've at last become respectable and rich. But move over, you no longer shock us or amuse us or make us think in new terms." In fifty years, maybe less, Picasso will be left over wall decoration resting next to Whistler's Mother and the old lady will be smiling sweetly because one of her boys has come home, just as she knew he would.'

'You mean I better unload my Picassos before the bottom drops out of the market?' Ned said dryly. 'Sunny, do you hear this?'

'We better not dump them all on the market at one time,' she replied. 'I'll call my broker in the morning.'

'Where was I?' asked Sunny,' I said good naturedly.

'How is it that you pick up on movies so much? That's about as filtered down as you can get, isn't it?' she asked.

'Movies are like a salad,' I began. 'You start with plain lettuce, olive oil and vinegar, the old Hollywood formula. Then you get fancy and start adding things; wild eyed Caesars, throw in crumbs and garlic. Then frustrated, insecure housewives tease the appetite with eggs and sour cream, onions and tomatoes. You start importing anchovies, peppers and cheeses, until it's loaded down with ingredients. It's still the same old salad, yet people have a sense of getting something bigger and newer for their money. The movies give you everything you ever wanted out of life, but more important, they satisfy that insatiable dream hunger. You get a lot for your money in a movie house, just as you do in a chef's salad. Listen, a whole book can be written about salads and class stratification. A snobbish business, don't you think? And there's nothing wrong in being a snob or being a Republican or anti-union or anti-semitic except the wrong people are and for the wrong reasons.'

'Wow! Now that's about as snobbish as you can get!' Jan replied.

'We're all snobbish, don't kid yourself. We're dull snobs or corny snobs or smart snobs or invert snobs, like that guy who wrote the book on snobs. He's a combination of them all, except he's not a smart snob. If he were, he wouldn't have exposed himself to begin with.'

'May we smoke, Professor?' Ned broke in.

'Yes. Class dismissed.' I got up and poured myself a drink. 'But don't get me wrong; I love Hollywood. I think I'll go up and say goodnight to the kids.'

Both kids were sitting in bed, leafing through a worn picture book. They seemed so content, I almost felt superfluous but I moved in and sat at the foot of the bed.

'What's cookin'?'

'Nothing,' Cunningham calmly answered. 'Peter Cottontail is hoppin' down the bunny trail,' he added, pointing to Peter himself.

'He's a crazy rabbit, ain't he?'

'Yeah,' Wabash volunteered. 'We have a record of Peter Cotton-tail.'

'I must hear it sometime. Who sings it? Liberace?'

'No, silly,' Cunningham said.

'Superman?'

'You're silly,' he repeated.

'You like to sing?'

'It's alright, I guess.'

'What do you like to do best?' I asked.

'I like to holler best,' Cunningham said with a certain amount of frankness.

'What do you like best, Wabash?'

'I like to holler too,' he answered.

We started laughing and they gave me a sample of their favorite occupation. 'Hey fellers, you'll get me into trouble. Have a little mer-cy, boys. I'm only going to be here a little while longer.'

'Where you going?'

'Jan and I have to get back to New York.'

'You got any children in New York?' Cunningham's little face screwed up. I noticed Wabash put his chin in the cup of his hand, looking like a tiny-tot juror waiting to pass sentence. I felt a little funny about having to tell them 'no'.

'Why don't you?' Jesus, I thought, I should have stayed down-stairs. I prepared hastily a scientific retreat.

'We've only been married about a year,' I said, giving him a sly wink.

'That's long enough,' he said sternly. 'Sunny said it only takes nine months after you plant the seed.'

I stalled for time. 'Is that what Sunny said?'

'Yep.' I looked over at Wabash. He just nodded, his chin still resting securely in his palm.

'Well, she's right.' I hoped it sounded final enough to satisfy him. It worked out and I went about tucking in the blanket around their feet.

'Listen, kids,' I said in a conspiratorial tone, 'I've got to get back to the gang, they're waiting for me.'

'You ever coming back?' Cunningham asked.

'You mean tonight?'

'No, silly. I mean are you ever coming back to live with us?'

'Would you like that?'

Yes,' they both said. 'You're silly.' They both laughed.

'I'm pretty silly. I'll see you tomorrow. Goodnight.'

'Good night,' they whispered.

'Later,' Cunningham said.

'Shhhhhhh. And good night.'

'Bye,' I heard Wabash say. Buy is right, I thought. I'd like to buy the whole set-up.

Sunny was gathering up the mess in the room when I returned: I offered her my assistance.

'Swell. You roll the tea cart into the kitchen and keep me company. I have a few chores to do.' She turned to Ned. 'Why don't you show Jan the collection of prints Jimmy the Picker sold you last week. Honestly, Jan, if you want to see the sickest prints of the Mauve decade, take a look.'

Jan and Ned went off to the Studio and I rolled the cart into the kitchen.

'Want a drink?' I told her I'd take a glass of milk instead. I never drank liquor in the kitchen. I helped myself to a glass and poured some while Sunny started to scrape the dinner dishes. 'How were the kids?' she asked out of habit.

'They're tucked in for the night. They're pretty sharp kids. You know what Cunningham asked me? When I was coming back to St. Louis and stay.'

'Good question. When are you coming back? We've missed you.' She came over and touched me affectionately. 'Isn't New York getting a little too much? It was for me. I always felt like an outsider.'

'A lot of excitement in New York but it does seem to be a little too much for Jan at times. She splits early.'

'It's her town, born, raised there: she should be at home there.'

'It's her town alright but sometimes I get the feeling she thinks I've taken it over, or away from her. I mean it's all my crowd of friends, everything, including all the conversation. It seems everything revolves around my work and writing: instead of feeling like an outlaw, she feels outlandish, almost superfluous.'

'That's a terrible feeling. It's bad enough to be out of touch when you're single, but to feel superfluous when you're married is really sad. I like Jan. I think she'd be a real addition here. Seriously, don't you ever think of coming back to stay?'

'I've thought about that, but I've never gone over in this town. It's always been a hard town for me to play. Too many adolescent rejections lingering. I'd run into the old crowd and they'd still be putting me down. No matter how much I've accomplished or what I've done, they could never accept it. They'd accept me alright if I played it straight and bought their values but I could never do that.'

'I know what you mean.' Sunny slammed the dishwasher cover shut with a little more zip than necessary. 'I have the same problem. I was a misfit kid and nobody wanted to play it my way either. I staged my abortive attempts at middle class rebellion and thought I was beating them. Went to smart schools, had my own apartment in New York and what passed for a glamorous job. I was kidding myself; I wasn't kidding them. Even today, when I run into those girls I grew up with its the same deal. There they are, in their Peck and Peck clothes pushing baby carriages. They've never been further than French Lick, Indiana and their husbands are section managers of the May Company. But those girls knew at sixteen what it took me ten years to find out.'

'I've got the message, but could you have made it without two years of psychoanalysis? And has it really worked out for you? Are children, a husband and the rest of the show really enough for you? Don't you ever get restless?'

'No, I'm not restless. The kids, Ned, this house – sometimes it all drives me crazy, but it's all-consuming. It's what I want and get the most pleasure out of.'

I couldn't have agreed with her more.

9)

THE NEXT MORNING I HAD a slight hangover; it was almost friendly, no anxious New York head. I felt good about it.

'What are your plans for today?' Sunny asked at breakfast.

'I think I'll show Jan around town. As Thurber says, 'take me back to the boyhood haunts of coot and hearn'.'

'God, Jan, if you're going to get the tout that Ned takes me on once every five years, bring along a handkerchief – the boys ham it up pretty much when they see the old homestead and the old school. Oh, it's too funny.'

'It's tradition, Sunny, you can't escape it.'

'Let's face it, it's the most broken-down shaggy dog tour since Lassie came home.'

'Come, my dear.' I got up, extending a wing to Jan. 'Are you ready?'

'Ready, but wait a minute while I get a couple of hankies.'

It was a typical spring day in St. Louis. The sycamore trees looked a little strained and the warm smell of Monsanto chemicals charged the air around us, torturing sinus sufferers.

'It smells like Donara, P.A.,' Jan said. 'Smogville – a nice place to bring up kids.'

'It clears up later in the afternoon, if we catch a north wind.' We walked down the steps holding hands. 'The tour starts directly over there,' I said, pointing to a neo-Georgian brick house where T. S. Eliot spent his formative years. She was impressed for a second.

'The trees look a little moth-eaten.'

'No trees on West 53rd Street, our little block,' I reminded her. 'The fellow who lives in the house now is a dispossessed poet from

San Francisco who claims he bought the house because of its rich, poetic heritage. He's really in the scrap metal business. Poetry in iron, like Max, the millionaire. Across the street lives a Dr. Hirschfield, near-Freudian with an ominous tic in his left eye. Spends his spare time re-gilding antique pier mirrors.' As we passed the guarded entrance of Leroy Clement Lindell, arch snob and silly remnant of St. Louis society, I told her how the rabble is allowed to look upon the well lit trees and the family portraits decked with holly, assuring her that tradition is still revered in St. Louis. 'Notice that miniature Swiss chalet over there. Two semi-intellectual socialites hold forth with country club violence right out of John O'Hara. A charming couple. They used to keep a hipster in the basement for laughs.'

'What do you mean?'

'He was some goofy musician that he was in the army with. He visited them and they picked up on him, touting him around to liven up their dull parties. They threw him out when they discovered he was peddling marijuana to their friends.'

'Nice people.'

'Talk about nice people, there's the town's busiest fellow. He's a classy abortionist with the finest trade from coast to coast. Has a sweet house, doesn't he?'

'A psychiatrist, a poet, an abortionist, the violent set; what a cosmopolitan town.'

'Well, at least a block of it anyway.'

We were walking past a row of little junk shops and I was carried back to my childhood days of ash pit picking: I must have spent half my childhood collecting things and the other half selling them to little shops along this street. They didn't have ash pits in New York so I didn't go into this with Jan who had wandered off to gaze in a window of junk jewelry. She wouldn't have understood my world of evil and luxury.

'Come over here a minute,' I heard Jan call out; it broke a nostalgic moment for me.

'What's up?'

'Let's go in and see how much they want for those ear-rings.'

'Good. I know the chap who owns the shop. It's a front for the pornography he sells. I bought my first French post cards from him. He'll remember me.' I recognized him immediately. He was still wearing those dime store spectacles which always made him look like an old man although he was only about fifty. He was completely bald now and his soft moon face seemed more genuinely obscene than before. He remembered me right off.

'Hiya punk,' he said as he got up from his trash-ridden desk. 'Is the lady wich ya?'

'Yeah, Frenchy, she's my wife.'

'Excuse me,' he said to Jan. 'I knowed this guy since he was a little punk trying to sell me fake South American stamps. Where you been? I heard you was in New York being a writer or somethin'. So how's he treatin' ya?' he asked Jan.

'Oh, just fine,' Jan said. 'How much is the pair of green ear-rings you have in the window?'

'Too much, Frenchy. Give the girl a break.'

'Go on, ya cheapskate. Those are classy pieces. I paid a lot of money for those. Say, you want any books, you?' he asked in his sotto voce, hitching up his pants at the same time.

'I'm too old for that stuff now.'

'What do you mean, 'too old'? Ya never too old. I got a deck of cards wid some beautiful photographs on the back. My best seller; let me show ya.'

'Naw, Frenchy, I've seen them all. Whatcha got really good?'

'Boy, ya got particular, haven't ya?'

'Discriminating, Frenchy. How much for the ear-rings? Make 'em cheap.'

'Listen punk, lemme make a buck. Two bucks,' he shouted to Jan. She went over to the window and picked them up to try on. 'Do you have a mirror?'

'What does she think this is? Tiffany's? I'm only kiddin' lady.' He went into the back room and brought out an old glass handled mirror. 'Here, don't break it.'

'Pretty cute, isn't she?' I said.

'She's got a nice build. Look here,' he pulled out the deck of dirty cards. 'This is the real McCoy. I'm getting three bucks a deck. They cost me almost that. Take it for cost.' He shoved them in my hand.

'I'll tell you what I'll do. I won't even look at them and give you three bucks for the ear-rings and the cards. Take it before I back out.'

'Oh you cheap son-of-a-bitch.' I knew I had tempted him.

'Hurry. Yes or no?'

'Go on, you cheap mumser. I'll take it.'

'I overpaid,' I corrected him.

'Get out of here punk. I never made a dime off ya.'

I put three bucks in his grimy but steady hands. 'Now, howsabout a wedding present?'

'Sure, sure. Wait a minute. I got somethin' for ya.' He walked over to his desk and pulled out an old souvenir ash tray from the St. Louis World Trade Fair and handed it to Jan. 'This is for you. Don't let this bum sell it on ya. ' Jan was quite touched and thanked him enthusiastically.

'That's very nice of you. Thanks,' I said.

He shook his head several times. 'It's OK. He's a good boy. Knowed him since he was a kid.'

'See you later, Frenchy.'

We got out on the street and I asked Jan for the ash tray.

'You're not going to sell it on me, are you?' she said, looking afraid.

'I just want to look at it a second.' The slogan, 'Meet me in St Louis, Louis, meet me at the Fair' bordered a picture of the Fair's number one attraction – Little Egypt. 'I could get a nice piece of change for that.' I thought for a second. 'How'd you like to see the site of the World's Fair?'

'And skip the homestead tour? What will I do with all those hankies?'

'We'll catch it next time. Let's go. They have a beautiful zoo there now.'

'Goody. I spent my entire childhood in Central Park's zoo dodging sex perverts. Let's go.' We switched our course and walked briskly towards the park.

'How do I look in these ear-rings?'

'Not bad. Almost sexy. We'll see what my pals at the zoo think. There's one obscene gorilla I'm anxious for you to meet.'

'What did you have in mind?'

'Oh, I don't know. A little sodomy perhaps?'

We cut across gentle mounds, skirted leaky lagoons and laughed at the statue of General Sherman and his horse; the Iron Man in the middle of nowhere.

'If Sherman's horse can take it, why can't you?' I said. We paused before a Union cannon at his side to read the inscription. I was really searching for my initials scratched in its barrel decades ago; all I found was the provocative message: 'Beverly. Call Joe.'

'How's this?' Jan asked, jumping up on the cannon, cheesecaking beautifully.

'Hold it!' I picked her up at the bend of the knees, toppled her over my shoulder and kissed her full on the lips as I put her down.

'You're crazy. I didn't know you were such a powerful brute.'

'I think I ruptured myself. But those ear-rings I bought you are pretty sexy.'

'You sure it's not that artwork you're carrying around?'

I forgot all about those cards. I pulled the deck from my back pocket. 'Gin, anyone?' I shuffled them adroitly.

'Cut?' I dealt out a hand using the General's platform for a table. We played it cool; neither of us paying any attention to the artwork. Suddenly Jan knocked with nine and I was caught with a fistful of soixante-neuf.

'What have you got?' I said, rolling her over on the soft, chilly grass.

'Cut it out, you impetuous boy,' she said, playfully fighting kisses and hugs.

'Nature in the raw is seldom mild,' I shouted, getting in some extra feels before I pulled her to her feet.

'I've lost an ear-ring,' she screamed. She was down on all fours frantically combing the beaten grass. She found it in a second. I pulled her up again and stole another kiss. We took a short cut through virgin forest and memory served me well; we came out right at the beginning of the zoo.

'Gee, this is fun,' Jan said, breathing hard and a little flushed. 'I haven't had so much exercise since I marched in a May Day parade. Oops. I was just kidding. I didn't mean it.'

'Forget about your warped childhood, but I see what you mean about us.' I kissed the back of her neck. 'We're much too hip for this sort of thing in New York.'

'What a shame.' She looked at me quickly with serious eyes. She didn't have to say any more.

We were in front of the bird house, a huge dome, perhaps a city block long and five storeys high. Its wire mesh covered natural trees, flowing streams and art nouveau rocks for vain peacocks to exhibit themselves.

'Hey, this is pretty. I've never seen anything like it.'

In my best Chamber of Commerce voice I told her it was the largest outdoor bird cage in the world. 'Wonderful birds, too. Look at 'em!' A huge crane flapped towards the roof on impossible wings that looked like lead.

'You wouldn't think that bug guy could get off the ground.'

'I never saw so many different kinds and so many colors. It looks like a Shriners convention.'

'Alger Hiss and Whitaker Chambers would have had a ball bird-watching here, wouldn't they?' I said. I suspected something more sinister when I saw three elderly guards enter the cage.

'Feeding time?'

'What's the story?' I called to one of the guards.

'We're going to bring them inside. Too cold.' I noticed they carried long sticks.

'This we got to see,' I said. The guards started at the far end of the cage, lightly tapping strange codes on the ground with their sticks. The birds started forming ranks. Stately and dignified, their columns marched toward the doors which led to inside quarters. Jan and I stood open-mouthed as the parade continued. The guards moved slowly with their tapping sticks; the birds seemed amazingly docile. It was really a spectacle.

Suddenly the guards were in trouble. A group of deviationists made a sudden break for freedom, creating confusion in the ranks. The splinter group was led by a horned screamer that looked, I swear, like Leon Trotsky.

'Those goddam Trotskyites have infiltrated everywhere,' I pointed to Jan. 'Look how beautifully those obedient Stalinists are adhering to the line.'

Jan was laughing madly. 'I see, but I don't believe it.'

The guards were running all over trying to restore order but the rebel leadership was impressive. Trotsky's cohorts made bold raids on the line in desperate efforts to win converts. Several of the lieutenants resorted to hoodlum tactics: I saw a razor-billed curasso nip a blue heron on the leg. Finally the guard executed a counter attack. He went right after the cotton-pickin' Trotskyite who by now had climbed a high jagged rock, screaming obscenities at his enemies. Waving his stick skilfully but never touching a feather, he silenced the shouting leader of the mob; by God, if they didn't all get back on the train, including Trotsky!

'Magnificent!' I called to the guard. 'Well done. You've nipped the revolution.'

'Down with Trotsky!' Jan screamed.

'Every once in a while, either this one,' pointing to Trotsky, 'or that one,' pointing to his field lieutenant. 'Mean ones, Troublemakers.'

'Communists. Get them out of this aviary. Confine them behind glass walls. They're no good.'

The guard looked at us rather strangely, scratched his head with his stick, knocking his cap to the side of his head.

'You know, mister, I think you've got something there.'

10

THE NEXT DAY SUNNY MADE hasty arrangements for a luncheon for Jan. Ned invited me to join him at lunch downtown. We ate at a crusty old restaurant the town had almost forgotten. We had fresh channel catfish, very good, hot cross buns and Brown Betty for dessert (horrible). I kept washing it down with a local beer and barely succeeded in doing anything more than develop a dull headache. We didn't talk much during the meal; I concentrated on avoiding the bones in the fish. But there were times when I felt we both wanted to ask each other the same old question: 'How are things really going for you?'

That was about as intimate as Ned and I ever became with each other. Ned was drinking cokes throughout the meal and after lunch, added cream to the coke, giving it the look of a cup of local laxative, Saratan.

'How d'you like Jan?' I finally broke through the wall of silence.

'Who?' I laughed.

'Jan, you know, my new assistant?'

'Oh, excuse me, I wasn't thinking. Jan? Let's see.' He took a look at the check. 'Very pretty I'd say. I don't think you'll ever be bored with her.'

'The way it looks, I don't think I'm going to get to know her that well.'

'What do you mean?'

'Characters in flight from femininity are awfully complex. Eyes in the back of their head. Wants acceptance from everyone. I have a friend in New York who sums up the type: "She'd go down on King Kong if he gave her the nod".'

'That should be interesting,' he said with a curious smile. 'What's so complex about Jan? It's nothing that a lot of attention wouldn't cure.'

He motioned for the waiter. 'How you getting along in New York?'

'You mean us? Jan and me?'

'Well, yes.'

'Married people on the make don't make it together in New York. Let's get out of here. I'm feeling nauseous.' My dull headache pepped up and I had a beaut by the time we got home.

Ned was resourceful at night with his suggestions for parties and amusements. He left the serious talk to Sunny. Towards the end of our stay he suggested that a party be thrown for us. The theme was to be, 'Come as your wife's lover or husband's mistress.' He was unable to pull it off during our visit owing to strenuous opposition from nearly everyone.

He was unruffled at the rejection. 'Perhaps when you come back to settle down in a year or two we'll all be healthy enough to give that party.'

Sunny put him down with a light tap and turned to me. 'What are you going to do when you get back to New York?'

I told her I had a lot of writing to do.

'As a matter of fact I'm doing a series of articles on the homosexual conspiracy for some creepy popular magazine. The editor is a buddy of mine.'

'Which magazine?' I named Rick's magazine and she exploded. I had seen her do this before so it didn't bother me; it started Jan biting her nails.

'Why, that's a fascist publication. How could you write for them. You surprise me.'

'Fascist publication? What the hell kind of archaic word is that? What a hangover word, Sunny. Nobody talks like that any more. Come on, kid, you're not serious?'

'I certainly am. They're anti-semitic, anti-union, American First-ers, Red-baiters, the complete fascist line.'

'She can't be serious, Ned,' I said turning to him for help. 'I haven't heard anything like that since I left college. Listen, my dear,' I turned to her, 'if you're not pulling my leg, which I think you are, you're way behind the times. You're caught in a political lag, like your husband's clothes – five years behind the fashion. All that junk is dead, kid. I'm surprised at you. Get off that kick – it's stale. Even the young kids in liberal colleges don't buy that left wing schmaltz any more. They all make fun of it.'

'Perhaps I'm old-fashioned, but I can't use words like "nigger" without feeling shame. Who are these people that go around talking like that? Maybe a handful of arch-sophisticates and neurotic snobs but that doesn't give it validity.'

'That's a beautiful dream you're hanging onto. But this is 1950. It's not peculiar to any group. It goes beyond politics. Why, it's mani-fested beautifully right in your home. Ned and you with your col-lection of 19th century freaks – you pay homage to anything that's weird and off-beat. Why look at the names you give your kids? What do you think that really means? You know damn well it's break a heart to get a laugh. Another bit of nihilism. Yet you still retain one sore spot that needs constant attention and soothing: your liberal conscience. Get rid of it! Be liberated! I had the same indigestion about words like "nigger" and "kike".'

There was an embarrassing silence.

'It's like using obscenities for the first time. You know of course that obscenity is just a state of mind. There is no such thing as a dirty word. In fact, I consider myself more free of prejudice when I use a word like "nigger" to describe one. The same goes for Jews. A kike is a kike is a kike, as Miss Gertrude Stein would say.'

'Call a spade a spade, is that what you mean?' I'm sure Sunny didn't intend to be funny but I thought she summed it up pretty good.

'Spades have the privilege of using the sacred words and we're not supposed to. "It's too good to waste on the common people," as Victoria said to Albert.'

Jan said something uncomplimentary and I gave her a scathing look.

'What world are you living in, Jan?' I turned on her. 'Pretty hard to look around at life, at least the way we know it, and say it's the land of your dreams.'

'There is another kind of life besides the one we live. Everybody doesn't dwell night and day on 'what's wrong with American culture' like you and Yogi and all your friends.'

Jan started biting her nails. 'I can't enjoy anything any more without being accused of being square,' she said with a mouthful of fingers. 'If I wear your shirt or blue jeans because I feel more comfortable in them, you accuse me of being lesbian. I used to read murder mysteries, but no, I can't read them any more; they're violent and sadistic, and I'm a sadist.'

'How about a drink?' Sunny's suggestion was perfectly timed.

It was embarrassing. It somehow always was when Jan levelled her hostility my way. I had tried a score of times to point out to her the simple fact I didn't like to see her take an openly hostile attitude to me in public. If she didn't agree with me, I advised her to wait until we got home. It never worked though. There was too much resentment; too much concern with justice for her to let me get away with anything. It could only have got out of hand that night, so we had a couple more drinks in an embarrassed silence. We went to bed, but hardly kissed good night.

]1[

THE NIGHT BEFORE WE LEFT they took us to a party given by a friendly nobody from my past. Jan was putting on her make up by the time I was ready. I looked at her reflection in the mirror and told her how pretty I thought she looked. She gave me an affectionate squeeze before she returned to her artwork.

'You look handsome tonight,' she said. It was the kind of remark I like to have lingering in my mind when I'm going out in public. 'I feel a little nervous, but it's our last night in town and we'll have a good time.'

'I hope so.'

I was determined to hit it off with everybody there. Not so much for Jan's sake, or Ned's or Sunny's, but for my sake. I wanted to see if I could fake it with the natives. I stripped myself of all costumes and disguises. My first words would be 'Hi, neighbour'. Could I do anything more than that?

Jan was shaky as a Homesteader surrounded by Apaches. She had staked out a millionth of an acre of wall-to-wall carpeting and was feeding it its third dry martini. I looked over for a minute, saw her Shirley Temple eyes itching to do a shuffle off to a snake pit. I wanted to go over and put my arm around her and say something nice, but I couldn't take those glassy eyes loaded with loneliness.

The hostess dragged me through a procession of introductions and left me with a prize jack-off who looked like Andy Gump, the chinless comic strip character. I had never seen anything like him outside of a comic book. I asked him how he was doing and he said he was having 'oodles of fun', which sent me to dizzy heights of bewilderment. I stopped Sunny and told her I had to give the hostess credit.

'She's garnered the greatest collection of goofy-looking people I ever remember seeing under one roof.' She didn't have any sympathy for me and warned: 'You get what you give.' I watched her go over to Jan in an attempt to put her at ease. Sunny was right: I was playing the cultural hero role, which was not going over. I made it to the bar and started some serious drinking, alone.

I was struggling not to hear an emaciated blonde labor leader and his wife with prematurely gray hair setting up a cartel at the bar. They were ordering Presbyterian hi-balls and I noticed they were holding hands. I started laughing in a quiet drunken way, bothering no-one. A stark, attractive brunette, tall, skinny and sexy, appeared from no-where.

'What's funny?' she asked me.

'Look at the couple next to us,' I whispered, pointing at them. 'They're rebuilding San Francisco together. He's big in labor. What's your problem?'

'My husband.' I liked the way she said it.

'Which one is he?'

'When you hear a wrist watch alarm go off,' she looked at her watch, 'in about fifteen minutes, that'll be my husband. You'll recognize the face that goes with the joke.'

It was a harsh description of a mate, I thought. What a castrator she must be. I didn't smile at the remark, but looked her over, ounce by ounce.

'How deep is your depression?'

'Bottomless.'

'Why are you telling this to me?' I thought she said 'because you have balls'. After a second, I realised she had said, 'because you look like a good ball'. I was thoroughly confused. I asked her to repeat that.

'Because you look like a ball'. She said it plain and dirty. I was almost too drunk to do anything about it, except talk.

'Do you give or take head, Madam?' I thought it ought to put a stop to the conversation. It didn't; it only excited her.

'Both.' She laughed, tossing her drink down like a real lush.

So many wheels started spinning in my mind I felt like Charlie Chaplin lost among the cogs of Modern Times. I finally settled on a course of action.

'I never disappoint a lady.' We adjourned to the next room, a sort of nursery, doing things even married people don't do, when we heard her husband's alarm go off. We both laughed so hard it almost killed our fun.

When we came back, things were picking up; people were dancing. The skinny girl and I parted as unsentimentally as we had met. I didn't see her the rest of the evening. I saw Jan, though. She was sitting on the hall steps talking to Andy Gump. Suddenly she picked up a record and smashed it over his head. Nobody seemed to mind, including Andy. I went over to her and asked her why she did it.

'I was bored,' she listlessly replied.

What a pity. I took Jan under my arm and walked to the car.

'We're not going to make it, are we, Honey?' Her voice had a strange quality of hopelessness I hadn't taken seriously before. I almost wanted to cry.

They took us to the station after a Sunday champagne breakfast. Ned presented Jan with a bound volume of the *Yellow Book* for 1892. Sunny bought a copy of *Variety* at Fred Harvey's. We looked very smart as we boarded the Spirit of St. Louis. I had an arm around Ned, chatting lightly, he chuckling softly, when I noticed his fly was open.

Rick called a week after I got back to New York to find out how I was coming along with the articles. I had been working on them.

'I'll be finished with the first one in a couple of days.'

'Good. Bring it up and we'll go over it here.' The way he said it sent a little chill down my spine. I thought about what Yogi said regarding editors – 'the scum of the earth'. I quickly reassured myself Rick was different.

'Say, Rick, have you heard? I had a fight with Yogi about the damned articles. He heard about it from somewhere and accuses me of stealing his act.'

'It figures. Don't pay any attention to that madman; he's impossible.'

'I feel bad about it.'

'You're better off without him.' I knew it was true but, Jesus, the guy did teach me an awful lot about the conspiracy way of life.

'It sure makes it difficult to work with him now.'

'You can't work with guys like him. I know his kind.'

'That's what he says about you. He gave me the whole 'sell-out' business.'

'His kind of writing went out years ago. He belongs in a museum. He even looks like a museum piece.'

'He helped me get on the right track with the magazine.'

'Too bad.'

'You may be right.'

'Sure I'm right.'

'See you in a couple of days?'

'Good.' I put the receiver down a little too hard, feeling a little disappointed in Rick's lack of compassion for Yogi.

Between worry about Yogi's castration capers, both real and imaginary, and writing about homosexual coteries, I began to feel as though I were operating within a giant pincer movement and my new look became the anxious look. The swill of morning mail added to the trapped feeling and I had a vision of myself as a magnificent sterile porcelainized garbage pail, waiting for the city sanitation trucks to collect me.

I had been back only a week. But that week's mail told the whole story of why I was tired of editing my magazine. There were twenty poems dealing with death. Twelve pieces of fiction, three of them dealing with castration; one dealt with hair; the rest nonsense. There were four tawdry confessions, one from a voyeur who had a friend in the demi-monde who would let him watch: there was an exhibitionist who travelled the subways late at night exposing himself to deaf mutes; a small town nymphomaniac who ran out of local men and turned lesbian; and a flagellant who was lonely at the YMCA.

The checks from Harvard University Library were still coming in; their records had been snaffled and I was getting checks quarterly. (They had an unbroken subscription till about 1969.) This was topped by a threatening letter from a Reichian, one from a Dianetic faddist and the clincher: a personal request from a Midwest sex investigator instructing me to send his copies of the magazine directly to his house instead of his office; they were invariably lost, stolen or stained before he had a chance to go through them.

I took the first draft of the articles over to Rick right after a solitary lunch at Chock Full of Nuts. He had an impressive set-up in an office lined with peg board and pine. Screaming eagle lamps of Federal design reminded the editors of their American heritage. I could spot Rick's fine touch in choosing the dishy secretary; the exotic plants standing around were decorator-bought.

He had his feet on his desk and was shouting over the intercom for some Empirin tablets.

'Sit down, Tiger, I have a terrible headache. I'll be with you in a minute.' On his desk was a Bachrach photo of his wife and child which might have jumped out of *Harper's Bazaar.* It was shadowed by an old picture of Ezra Pound (circa 1914) with a dedication to Wyndham Lewis scrawled in green ink right under Pound's beard. He bore a striking resemblance to a young Yeshiva student.

I handed him the manuscript. He took out a Vick's inhaler and went through the ritual deftly with one hand while reading the script. Both eyes were open, if a little red from his cold. I was sorry I had dropped by with the manuscript on an afternoon when his health was obviously failing.

'Good. This is almost perfect the way it is. Suggest you emphasize or name three or four writers, novelists, whose first rate talent has been traduced by bad advice from homosexual editors.' I knew he had Bummy Carwell's editor in mind because I had told him the story.

'In general, be more specific about just how the corruption takes place. Elaborate on the idea that the quality fiction scene is wholly dominated by homosexual authors writing for women's fashion magazines. Effeminization of literature, etc. In short, Tiger, you've done a good job.'

I thanked him.

'Let's get together some night. Bring Jan over and we'll knock off a few reputations together.'

'Why don't you drive out to Connecticut with us some weekend. Get your health back.'

'I'd like that. Fix it up.'

'Right. See you in a couple of days. Call me.' A voluptuous non-literary secretary swung into the office as I was leaving.

'Take care of that cold,' I called back.

12

OUT OF THE BLUE YOGI CALLED BACK, gentle as a lamb; he almost apologized but naturally he couldn't pull it off. Instead he talked rapidly about tackling 'the big obstacle that is preventing me from pulling out the stops of the whole neurotic, moronic censorship law'. He was ready to let me publish the book that he had poured all his scholarship and seven years of his life in writing. He laughed triumphantly. 'We're going to jail together.' He had it all figured out.

Yogi had nothing to lose should he get indicted. He could take an oath of poverty, have the court appoint a lawyer and then spend the next few years appealing and appealing until he either won or was jailed. I was nervous, dedicated, awed with Yogi's brilliance or nerve (I don't know which). I thought we had an interlocking neurosis that spelled victory. Yogi worked furiously on the project. He bought special water-marked Indian paper and hounded type foundries in Brooklyn for umlauts, dashes and exclamation points more aggressive than the ordinary 20th century ones. He diabolically searched for obscure German dyes which would come off on the hands of infidels who guiltily sweated while reading his book. He drove the printers mad insisting on blacker than black inks. His proof sheets were masterpieces of Joyce-like corrections. He would crawl in one of the huge-mouthed presses with gauges to ensure correct pressures. He revealed a printer's thumb that rivalled the great technicians of Skira's press. The Bauhaus simplicity of the cover design ensured aesthetic recognition. Every delay was a printer's plot to destroy him. He was the talk of the Fourth Avenue printers, and he could be seen going home late at night with his manilla envelope clutched in ink-stained mitts.

Just as we were ready for the final run Yogi made crude changes to the original text to ensure, he said, a test case. It was the first time I ever dared to challenge him. 'Yogi, for Christ's sake,' I said when I caught the changes. 'What are you doing? Why these changes? Very poor taste.'

He was enraged. 'Poor taste?' he shouted. 'What do you know about taste? Don't start with me. You're a pimple on the moon of progress. If you hadn't met me, you'd still be playing at publishing. I knew you wouldn't have the guts to follow through. I know what I'm doing and I'm going to do it. I'm the only guy in the country who knows what censorship is about and I tell you I'm going to strike it down.'

'Listen, Yogi. You don't need those changes to strike it down; you've got enough in that book already to hang us both. Be reasonable, for God's sake.'

He was furious. 'I've heard that temperance lecture all my life. This is my one big chance to lance the boil and I'm going to stick that needle in. There's no compromising with those Post Office jerks. They're going to get both barrels. Now either you come along with me or get off the pot.'

'Have it your way but count me out. ' He quietened down for a moment when I called his hand. He started on a new tack.

'You're not so bad, really,' he said in a calm voice. 'You published me when no-one else would touch me and I'm grateful for that. But I tell you I know I can win this fight. The censorship law as it now stands is a ridiculous farce and I know how to kill it. Look, murder is a crime, describing it is not. Sex is not a crime, but describing it is. What are the rewards for the murder mystery writer? A colour spread in *Life* and lasting fame. The penalty for describing love? Jail and everlasting disgrace. Does that make sense? This book of mine is going to blow that stupid reasoning to hell.'

'O.K. Yogi. You've told me that a hundred times. I believe it and I know that censorship is stupid but why don't you listen to me and cut the rough stuff that's going to make your case that much more difficult?'

Yogi couldn't see it. 'Do it alone. I'm pulling out.' I was disgusted with his bull-headedness. 'It's all yours now.'

He looked at me with those torches and I felt the sparks fly but I was through. I began to realize why no-one could work with him. He couldn't afford to be accepted by anyone, including his friends. He figured if any of his friends or anybody else accepted him, he must be slipping because they were jerks in the first place and to be accepted by jerks was the end. He had to do something to bring the end about.

The book came out under his own imprint and was an immediate success with both the critics and the Post Office. The charge came through. Yogi was ordered to Washington for a hearing and a possible criminal arraignment. I called him a couple of days after I heard the news.

'How do you feel?'

'Lousy. I've got the gout.'

'What? You're too poor to have the gout. Are you in bed?'

'I haven't been able to move since I heard from Washington. My leg is swollen bigger than my head.'

'It's not psychosomatic, is it, Yogi?' I teased.

'Oh, no,' Yogi said, knowing damn well it was.

'What are you doing about a lawyer? Contacted any of the free speech brigade?'

'You bet,' he said with a slight bitterness. 'They asked me how much money I had.'

'What about the Civil Liberty boys?'

'You nuts? I talked to a couple of them yesterday. Those bastards will get me twenty years. Don't you know they hate free speech?'

'Yes, I know your pet theory. But what are you going to do? You've got to get counsel.'

'I'm working out something else for those Washington boys.'

'What kind of torture have you got in store for them?'

'I've got a little plan. Come up some time and I'll let you in on it. I don't trust this goddam phone. They're probably tapping this line now.'

'See you later.' I wasn't taking any chances either.

I went up to see him about a week later. He looked terrible. He was in a wheel chair practising hair-pin turns and sudden stops and making like Doctor Gillespie. His foot was wrapped in filthy rags and it gave off an odor not unlike the gangrenous cat I met on my first trip up there. I was pretty shocked.

'You're not going to Washington like that? Not with those rags around your foot? You actually stink, Yogi.'

'Fine. I'll smell them out. Part of my plan.'

'I've got a better one. Why not cut off your leg with your scout knife and wave the stump under their noses? They'll be stunned.'

'That's what the doctor wants to do now, so your plan isn't far-fetched, wise guy,' he said with some satisfaction.

'You mean you've seen a doctor?'

'You're right. I don't trust doctors. They're either sadists or homos. This specimen was both. I'm going like this and I'm wheeling myself to that court room if necessary.'

I pictured the scene. It was too much to resist. 'Yogi, I'll take you to Washington. I want to see those cherry blossoms wilt as I wheel you by.'

Yogi laughed. 'It's a date.'

I got up to go and he wheeled around to see me to the door. We shook hands. He looked up at me for a brief moment and I could see he wanted to tell me something nice.

'Thanks. You're not so bad after all.' I was really touched.

'I'll make arrangements for a hearse to take us to the station. Don't worry about a thing,' I said.

On the way down to Washington, I tried to get the plan from Yogi. He was very hazy about the whole thing. No money (I paid for the tickets), no briefcase with-important looking documents; just Yogi in a wheelchair with a gimpy leg. I pleaded with him.

'What do you have in mind? You've got to do something besides look beautiful.'

He didn't answer right away. Then after a while he said: 'I really don't know what I'm going to say or do but I'll tell you this much. I'll make those Post Office flunkies wish they'd never been born.'

I knew he would too.

We arrived for the hearing a smart twenty minutes late. I trundled him down the corridor past a few gaping clerks into a room marked 'Private'.

Yogi surveyed the assembled group. His inventory glance missed nothing; from the watery blue eyes and signet ring of the tall guy standing to one side of the table, to the overworked nose-stroking of the fat bureaucrat, to the dried-up, thin-lipped, frozen-eyed, bald specimen out of Grant Wood.

'What did I tell you. They're just a bunch of old tantes. You'd think we stumbled into the 'lavender brigade' from the State Department by mistake,' he said in a satisfied stage whisper.

I acknowledged his remark with a nervous grin, knowing well they had heard it.

'Good morning, gentlemen,' Yogi said in his silkiest voice. There was a rustling of papers and coughing which was out of all proportion to an ordinary greeting. 'I'm sorry to delay this hearing. I had to change the dressing on my leg.'

They looked down automatically at the filthy rags around his foot. Signet Ring cleared his throat.

'You are Alexander Laguerre?' he asked in a quiet voice.

Yogi nodded his head a little. 'That's right?'

'Are you represented by counsel, sir?'

'No, sir, I am not.' Then he added, 'I dismissed him at the last moment. I discovered he was homosexual.'

'I beg your pardon?' Signet Ring incredulously asked, turning to the others to be sure he'd got it right.

'I said, gentlemen, my counsel was dismissed because of security reasons; like the State Department does, you know,' and gave them an exaggerated grin showing every tooth in his mouth.

The Bureaucrat took over the questioning. 'Since you do not have counsel, I wish to tell you that anything you say here may be used against you.' He went on. 'This, sir, is a hearing before the representatives of the Post Office to determine, among other things, whether your mailing privilege will be revoked.' He held up Yogi's book with a thumb and forefinger as if it stank as much as his foot. I looked closely to see if his hands were spotted red but he sat down before I could tell.

'It is definitely our opinion,' 'the Grant Wood one began, 'that you have violated the obscenity regulations of the Post Office department. This is a serious offence in itself. The representative from the Justice Department would like you to answer some questions at this time.'

The attorney from Justice walked in through a side door. His timing was perfect. His pinched collar was a little too tight, which may or may not have contributed to his tomato-red face. Yogi looked up at me again with a grin. 'Where was he hiding? I missed him on my opening shot,' he whispered.

The attorney reached into his beautiful leather briefcase and fumbled for a sheaf of papers. Before he had a chance to get them out, Yogi let go another missile.

'I trust, gentlemen, that this is not a fairy inquisition. We're All-Americans here, aren't we?' Yogi put his hands on his hips and stuck his gimpy foot out a little further than necessary.

The attorney gave Yogi a scathing look reserved, I suspected, for communist defence attorneys and First and Fifth amendment lovers.

'May I remind you, sir, that I represent the United States government.'

'Yeah?' Yogi replied, affecting the growl of the hood. 'Then who do those flunkies represent? Amerasia?'

'What did you say?' the Attorney asked petulantly. 'Repeat that, please.'

'Which one? The part about fairies or about flunkies?'

'That is what I thought you said. You are in serious trouble. Watch your language,' he warned and actually took off his glasses.

'You big men are watching it for me, aren't you? Isn't that why I'm down here? Put your glasses back on, big shot. I'm not going to hit you.'

The Signet Ring quickly stood up. 'I think, sir, in view of your actions here before us, we must ask you to be represented by counsel for your own good as well as for the dignity of the hearing.'

Yogi pulled in his leg and pointed his finger at the collected group.

'Who in the hell are you to tell me to get a lawyer?' Yogi shouted. 'I don't need to hide behind any shyster at a kangaroo court like this. Now let me tell you something. You're not dealing with a frightened little writer of dirty comic books, 'the kind men like'. I spent my life in fighting for the right to think and write as I saw fit and to try to defend that right before your twisted minds would be a waste of my talent and your time. I may be a nobody without a penny to my name, but I wrote a book for scholars and serious men – a reference for the future – a book that spoke for love and against death, and you have the nerve to object to a few 'nasty' words. That isn't the real reason why you hate my book. It's because your narrow perverted minds can't stand the truth about your miserable, shabby, lying exist-ence. I've been waiting for a chance to expose you in open court for ten years, and you're giving me the chance. Without your summons I would have been nothing more than a lunatic with a sandwich board around my shoulders picketing the hurried shoppers of Main Street with my little gripe. You, gentlemen, are going to lift me out of that ignoble role and give meaning to my life's work for the first time. Now throw me in jail, you fakers, or let me go home.'

Yogi slumped in his chair, spent. I could hear the bars closing around him and the key dropping down the well. The four of them spontaneously huddled around the table. Bureaucrat spoke.

'You may go for the time being. Rest assured, sir, you will hear from us again.'

Yogi had done it! I shook hands with him and whispered, 'Great speech, Yogi. Let's leave quick.' I wheeled him out fast, concentrat-ing on getting him away before he could say another word. I wasn't fast enough. As we hit the door, Yogi turned round to those dazed inquisitors and screamed: 'Don't call me, I'll call you.'

13

ONE OF THE FIRST THINGS I did when I got back from Washington was to stop off at Clark's for a drink. I felt so relaxed after a couple of scotches, I decided to give Sari a ring. What would it hurt? Clark's was empty; she could come down and have a drink with me, it was only one-thirty. I was wondering how she was getting along. I got her number from information and dialled it quickly before I forgot it.

'Yes?' Her voice was brisk, almost salty.

'Did I get you out of your Orgone box?'

'It's you. How nice.'

'Well, that's good to hear.'

'Where have you been?'

'Out West. Visiting zoos. What are you doing?'

'Nothing.'

'Come on over to Clark's and have a drink with me.'

'It's too early to drink. Why don't you come over here?'

'Sure it's alright?'

'Why not?'

'Where's that science fiction character?'

'Don't be mean.'

'No more homework with him?'

'No more homework.'

'I'll see you in about five minutes. Got any Pernod?'

'As a matter of fact I have, smarty. Bring some rocks.'

We both laughed.

After complimenting her on the nice pad, I checked out the bookshelf. In between a key to Ulysses and the Random House edition of the same, some Burns Mantell anthologies of plays, year by year. There were three Max's: Lerner, Eastman and Schulman – but no Max Nordau. WQXR's program guide for the month was within easy reach on the pine cobbler's bench opposite the chintz-covered sofa.

She handed me my drink with a beguiling smile. 'Are you checking my shelves for subversive literature, you stinker?'

'Just checking to see if you have any copies of my magazine. I hate to go places and not see it prominently displayed.'

'I've got a couple of issues. I always hide them when I'm expecting a visit from my mother.'

'What's your mother like?'

'Beautiful and innocent.'

'What an unfortunate combination for you.'

'Don't I know it. It's cost me a fortune in analysts. Tell me, how was Washington?'

'A small but unappreciative audience. Stix Nix Hip Trip,' I said, paraphrasing the classic caption in *Variety*.

Her laugh at that moment made me feel careless in an old fashioned way, and I realized if I weren't careful I would be finishing that lay I started in the sunken swimming pool many nerves ago. She talked on effortlessly, at times humorously, about the role of being an actress. She painted a picture of a creative jungle of double-crossed psyches where all who enter were doomed. The lyric was pure corn but the melody of little-girl-lost was easy for me to transpose.

'Why do you stay in the business?'

'Who knows?' she said, as if it didn't matter.

She made me another drink. She had excellent time lapses.

'I tell myself I want to get married and take care of a man. Do you think that's my trouble? I mean, because I want to take care of a man?'

'Let him take care of you. Why do you want to do the taking care? Is it easier than loving?'

She came over and sat next to me, her head against my chest.

'How do you love?' she asked hopefully.

'Sari,' I said softly, 'If I knew the answer to that I wouldn't be here.' It was the first honest thing I'd said in years.

'Mean, mean,' she cried, shaking her head, trying for tears. She closed her eyes. 'I didn't want to hear that answer.'

'No, Sari, not mean.' I lifted her chin with my finger. She opened her eyes; the making of tears were there.

'Be nice, please be nice,' she pleaded.

I dropped her face, got up and walked over to the window. I couldn't help recalling a similar scene some time ago with a frantic Reichian lay who kept telling me all through the act to 'relax, boy, relax' until all desire left my body. Women who beg to be treated 'nice' obviously don't want to be treated 'nice'. 'Make me pay for this affair, please' is what she was telling me. 'Punish me, its the only chance I have to ease the guilt'. I quickly turned to her.

'Do you really hate yourself that much, Sari?'

'Yes,' she screamed at me. 'Yes, yes,' she cried, her damn eyes spilling tears. She turned over on her stomach, pulling the pillow over her head, muffling uncontrollable sobs. Her shoulders shook rhythmically and her feet dug deeply into the foam rubber seat. I didn't make a move. I was thinking if we were only on street level instead of five storeys up, I would jump out, brush myself off and get as far away from the scene as possible.

As quickly as she started, she stopped. She lifted the pillow from her head and turned her face to me. It was the look of a raped Madonna who had enjoyed it. Exquisite.

'Golly, I'm sorry,' she said. 'I don't know what got into me.'

I smiled for both of us.

'Nerves, I guess,' she added, smiling back. 'I've missed you.' She picked up the empty glasses and without asking me, made another drink. I followed her into the kitchen, marvelling at how quickly she'd mended. By the time I left her apartment, I knew I was booked for spring.

14

'HELLO. MONSTER!' It was Rick calling, catching me in the middle of a shower.

'Call me back. Showering.'

'I'll hold on a minute; got a fun deal coming up.'

'O.K. Hold it.' I went back, turned off the shower. 'What's up?'

'Did you ever hear of Katherine Sloan Whitaker?'

'Is she the society quiff that's always selling Lady Esther face powder and smoking Herbert Tarreytons?' I lit a cigarette.

'The same. She's very literary this year, running a salon on Beekman Place for one-shot novelists, moss-draped young 'uns and lecherous old queens. I have an invite for tonight. Want to make it?'

'I'll fake it.'

'Can you fake it without Jan? She dislikes wives.'

'Jan's with her mother tonight, sewing hems.'

'Talented girl you have. I'll meet you at your place at eight.'

'Good. See you.'

'Later.'

I killed the shower but was caught at the shave. It was a call from Danny.

'Where you been, man?'

'I'm broke, Danny.'

'How you fixed for pot?'

'I'm not.'

'No, I mean you want some?'

'Wait a minute, Danny. What kind of pot are we talking about?'

'What you think? Charge, pot, gage, vance, hemp, top quality shit!'

'You loaded?'

'Loaded? Man, I'm in business.'

'Danny, I'm happy for you. Wholesale or retail?'

'Strictly retail; no discount house operation, chum.'

'How much?'

'What are you doing now?'

'Shaving.'

'I'll be right up.'

To the tune of Gillette's theme song, he sang: 'How are you fixed for gage? How about that for a commercial?' He laughed.

'You got talent. Come up.'

'It's a beautiful day. I'll be right there.'

I finished the shave, nicking myself every time I smiled thinking of Danny turning into a merchant prince. I finished dressing just as he hit the buzzer.

His green eyes were burning; his small frame was packed tightly into a black hopsacking suit and a blue Oxford button down shirt. He was carrying a new smelly leather Brooks briefcase, looking every inch the successful young bond salesman.

'Sit down, Danny, take it easy.'

'Can't stay long, man. Have other clients to see, y'know.'

'Aw, relax. Wait till you hear this new record. Real head stuff.' I watched him twitch in time to the music.

'How about a beer?' I asked.

'Not lushing any more,' he said disdainfully, studying the crease in his black pants. 'How do you like this new outfit? Sheer poetry, no? These pants are lined with white raw silk. Notice the jacket, two vents. All my life I've wanted a two-vent coat. Sounds like an echo of corny Clifford Odets, doesn't it?'

'You're not high or anything, are you Danny?'

'The stuff doesn't affect me. It's night and day, I'm away. Dawn to dusk, it's high finance all the way. Love me, kid, I've got the goodies.'

'Take it easy, you flip,' I said. I turned down the volume of the record machine. 'Is this the one time big time fair-haired boy of the avant garde? Where is the hungry poet of yesteryear? What happened to him? How in the hell did you ever get into this deal?'

'I applied for a G.I. Loan to open a fake appliance store and through some fluke I got it. The next day, I made contact with Bunny – you remember Bunny from the Dance Palace – and bang, I'm in business in a big way.'

'What made you do it?'

'I told you that night with Max I wanted money. I figured the whole thing out. It was like constructing a tone poem; I'm just utilizing my sublime technique on a different level.'

'You're not making sense, Danny. You're a bankrupt poet.'

'No, I'm not bankrupt. I'm a referee for bankruptcy. Let's get down to business.'

'How much?'

'How much do you want? A match box will cost you five, a lid twenty. Quality is the keynote.'

'I'll try a box.' Danny opened the briefcase and picked one out.

'Careful. Don't spill it,' he said as I gingerly opened the box.

'Looks good. Will your firm honor a check or do you prefer cash?'

'Are you kidding? Cash, man.'

'O.K. Big shot.' I handed him a five spot. 'Well, Danny, success to your new career.' There was a moment of embarrassed silence as we both looked down at the floor.

'I know, baby,' he chuckled, 'but does it matter which way you sell out? Me? I'll take the high road.'

'Lousy pun.'

'Lousy life. So long, baby, call me; let's have a social evening some time. Give my love to Jan.'

'Sure,' I said as he closed the door. Well, what are you going to do, I thought, when the little vented jacket had disappeared. You got to help a friend starting out in business. Christ! He'll be on 'H' in a month and that'll be the end of social evenings with the poor bastard. I threw the box on the mantelpiece and pulled down the shades out of habit.

Jan came in about five-thirty and woke me up.

'What have you been doing all day?' she asked.

'Will you ever stop asking me that question?'

She didn't answer, which was wise of her. I got up and brushed a kiss across her cheek. 'I'm sorry. What's for dinner?'

'Who knows? I didn't plan anything. Would you like a cucumber sandwich?'

'Naw, I had one for lunch. Give me variety in my meals, please,' I begged.

'How about a bean sandwich?'

'I'll get gas. I'm going out tonight and I can't afford it.'

'Where are you going?'

'That's two questions I'm beginning to dislike. 'What do you do all day?' and 'Where are you going?'

'I'm going to a dog show with Rick.'

'Isn't it usually a dog fight that one avoids, like, "I wouldn't take her to a dog fight"?'

'Uh huh.' I started combing my hair looking in the Venetian mirror above the mantel. 'Say, honey, I wish the hell you'd dust this mirror. I can hardly see myself.'

'Quel nerve,' she said from the kitchen.

'Why don't you get a maid?'

'You wouldn't let me, remember? You said she'd disturb your sleep.'

'I'll have to reconsider.'

'You're impossible.'

'Reminds me. Danny was by today.'

'How exciting,' she said flatly.

'Yeah, well, he's turned pusher and I bought a fresh box off him.'

'Oh, that's good news. That last stuff was catnip. So Danny's a pusher. What a joke.'

'Is it?'

'You know what I mean.'

'Yeah, I do. What's happening to this town?'

'Are you bitter?'

'Aw, more bored I guess. Aren't you bored with that job of yours?'

'What would I do without it? Lecture?'

'Why don't you get a more interesting job?'

'Thanks. Here's some melba rounds.'

'Thanks. What comes after this course?'

'What do you want?'

'Fry a couple of eggs.'

'Coming up.'

'Am I getting bored, honey?' I shouted to her in the kitchen.

'No. You're just impractical.'

'That's a relief. What are you eating?'

'I've got an old steak bone.'

'When did we have steak in this house?'

'I brought it back from the country.'

'Jesus, you're cheap.'

'Aren't I, though.'

'You still going to your mom's tonight?'

'I guess so.'

'Going to sew an awful lot of hems?'

'Tonight I think we're letting things out.'

'The change should do you good.'

'You are funny,' she told me, darting out to give me a kiss.

'Aw, well, we'll get together one of these days.'

'You think so?'

'Can't miss. I've got a few more things to do.'

'Are they marriage-building?'

'They might be.'

'Do you love me?' she asked.

'Yeah, I think I do.'

'Don't commit yourself, you old bastard. Here are your eggs.

Choke on them, please.'

'Come over here,' I said. She came around the table and I put my arms around her waist, my head against her stomach. 'I love you, you'll see.'

'I'm late.'

'You're what?'

'I'm a couple of weeks late.'

'Well, what's wrong with that? I think it's great.'

'Not with me.'

'You know millions of people get pregnant in New York every day.'

'Yes, but we're not people.'

'But what if we tried?'

'You wouldn't know where to start and I can't see where it would end.'

There wasn't much I could say after that.

15

'WHO'S GOING TO BE THERE TONIGHT, Rick?' I asked as we taxied to Beekman Place. We were very high. Danny's merchandise was superior.

'Mabel Dodge Luhan, perhaps Peggy Guggenheim, you never know. Kathy runs a real Parisian style salon.' Suddenly pointing to the cabbie's license Rick laughed. 'Get a load of the monicker: 'Ethan Allen Rifkin.' That's superb. And the horn rim glasses, the intellectual hackie. Lectures twice a week at New York University.'

'CCNY. He's more the academic type. Let's ask him.'

'Hey, Rifkin,' Rick called. 'Read any good books lately?'

Rifkin didn't say a word or look around. He just reached over and held up a copy of William Empson's *Seven Types of Ambiguity*. I leaned over the front seat and spotted a stack of books which would stagger a heavyweight.

'What a thinker,' I said. 'What else have you got there?'

'Classics, sirs,' he answered in a distinguished voice.

'A real pedagogue,' Rick said. 'What did I tell you? You live in the Village, Rifkin?'

'Sutton Place, if you please.'

'What?' we both said at the same time.

'A pusher, Rick. See, he doesn't have to hack; he's a dealer.'

Rifkin broke into a downright friendly grin. 'Don't get excited. I've got basement quarters – the janitor's a pal of mine. He writes for Encounter.'

'It figures,' Rick said. 'Who are you, Rifkin?'

'I ain't Joe Gould,' he growled good-naturedly. 'Where you characters going?'

'To Katherine Sloan Whitaker's. Would you care to join us, Mr Rifkin?'

'I might do that. Who is the broad?'

'She's beautiful, if forty; she's talented, if limited; and the Chief and I are going to turn her on. Are you with us, Rifkin?'

'To the death, gentlemen, if I didn't have to work tonight.'

'Hey, Eth,' Rick said, 'do you mind if we turn on in here?'

'Be my guest, fellows,' he said, very much in the swing.

'No, you be ours.' Rick lit up and passed the joint to Rifkin.

'Great shit,' Rifkin said. 'Who's this lady again?'

'Top drawer stuff.'

'You know her personally?'

'Never met her. A friend of a friend deal.'

Rifkin's voice went up a couple of decibels after a few more drags. 'I think I'd like to meet Mrs. Whitaker.' He hesitated. 'Would I?'

'Sure, Rifkin,' Rick assured him. 'You're bizarre enough for her.'

'This is too much,' I volunteered. 'Let me have another hit; it's the last drag that gets you high.'

Rifkin recklessly pulled into the kerb, his tyres taking outrageous punishment. 'Here it is, chappies,' he said. 'I'll be quitting this job soon as I can live again.'

'Sure you don't want to live it up with us tonight?'

'I've got a consciousness about any job I take no matter how short it lasts. But I feel great about everything now, thank to you gentlemen.'

Rick handed him a couple of bucks.

'Before you leave, roll down the windows and get the smell out of my cab, if you don't mind.'

'Adios, Senor,' Rick called out, slamming the door, ignoring his request.

We were sky high going up in the elevator. It seemed like a two hour ride; everything was like a movie in slow motion. Ushered into a drawing room of weak chins, pointed chins and one lovely chin that I was sure belonged to our hostess, I felt as though I were in a wax museum. In my peculiar condition, the eyes coming toward me loomed as large as the optometrist's sign discarded years ago in The Great Gatsby. Up close, a pair of grey eyes floated gently in a classic face, fair and clear of almost everything, including expression. But her body twisted like a blue marlin on a hook as she moved towards me.

Her handshake was a surprise; it was as powerful as a gym instructor's. 'How do you do? I'm Katherine Whitaker,' she said simply, her handshake almost drawing me to my knees. Rick withstood her grip by putting his free hand on her elbow, adjusting her pressure by deftly fingering her funny bone. He had obviously been training for just such occasions; I had to call the contest between them a draw.

'I'm Rick Davis, Connant's friend. It's extremely kind of you to invite us. This is my friend, Brad Blisberg, the editor of Nerves.'

'Connant told me I ought to have someone to represent the North, there are so many Rebels with us tonight.' She turned to me. 'I adore your magazine. Everyone's talking about it. I'm so pleased you came.'

'I adore this little set-up of yours,' I said, looking around and snatching a drink from a passing tray. 'Do you think I could drum up any subscriptions here tonight?'

'Put me down for one. I've been meaning to subscribe.'

'Chief,' Rick said, his eyes restlessly searching the room. 'Go check the natives and report back any signs of life.'

'Got you, Ace,' I said. 'I'll be back in a year.'

I left him with that blue marlin, preparing to reel her in on his line. I walked over to the tight group of boy wonders with my sack of marbles in my little hand, waiting to be asked to join their game. I recognized two or three of the faces from years of studying *Harper's Bazaar, Town and Country* and a brief fling with the hole in the cover of *Flair*. Every spastic and his brother was in the circle, led in discussion by a famous hair-lipped boy novelist from the south. He was unfolding a current tale of Hollywood intrigue, holding the group spellbound with his witty lisp.

'Can I play, fellows?' I pleaded at a break in his vignette. I introduced myself with as much savoir-faire as I could muster. Three refused the introduction, two recognized my name and then asked to be dis-introduced.

'That leaves you and me,' I said to the rising star, Woodrow Montgomery. 'If I be quiet, can I listen?'

Woody was a trifle embarrassed at the cool reception I had received and was determined to make me feel at ease. Perhaps his years of hare-lipped rejection had mellowed him and he rose to my soggy opening gambit. More delicate than his famous life-size picture on the back of his first book of short stories, his finger nails were bitten to the moons. His Tattersall waistcoat was slightly soiled from years of spillage of Ramon Gin fizzes he was famous for drinking. Otherwise, he presented a perfect picture of a well groomed office boy for the Smart Set.

'Why does everyone dislike you so?' he asked, leaning eagerly toward me with his Sen-Sen breath. 'It's such an intense dislike, I almost feel you're the only exciting person here. Are you a critic? I can't understand the unanimous disdain if you're not.'

Somebody got to his ear before I had a chance to reply. I didn't catch what was said but Woody let out a shriek of girlish laughter, which surprised both his informer and me.

'So,' he lisped, 'you're the one who's going to expose homosexual writers. How delightful! Would you start with me? I love to be exposed.'

'So I've been led to believe, Woody. Is there really so much to expose? Do you do outrageous things?'

'Forever doing outrageous things. It's the only way to establish a reputation, and saying outrageous things is the only way to insure it.'

Everyone laughed and the group around us relaxed. I had to hand it to the little tike; he certainly had stolen the offensive.

'The first question, Woody, is what do you do when you're in bed with your lover?'

'Delish question. Oh my, what a delish question. You are worth cultivating!' He waited a second for the laugh like a pro and then went on. 'I was going to save the answer to that for Dr. Kinsey, but you're infinitely more attractive and he's never asked me, so I shall tell you instead. I just want my lover's arms around me; I just want to be held and told that everything is going to be alright. By the way, what are you doing later on?'

This brought down the house and people from the corners of the room came alive and looked over to see what had happened. I didn't laugh nor did he until he realized what a hit he had made and then he broke a high C, high enough to make a dog howl.

'What's happening?' Mrs Whitaker shouted from across the room. Rick was lighting her cigarette.

'Woody is priceless tonight,' someone shouted back.

'Oh, nothing more than that? Woody's always priceless.' She went back talking to Rick.

'Woody, are you really priceless?'

'No, of course not. But I have a price. We all do. Mine is reasonable.' He put his little finger across his hare-lip. 'I want people of taste and manners to like me. I try to amuse them without dancing. I try to teach them tolerance without patronage. I'm forever reminding them of loneliness in a world without beauty. I am always pleading with them not to trample on delicate things like one another's feelings. Is that too much to ask?'

'No, that's not too much to ask. If that were all homosexuals asked, I'd be out of a job. Woody, has it been fun being famous?'

'Yes, it has. I am peculiarly equipped for fame. First, I am rich ,which leaves me free of economic ridiculousness. Without obligations, I am free to travel. I see the Luxembourg Gardens when the roses are in bloom. I go to Epsom Downs and sit in the Aga Khan's box. I skip to Minorca or Ischia to catch the soft Mediterranean breezes; see my friends in outlandish Capri. Free to travel and I travel to freedom!'

'Is it always beautiful at the other end of the line?'

'My kind of beauty, yes. I know a score of cardboard villages where I can seek instead of hide. People like me and I like them and I have found contentment in the arrangement. I am a homosexual who tries to build on love, not hate as so many do. I know people laugh at me but when I open my heart their laughter turns to tears. I feel then I have sown love where ridicule and hatred once thrived. I'd make such a gorgeous bishop, don't you think? I'd love to wear those flowing capes and light those lovely candles. I used to wear cousin Rutherford's cape when I was a child.'

'With an act like that I can book you into the Blue Angel. You'd be a star with that special material,' I assured him.

'Oh, do you really think so?'

'Well, if you ever want an agent for cabaret, I know an ambitious pioneer who'd love to have you.'

'And I him,' he replied. 'Do join us again; you're terribly amusing.'

Sad little fellow, I concluded, but not so dumb. I was all set to crucify him but it was me who ended up on the cross. I shrugged my shoulders helplessly and moved into the library, still a fighter without a challenge, but not for long. I spotted two rotten faces by the window and moved in cautiously.

His was a classic queen's face. The eyes were so watery and his facial lines so deep, I thought I was looking at a relief map of a dried-up river bed with a slight trickle of moisture running through. He was talking to a frail, tubercular-looking woman with a black Sobranie cigarette in a long tortoiseshell holder. She looked starved for the needle. Her pale thin lips could hardly smile from years of controlled aggression and the stretched neck muscles confirmed my judgement.

'Who are you?' I asked. She seemed stunned, or offended; it was hard to distinguish which.

'What?' she said indignantly.

'I'm sorry,' I apologised. 'I'm Goose Goslin, Washington Senators, 1931. How do you feel?'

'That's a baseball player, darling.'

'Oh, so you remember me? So few do any more. What a novelty to meet a Goslin fan these days.'

'How do you feel?' he asked suspiciously.

I had to be honest. 'Schizophrenic,' I shot back.

'Oh dear, another poet.'

'Yes, a poet this spring.' I was trying to recall his companion's face. Had it adorned a dust jacket I discarded ten years ago? I extended my hand to her, trying to start all over again. She took a dim view of it and decided to drop her ash on it instead.

'Aw. Now I remember who you are,' I said, rubbing the ash playfully in her henna rinse. 'You're Ashes McNiece from the Carolines. You slept with the giant writer from Ashville in a Times Square hotel a month before he died. Confess!'

'He's mad, darling,' the queen said. 'Humor him.'

'He's humorless and quite mad,' she said, peeved beyond further words.

'So you prefer anonymity; your privilege, but I shall probably forget my manners tonight and expose you.'

'Go fuck yourself,' she said, turning away.

'So it's true, you did sleep with the giant. I understand, darling. I'll go; don't call the bouncer.' To her friend, I whispered, 'Who's the darling?'

'Run along,' he said. 'You're making her unwell.'

'I understand. It's been ten years. That's a long time for anyone to cherish a one-night stand. See you at the penny arcade, and don't be late.'

Nick was still talking to Mrs Whitaker as I went up and showed them my bruises. They were in the hall and I don't think Rick had moved two steps. What a fisherman!

'I need a drink to heal these wounds,' I pleaded.

'Not a bad idea; we could all use something,' Rick added.

'I'll see what I can do,' Mrs W. offered politely, leaving us together.

'How are you doing with her?'

'Not bad, not bad at all. Workable, I would say. She has an insatiable curiosity.'

'I'll say. What do you think? Should we turn her on?'

'Soon, sonny boy. She still needs a little priming.'

'Good hunting. I'm off to torture that little spastic in the corner. It's one of the few contemporary experiences one can indulge in without feeling shame. Tell Kathy I'll be back later, should she miss me.'

'O.K. But knock before you enter. We'll be in there.' He pointed to a baroque door.

As I sauntered back to the scene of ferocious inarticulateness, a wave of longing for Jan hit me. This tableau had suddenly lost its lustre. I could only think of Washington Square Park and playing sidewalk tennis in the spring. I went to the phone and put in a call. It was early yet and Jan had just got in. I told her what was happening.

'If you don't like it, come on home,' she said, as though she didn't really care. I thought it was a good bit of advice, but her tone put me off making a decision.

'I'll see you soon, honey.' I hung up, feeling guilty. I poured myself a hi-ball glass of madeira and headed for the bathroom to gargle. Madeira made a good mouthwash; it left the breath insidiously sweet.

The door was unlocked and I had started to unzip my fly when I noticed a young girl putting the finishing touches to a country club face. I didn't know whether to zip up or down, the face looked so enticing. It was tempting but I started to back out, securely zipped.

'I'll be through in a minute,' she said. It sounded so friendly, I hesitated closing the door.

'Sure you won't mind?' I thought I had seen her a minute ago in the library.

'Are you with anyone?' she asked.

'No,' I lied.

'What do you think of it out there?' She pointed with her lipstick brush.

'Sick,' I said calmly.

'Lock the door, will you?'

'Sure.' I came back and sat on the edge of the tub, watching her calmly squeeze an imaginary blackhead. Her face looked about sixteen and strong willed. Her hands were pudgy and childish but other parts of her looked more mature; it was an extremely provocative combination.

'Mother is making a fool of herself with these parties, don't you think?' I was shocked that Mrs Whitaker could have such a grown-up daughter. They didn't look more than ten years apart. She didn't give me a chance to answer even if I had been able. 'This literary riff-raff is nauseating, don't you think?'

I said yes with a nod of my head; I supposed she wasn't going to let me talk. I was right.

'I've been watching you,' she went on, not once taking her gaze off the mirror. I wondered if she could see me. I was beginning to feel silly with that glass full of madeira, taking a piss.

'I liked what you said about that awful woman. She deserved it. I've always hated her. She's a lesbian, you know, and mother won't get rid of her. Do you think it's shocking of me to talk like this? Are you a writer? It really doesn't make any difference; you have a kind face.'

She turned around quickly.

'Would you like to kiss me before I put my lipstick on?'

There was a pause while I gave it serious consideration. There was no telling what this neurotic Junior Miss had in mind.

'Something friendly,' she suggested.

'Okey doke,' I said, trying to high school it all the way. I put my glass down and started kissing her quietly, almost paternally. She would have none of it. She tongued me until my ears rang. Then she slipped her hand inside my shirt around my nipple, and then broke off abruptly.

'God, you're wearing an undershirt,' she said in disgust.

'What did you expect, King Kong?'

'Men who wear undershirts are unaesthetic.'

I picked up my glass, took a couple of swallows, rinsed my mouth with what was left and spat it out in the toilet.

'Well, Miss Whitaker,' I said, slapping her friendly bottom. 'I'm sorry about the undershirt.' She didn't bother to answer. 'Take care of those blackheads' was my parting bit of advice.

The daffy experience cheered my spirits and I went back to find Rick and Mrs. Whitaker. I knocked at the door and Rick shouted to come in.

'Tea anyone?' I asked, posing in the doorway. Rick had done some neat priming; she looked surprised and slightly silly. It was in keeping with the room; a Hammond organ in the corner looked equally silly. Rick gave me the nod. I moved in and started rolling a joint.

'This doesn't shock you?' I asked. I was doing a one hand roll, not spilling a grain.

'Not at all. It's a funny thing isn't it?' She was apparently fascinated by my deft finger work.

'Nice job, Rilke.' Rick applauded.

'A touch of the old West,' and handed her the joint.

'What do I do with it?'

'Inhale it, darling, and hold the smoke in your lungs as long as you can. Like this.' Rick did an exaggerated version of a tea-head. She took it to her lips.

'How fascinating,' she said before inhaling deeply. It choked her and she coughed, aristocratically, of course (perfected by years of boredom). I couldn't help thinking she had encountered the experience somewhere in the past and was pulling my leg.

'Is this very widespread?' she asked innocently, inhaling magnificently, 'I mean, what are the figures on dope addiction?'

'Kathy, this isn't 'dope addiction'. This is clean American sport. 'Every day in every way, it gets better and better' to paraphrase some Frog. Everybody picks up on it these days.' Rick sounded very sincere.

'How intriguing. What's it supposed to do? Will I get sick?' Her virginal enthusiasm was touching.

'Not tomorrow,' I said.

'No hangover? That's rather un-American, isn't it? Aren't I to pay for forbidden pleasures? I always have. Let's absolve ourselves immediately.' She got up and walked very quickly to the Hammond and struck a cleansing chord. 'Who's for hymns?' she asked, giggling slightly.

'Do you know Throw Out The Lifeline?'

Rick turned to me, whispering, 'someone is sinking tonight'.

'Quite appropriate,' she enthusiastically said, going right into the chorus. She had a sensational contralto. Rick and I walked over and raised our voices in splendid off-key solemnity.

What a charming picture the three of us made around the organ, the joint hanging Bogart-like from her lips. Rick started to massage the nape of her neck, singing in his sweetest choir boy voice. After the song ended, he leaned over, took the joint form her lips, kissed her hard and dragged deeply from the joint.

She ran her fingers through her hair in a desperate gesture which suggested she knew she was about to pass the point of no return. Her curiosity, so noticeable from our first meeting and confirmed by her daughter, had done her in. She was hooked. She looked up at rick with frightened, middle-aged beauty. Rick was eyeing the gilt-framed icon dangling solemnly above the organ. She noticed him staring at it and casually mentioned that it had been a gift from an archduke's son.

'Tell me, Kathy,' Rick asked, 'do you think Christianity is as constructive as marijuana?' Without waiting for a reply, he gave me a look I was quite familiar with. I struck an ominous bass chord and slipped out of the room.

16

By the end of the next month, Jan and I both knew she was pregnant. Her mornings of nausea and nights of restlessness changed our significant lapses of communication into noisy skirmishes of aimless abuse, never violent, but always disturbing. I tried to give the coming event favorable odds but couldn't get her to lay her resentments down. In short, she felt trapped and I began to feel superfluous, an unbeatable combination for disaster.

I saw more of Sari than I should have, I suppose. We tried to make our love scenes convincing, but we only fooled each other, not ourselves. After a while, the extra work became so classic in its middle class conception, I began to feel the summer's hot air blowing away springtime's promises and I slowed down, satisfied with telephone calls from public booths and sharing an occasional drink.

I saw Jan's pregnancy as our only hope of ever getting out of New York. I made some quick decisions. I had Jan quit her job. I gave Yogi the job of editing the magazine; I was sick of it. Jan and I hid out at her folk's place in Connecticut. You'd think it would be hard to put down rolling hills, a natural private lake and martinis close at hand all afternoon. At sundown, we'd barbeque chickens or thick steaks and eat on a terrace enhanced by candlelight and Bach's harpsichord and flute. You'd think that would be hard to put down, but we managed to do it at the end of two weeks. We then knew it was something more than New York. I couldn't help but feel Jan resented me for knocking her up.

The first of my series of articles appeared in Rick's magazine, and much to our surprise, it laid an egg. Everybody was embarrassed by it, including the magazine. It was too early for our exposé; only a handful knew what we were exposing and the rest thought we were too hysterical. Rick was fired before the final article appeared. I saw him right after it happened.

He told me of grandiose plans to start a big circulation magazine utilizing his theory of literary violence. 'Now's the time. Violence has become the new American characteristic, and to be contemporary, one cannot ignore it any longer. Listen, boy,' he said, giving me a startling slap on the back, 'the nightly muggings of New York are being duplicated in big towns across the nation. Mugging has ceased to be an isolated expression of a few neighborhood toughs; it has become an accepted form of social intercourse.'

I ignored his dreary analysis. 'Where are you getting the money and backing?'

'That, my boy, is Kathy's job. She and I have become very close.' I wasn't at all surprised.

'So what are your plans?' he asked, adroitly changing the subject.

'Hazy,' is all I answered.

'I'll keep you informed.'

I did see a columnist's item – it might have been Cholly Knickerbocker – some weeks later, intimating that Katherine Sloan Walker was backing a new literary magazine, 'something like the Saturday Review of Literature' is the way it was described. I could see Rick going into a deep funk at the comparison of his violent baby and that old rag.

I decided to give Yogi my magazine outright. I met him some time after we had made the deal. We had lunch in a delicatessen around the corner from his printer.

'How are you doing with the magazine, Yogi?'

'You should be paying me,' he suggested with dry humor. 'I haven't any money to pay the printer and the distributor won't give me the money for the last issue until I get this one out. That's American finance; I never could understand money matters.'

I didn't think he'd have the nerve to ask me for money after I'd given him the magazine, all the money due from the last issue, all the office equipment, paid his rent, bought him some coal, given him the use of my car and practically turned over my life insurance to him. But he did.

'Yogi, don't you think I've done enough for you and the cause?'

'Yeah, yeah,' he reluctantly conceded, 'but that was last month! What have you done for me lately?'

'Good luck, Yogi. I'm pulling out of the racket. I've had it.' We shook hands. 'Send me a few free copies of the castration issue, will you?'

'Sure, just let me know where to send them.'

I got up to pay the check and left a tip.

'Hold it a minute,' he whispered to me. 'Hey, you,' he motioned to our waiter. 'Are you a union waiter?'

'You bet I am,' the waiter proudly said.

'Good, then you don't need our tip,' Yogi replied, picking up the half-buck and pocketing it.

17

'HEY, WAKE UP. Talk to me a minute.' Jan was shaking me by the shoulder.

'What about?' I was very sleepy. It was the day I promised myself to look for a job.

'Do you want to go to Connecticut this weekend? Mother wants to know by noon.'

'Call me at noon. I can't think now.'

'Listen,' she pleaded. 'I haven't seen you all week. Let's get together this weekend. I've something important to tell you.'

'Call me at noon,' I repeated, a little irritably.

She fled out of the room, slamming the door. For a moment I thought how inconsiderate of her. Then I felt maybe I had handled the scene badly. Something was wrong. I reminded myself to think about it later.

I awoke about twelve thirty but Jan hadn't called. I started off the morning sucking on some left-over Tums for the tummy; I had a terrible case of acidity. I showered and shaved. The fluorescent light over the sink was flickering, contributing to an already uncomfortable feeling. I messed around the house, waiting for Jan's call. I considered a legitimate breakfast. The icebox harbored a surrealist array of two broken eggs, some horseradish, a few wrinkled Greek olives, Major Grey's chutney (a gift from last Christmas), some non-fattening bread and three cokes. I settled for the coke, wondering what the hell we ever ate round here.

I put on the Mulligan record, but the cool sounds did nothing for me that early in the day. Peeked out the shaded window to see what was happening in the outer world; it was crowded. The most satisfying event while waiting for Jan's call was a full-throated coke-belch. Heartened by the physical exertion, I made up a crazy little speech full of good intentions and meaningless remorse that I delivered with flawless Leslie Howard inflections before the Venetian mirror (it still hadn't been cleaned). The phone rang, pleasantly applauding my performance. It was Sari.

'Surprised?' she asked. I hesitated before answering. She repeated it. 'I said, are you surprised?'

'Not exactly.'

'Oh.'

'How have you been?' I asked. I hadn't seen her in a couple of weeks.

'Pretty good, and you?'

'A little more disorganized than usual, nothing serious.

'Can you drop by this afternoon? I'd like to talk to you.'

Everybody seems to want to talk to me these days.

'I'll drop by.'

'What time?'

'I'm expecting an important phone call. I'll be by about three. O.K.?'

'Fine. See you then.' We hung up.

I waited till about three for Jan's call. I finally called her at work; she hadn't come back from lunch. I didn't think too much about it at the time. Hopped a cab to Sari's.

I smacked her cheek with a kiss; she returned with a playful embrace. The apartment looked disordered, which was rare for her. She was in shorts, shirt, no brassiere, drinking gin and tonic. I went to the icebox and got a beer. Neither of us had a hell of a lot to say. I resorted to reminiscing about our first meeting in the swimming pool, the Museum of Modern Art and Pernod, rocks on Sixth Avenue, but our affair wasn't old enough for nostalgia. She started to straighten up the place.

'Come on over here and settle down.' I was a little annoyed at her straightening up on my time. She turned on the radio and we listened to the music for a while, slightly embarrassed at having nothing to say.

'I just wanted to be sure that it's all over,' she said out of the blue. I couldn't deny it and didn't try.

'I've been worried about you lately. What's going to happen to you?' She stood over me, setting her cold drink on my shoulder, rubbing my neck innocently with her free hand. It felt good.

'Who knows?' I said, setting my beer on the floor and wrapping my arms around her tiny waist.

'Is there another girl?'

'Yes, I suppose so.'

'Who?'

'Well, I'm working on one.'

'Do I know her?'

'It's Jan,' I said. She flopped on my lap and crossed her legs. I tried to get my beer up from the floor but couldn't reach it. Her hand was still around my neck.

'You know,' she whispered in my mouth, 'I hope you make it with her.'

'Sari, I'm glad you feel that way because I've just realized that if I can't make it with Jan, I can't make it with anybody. That's not a pretty picture to look forward to.' I said it with a kiss only an inch away. She held the kiss longer than I expected, even wrapping both her arms around my neck. I could hear the ice cubes of her drink clinking in my ear.

'I'm going to miss you,' she said. I was pleased about her taking her time in breaking away.

'Where are you going?' I asked out of habit.

'That's what I wanted to tell you about, why I called. I got an offer to go to Israel and make a movie. My producer friend in Hollywood got religion.'

'What's it about? *Birth of a Nation*?'

'You won't believe it, but he said it was a musical.'

It struck me very funny. 'A hundred rabbinical students and a girl-type picture?' She thought it was amusing and she gave me the story line just as it must have been told to her with that peculiar brand of Hollywood sincerity. I interrupted her.

'Listen, Sari, I got a great title. How about calling it 'Song of the Kreplach.'

'Oh, you're hopeless,' she said setting down her drink and falling into a chair, stretching out her long white legs. She kicked off her flats and studied her toes, a bit of staging that didn't go unnoticed. I finished off the beer, got up and turned the music up. I pulled her up from the chair and we started dancing on a dime. We lost the rhythm when I accidentally stepped on her toes and we broke a foot apart. I was the first to look away. It was foolish.

She walked me to the door.

'So long, Sarah,' I said. 'It is Sarah, isn't it?'

'Get out of here, you rotter,' she said good-naturedly, giving me an extra push.

It was a few minutes before four when I left Sari's. I ducked into a phone booth and made a call to Jan's office. Decided to have a quick drink at Clark's and then try calling home. Clark's was very quiet; a few neighborhood regulars, a re-write man from the Daily Mirror (a Clark fixture) and a couple of ancient biddies drinking half and half at a table in the rear.

I noticed for the first time a discreet sign at the back of the bar that discouraged men unaccompanied by women; it was the owner's gallant way of saying 'no pixies served'. A true sign of the times, I thought. The rest of Clark's décor was pictures of Irish democrats abroad, shillelaghs, Irish sweepstake posters, Roosevelt's rotogravure photographs, World War i souvenirs, and a little private joke of the Irish: photographs of twenty-nine vice-presidents, the underdogs of history. I had another drink, dark beer, nothing serious, killing a little, working up a little anxiety. I ordered a Jack Daniel's chaser with my next beer. It helped. The telephone booth was occupied, as it always was, which increased my mounting restlessness.

A beefy-faced half-drunk square sat himself down next to me and threw out a few remarkably dull lines aimed at no one in particular. I did my best to look preoccupied. I switched to straight shots. The dullard couldn't take the silence that sang up and down the bar and insisted on some friendly mutual lower class drinking.

'Too much loneliness in this town.' He spoke in my direction hoping to get a rise out of me. It surprised me when I heard poetry out of place, but from bitter experience. I have adopted the wise policy of ignoring poetry emanating from unlikely sources because it has invariably turned out to be a mistake and eventually creates fear if not embarrassment in the 'poet'. In a bar, this kind of rejection always leads to alcoholic aggression, which in turn seems to be beamed my way. Sitting next to me was a tureen of tension and I begged off, pleading and hinting at uncommon sorrows.

As I expected, he took this to be the brush off and crowed about it to the bartender, a stately-looking, thin Irishman with glasses, not unlike Joyce in figure and speech.

'Be easy there, fellow,' he cautioned. 'The gentleman wants solitude, not uncommon in this bar.'

The drunk pointed to the sign at the back of the bar. 'If you ask me, he looks like one of these...'

I didn't let him finish the sentence. I threw about three quarters of an ounce of sour mash right in his eyes and gave him a dark beer chaser; it temporarily blinded him. I pulled the bar stool out from under him, grabbed him by the hair and dragged him over the sawdust covered tile floor, leaving a trail of stale beer and confusion. As he struggled to collect himself at the door, I kicked him in the face with my continental heel, which left a cat's paw tattoo that looked better than his ugly red face.

By this time the bartender took over, slinging him across his skinny shoulders and dumping him in the hallway next to the bar. I tried to apologize but he would have none of it.

'Forget it,' he said, 'come back in and have one on me.' It was the greatest vote of confidence I had ever received. I felt for the first time what it was like to be a physical winner. I liked the feeling. I ordered a rare hamburger and ate it with a strong appetite and a shaky hand.

The telephone booth was empty and I tried again to get Jan. No answer from home. I didn't care too much by this time. It was close to five thirty and within fifteen minutes, the bar had changed from a Third Avenue saloon where Irish washerwomen, neighborhood alcoholics, TV repair men and beer drivers drank in friendly solitary harmony (violence of the kind I had created was rare) into a college reunion. Madison Avenue had taken over completely, unchallenged.

I retreated to the back table and rang the buzzer for another drink. The juke box ignited with songs no one familiar with a Third Avenue saloon ten years ago would ever dream of hearing: Mabel Mercer, Edith Piaf, musical comedies of yesterday and today; mambos, Sumac and for the sloppy cornballs, Gordon Jenkins' Manhattan Towers.

I was fascinated with my swelling hand, relishing the thrill of victory when I spotted my friend, Johnny. I nodded for him to come over and join me. I hadn't seen him since the pogo stick party early in spring that was supposed to celebrate the publication of his book. Nobody had paid any attention to his book since but I have always looked upon him as a genuine talent and warm friend, although we didn't get together often. That's the way it goes in New York.

He was very depressed and jumpy and ordered a double scotch. He asked about Jan, which showed some decent feeling. Usually, when we meet someone after a long quiet, the conversation consists of the clichés: 'What's new?', 'How you doing?' and 'I've had it!' Johnny always made it a point to enquire about you which made him a conversational rarity. I told him about the fight I'd just had.

'Great!' It was probably his first smile in a year. 'There should be more action of that kind. I find myself wanting to mix it up a little. I almost had a fight with Bummy Carwell last week.'

'What happened to him?'

'His new book was brutally rejected by his publisher. They

claimed it was phoney. He flipped.' He stopped a minute as if it was too painful to go on. 'He resented my book and accused me of turning on him. I kept trying to tell him how big a flop my book was but it wasn't a big enough flop for him. Now he's fled West to look for shades of Walt Whitman.' We drank to Walt and Bummy.

I asked Johnny what he was going to do to change his luck.

'I'm writing a new book about Uptown Bohemia,' he said wistfully.

'That'll do it every time.' We both had a good laugh. 'Get on the phone. Let's get this thing rolling.'

He looked over at the phone booth; it was still busy. While he was checking his address book, I watched a loosely attractive solo dame at the next table who was flipping through her address book. I looked at Johnny and then looked back at her. It was a familiar sight to see them both running through the possibilities for the night.

'Hey,' I called over to her. 'Why don't you come join us. Johnny here has a book of fresh numbers. Perhaps you can swap.'

Johnny looked up and gave her a harmless smile. She returned it but made no further move. I nudged Johnny into action.

'What's the story?' he asked me out of the corner of his mouth, pointing to the girl.

'East Hampton type on the prowl; been around; probably a weeper when tight,' is the way I summed her up.

'Very astute.' He patted me on the back. Encouraged, he reached over and hooked the leg of her chair with his foot and dragged her and the chair all the way over to our table. She seemed to enjoy the slide.

We skipped introductions; Johnny commandeered her address book, casing it casually.

'Do you really know Cholly Knickerbocker?' he asked. 'I thought that was a made-up name.'

'Yes,' she said with an accent straight from Vassar. 'Isn't he divine?'

'What would you like to drink?' Johnny asked, 'We're ready for another.' We all ordered scotch.

'Make it Chivas Nerves,' I called after the waiter.

It wasn't long before a couple of personable strangers, living it up too, joined us and soon we were rolling. East Egg turned out to be as fast and low as a Jaguar ride. She attached herself to a hard-drinking Armenian who was complaining about his unpaid tailoring bills.

I told Johnny to give Danny a ring. 'I think this crowd is good for the night. Tell him to bring his briefcase.' Johnny went out singing a snatch of I Understand. He came back a couple of minutes later whistling Tumbling Tumble Weeds. 'I was made a hit parade,' he said.

The cocktail hour was thinning out, leaving a few die-hards (the *Daily Mirror* rewrite man was still there), some displaced persons and our table. East Egg, bored with the woes of the well-dressed Armenian, collared a tipsy D.P. on his way out. He turned out to be a famous band leader from the early swing days. We all recognized him once his name was dropped. He was pretty surly to begin with, but cooled the act when he found out Johnny had written the book he had just read. We couldn't get him and Dostoevsky off our back after that. He became a brooding literary figure, Johnny wanted to talk big band lore; he insisted on exploring Chekhov parables. We had to fluff him in the end – no sense of the ridiculous. Danny shuffled in with two of the most aristocratic women I ever saw outside the pages of *Town & Country*. He was certainly travelling in high society. He was flustered at seeing a sea of unfamiliar faces but I made elaborate introductions the minute I found out their names. One was a Hungarian countess and the other a red-headed young edition of Lady Peel, complete with monocle hanging down her cleavage. Somehow everything ceased to look ridiculous amidst such overwhelming absurdity.

It was about ten-thirty when we decided to get something to eat. We didn't lose anyone with the suggestion.

'Hey, man.' Danny came alongside of me as we were going out. 'I saw Jan today. She seemed strange.'

'What time?'

'In the afternoon, about three o'clock. She was down at the circle in Washington Square.'

'Was she with anybody?'

'Nope.'

'What made her seem so strange, Danny? Was she high?'

'No, maybe she wasn't so strange.' Danny reflected for a moment. 'It's just that I went up to talk to her and she either cut me dead because of my new business connections,' he stopped for a smile, 'or she didn't recognize me in my new uniform.' He noticed my worried look. 'Say, man, I'm sorry I brought it up.'

'Did you try to talk to her? What did she say?'

'I cut out; there was nothing to say.'

'Danny. I'll meet you all at Squire's for dinner. I'm going to try to contact her. I'm a little worried.'

She wasn't at home. I called her mother. No-one answered. I had forgotten they were in Connecticut. I called there; no luck either. Her mother gave me a quick grilling which I didn't appreciate. I tried Joan Beardsley, her dikey friend (it hurt). Her husky-throated room-mate said she had gone out to dinner with Jan. That was a relief, I thought, or was it? Half a dike is worse than one, I mumbled to myself.

I should have gone home right then, but once you get rolling, it's hard to stop. I joined the wolf pack for dinner, fell into some soup and snails and, by the time we were ready to leave, someone invited everyone to a friend's apartment up the street. An hour after we were there, everybody was out of their head. I had witnessed the journey to the end of the night so many times, it never occurred to me this third act would be any different from a score of previous ones. Everybody was mixing in and out of each other's pants with professional pride. It was about twelve-thirty when I gave the house another ring.

It was then that I experienced the feeling of being really lonely in a frantic lonely crowd. I felt I wanted Jan and I couldn't hold back a flood of soul searching. WHY DO I DO IT? The patterns of the past were not working for me tonight. I felt I needed her.

The drinking and the violence of the afternoon were beginning to wear me down. When Danny wanted me to join him in lighting up, I begged off, claiming I was too lushed to enjoy it, and I was. He gave me a peculiar look, shrugged it off and made an attempt to pick up a couple of other passengers. He landed with the Countess and the East Egg.

Things got worse. I let myself be carried off on a whirlwind tour of Village bars. In one of them, I remember a drunken old poet (long past the stage of being a has-been) coming over to our table trying to sell an 'original poem' to the Countess for the price of a short beer. Danny, who was making a brilliant defence of dynamic capitalism, told him to get lost.

More people joined us. We got outside when the Lady decided she wanted to go to a Village tourist trap. At this stage anything sounded like a good idea. The club was right around the corner.

The place was filled with sour-faced waiters and a nervous proprietor. The first show had closed to an empty house so we had the run of the place. They moved us around an interminable banquet table and somebody sat me at its head. I marvelled at everyone's stamina and good humor. It was a shame I was in such a funk.

'Wake up, man,' Danny was nudging me, 'say a few words for posterity.'

The Armenian seconded the motion and East Egg got up and started applauding. You know how these things get going, and before I realized what had happened, I was standing up unsteadily, as I recall, acknowledging the plaudits of the mob.

'As your good friend Marcel Proust would say, 'Where's the urinal, I think I'm going to be sick.' I excused myself and made it just in time.

I must have blacked out because the next thing I remember was the Negro midget wash room attendant helping me off the floor, wiping off my clothes, and giving me a great big toilet-tip smile.

'What happened?' I asked him.

'You was sick, sir, but you all right now. Yes, sir. You look fine. You must have taken a nap, sir.!

'How long was I out?'

'About twenty minutes, sir, yes sir, about twenty minutes, sir.'

I looked bad in the mirror for the first time. I knew I had something to do but couldn't think with that midget 'sir-ing' me out of my mind. I staggered back to the table; the place seemed suddenly filled. I must have been out longer than twenty minutes. (It was swell of the gang to check up on their pal.) I threw Johnny some money that more than covered my share of the bill, and split.

I sneaked into the apartment out of habit. I could see in the dark that the shades were still down from the morning. Groped for the light switch and finally hit it. Jan was asleep on the couch with her clothes on. She hadn't made the bed. I peeked at her face for a second; she seemed to be knocked out. I ruffled her hair, picked up her arm and let it drop – it was like lead falling. I bent down to smell her breath to determine if she was drunk. A light bourbon smell. I rubbed her stomach; it was a little larger than I remembered it.

I started undressing, sitting on the edge of the couch, staring at her, debating whether to wake her up or undress her asleep. I hadn't remembered seeing her so relaxed; it was a shame to disturb such a peaceful sleep. I decided to let her sleep it off.

I got into bed, turned off the light and tried to forget a horrible day; I'd forgotten to brush my teeth. I got up and went to the bathroom. The mirror door of the cabinet was open; I gave it a casual glance. There was nothing extraordinary about it. Spotted some Pepto-Bismol and took a couple of large swigs, hoping it would settle my stomach. I finished brushing my teeth.

On my way back I stood over Jan, fascinated with the contented look on her face. I picked up her arm again and let it fall, hoping she would wake up. I wanted to talk to her. Wanted to tell her what a lonely time I had. The arm was disturbingly limp. I picked up her leg. One shoe fell off. The leg was as light as a feather but fell like a lead balloon. Sat down on the edge of the couch again, gently shaking her shoulders. There wasn't an ounce of resistance or a hint of being disturbed. I gave her a kiss; her lips were dry, her breathing sounded heavy.

'Honey?' I whispered. 'Honey, you asleep? It's me. I got something to tell you.'

When she didn't respond I lifted her head but it fell back before I had a chance to hold it. I began to shake her all over. I tried to pick her up, but couldn't get more than a few inches in the air. She was like a limp, wet rag; nothing held together. She fell back on her side and then I saw the bottle. I recognized it immediately and knew it was empty before I gave it another look. It had been full a month ago and I never used them for sleeping, she but rarely. Tried to control myself but couldn't; heaved up the Pepto-Bismol as I crawled towards the phone. I could hardly dial O. I forced myself to be coherent and finally got through to the emergency operator who was reassuring. I threw the phone away and rushed over to Jan. I tried to shake her some more but it was no use. I listened to her heart; it was still beating.

I searched the room for her pocket book, in case she was carrying any pot. I found the purse in the next room, dumped its contents on the floor; she was clean. I tried to remember where I had hidden my stuff and automatically went to the mantel opening, reached underneath, retrieved the box and practically on hands and knees made it to the toilet. Threw it in the bowl, box and all and flushed the toilet. I was head level with the toilet seat as I dry-heaved my guts out.

I forced myself up and threw on some clothes. I wasn't going to make it, I kept telling myself; then I heard the siren wailing down the block. I had the door open before they stopped. I stood in the doorway, shaking, helpless, waiting.

'Up here,' I hollered. Two of them rushed up the steps and started working on her with such professional zeal, I straightened up, praying, hoping I'd be able to carry it off.

'Is there anything I can do?' I asked one of them.

'Take it easy,' he said, 'nothing to worry about.' They had her on a stretcher in a minute.

'Wait, I'm coming with you,' I hollered.

'Put your shirt on then, let's go,' he said.

I tried not to look at Jan on the stretcher but as I saw her being carried around a tricky turn in the stairs, I mumbled a little tag line from a childhood prayer.

Just before the driver slammed the door of the ambulance, I caught a glimpse of his face. I held the door open with my foot.

'Is you name Rifkin?' I asked. 'Ethan Allen Rifkin?' I was almost positive it was the hip hackie who had taken us to Katherine Sloan Whitakers a few months back. There was no mistaking those glasses and that gravel voice.

'That's right,' he said proudly. 'Hi. Do I know you?'

It was a hell of a time to go into it, so I dropped it. 'Let's really go on this ride. I'll talk to you later.' I never knew if he recognized me or not. He slammed the door.

The siren sounded like seventy-five, and the ambulance lights threw a Martian glare on the suddenly motionless streets. I made a check of the speedometer as we screeched around Columbus Circle up into Broadway. We were going fifty-five. I caught the lights of the other car and wondered why it hadn't pulled over to the curb. It was too late.

Rifkin did all he could to avoid him, but he got us and knocked us into a plate glass window of a liquor store. I was thrown against the ambulance's side. An oxygen tank above Jan's head broke loose, stabbing her across her skull. I watched it happen and couldn't even scream.

Rifkin was slumped over his wheel, his horn-rimmed glasses smashed and there were pieces of glass sticking in his forehead. Blood was dripping over a copy of the *Partisan Review* that was lying next to him, like a bible.

I watched them take Jan away in another ambulance. I forgot to cry.

I was packing Jan's things to return to her folks when Danny dropped in on me. He didn't have much to say. He started to read the *Journal-American*. I was almost finished with my packing.

'Hey,' he said, looking over the edge of the outstretched paper, 'Here's something you'd get a kick out of.' He started to read.

'Elsa Maxwell says, 'I'm sorry to leave my favorite jungle, New York. Lawless, careless, casual, terrible, electric, thrilling, murderous, heart-breaking, gay, fascinating, divine New York!' There was a moment of silence.

'That's a laugh, Danny,' I said, 'do you remember when laughs didn't cost a thing? Got a light?'

THE END

Index

TIGER OF THE STRIPE

Typeset by Tiger of the Stripe
in Adobe Garamond Premier Pro
with chapter numerals in
Monotype Colonna

www.ingramcontent.com/pod-product-compliance
Lightning Source LLC
Chambersburg PA
CBHW071221290326
41931CB00037B/1598